UNION OF SOUTH AFRICA.

REPORT

OF THE

Native Grievances Inquiry

1913-1914.

Presented to both Houses of Parliament by Command of His Excellency the Governor-General.

NEGRO UNIVERSITIES PRESS
WESTPORT, CONNECTICUT

Originally published in 1914
by Cape Times Limited; Goverment Printers

Reprinted in 1970 by
Negro Universities Press
A Division of Greenwood Press, Inc.
Westport, Connecticut

Library of Congress Catalogue Card Number 77-109362

SBN 8371-3851-5

Printed in the United States of America

REPORT

OF THE

NATIVE GRIEVANCES INQUIRY,

1913–1914.

PART I.

INTRODUCTORY.

UNION OF SOUTH AFRICA.

REPORT

OF THE

NATIVE GRIEVANCES INQUIRY,

1913-14.

Presented to both Houses of Parliament by Command of His Excellency the Governor-General.

1914.

PART I.

INTRODUCTORY.

1. By Government Notice No. 1074 of 1913 I was appointed as a Commissioner with the following reference : —

" To investigate the conditions under which natives are engaged for and employed on the mines of the Witwatersrand, and if any grievances or abuses be found to exist to make recommendations with a view to the removal thereof; to inquire into the control capable of being exercised over natives housed in compounds in the Witwatersrand area and to make recommendations as to what measures should be taken with a view to safeguarding life and property in the event of any industrial or other unrest or disturbance."

2. The purpose of the inquiry seems to have been misunderstood by some witnesses. There was no intention of investigating the truth or falsehood of individual complaints: the Commission, having no power to compel the attendance of witnesses or to administer an oath, could not do this effectively. The object was to ascertain whether the native mine labourers, as a class, suffered under any generic disabilities and, if possible, to suggest means by which these might be remedied in the future. Accordingly, whenever I have met with specific individual complaints, I have called the attention of the local representative of the Native Affairs Department to them and left it to him to set them right.

3. The procedure of the inquiry was as follows. First of all, with a view to getting a general idea of the subjects under investigation, I got some officers of the Native Affairs Department to tell me at secondhand the grievances of which the natives mostly complained to them. After this, I went to the compounds to hear what the natives had to say for themselves, or met their delegates at the neighbouring Pass Office. Before each visit, the Native Affairs Department had arranged that the labourers should select their own spokesmen. A shorthand note of the evidence was taken, and a transcript or summary was sent to the management of the mine concerned and the expression of their views invited.

4. This necessarily occupied a great deal of time, as I visited practically every compound on the reef, and much time was consumed in mere repetition. Undoubtedly, I might have obtained the same amount of information in a much shorter time, had the obtaining of information been the sole object of the inquiry. Since, however, it seemed to me desirable not only that the natives should have a free and full hearing, but that they should feel that they had done so, I do not consider that this time was wasted.

5. After the management of each mine had had time to consider the transcript of the native evidence, I gave them an opportunity of putting forward their evidence and views on the points raised or on any others falling within the terms of reference. I also heard witnesses who put forward the views of the Native Recruiting Corporation, the Witwatersrand Native Labour Association, Mr. Mostert and others interested in recruiting.

6. In March, 1914, I was instructed by the Minister to go to the Transkei in order to take evidence in reference to the system of making advances to natives recruited for the mines. I visited Kokstad, Bizana, Flagstaff, Lusikisiki, St. John's, Umtata, Idutywa, Butterworth, Queenstown, Kingwilliamstown, East London, Durban, Maritzburg and Vryheid, and heard evidence from magistrates, merchants, recruiters, traders, natives and others interested.

7. In addition to the classes enumerated above, I have heard various individuals who are interested in the matters under inquiry, missionaries, medical men, officials, etc. In all, I examined 1,144 witnesses and held 87 sittings.

8. Apart from the evidence formally taken, I have received many statements by way of letters from mine managements and others. I have also gathered a good deal of information from informal conversations. Where these sources have seemed to me reliable, I have not hesitated to base my conclusions upon them as well as upon the recorded evidence, since the latter was not given under the sanction of an oath or subject to cross-examination by opposing parties.

9. A great part of the evidence has been given by natives. I have not previously had any wide experience of native evidence, and I was, at first, a good deal puzzled by some of the stories I heard. I now think that, while the native does not very often invent a story entirely, he will frequently, upon a very small foundation, build up a magnificent superstructure of fiction. At one mine there was, a week or two before I heard the complaints of the natives employed thereon, a disturbance between the natives and the police, in which one of the former was, unhappily, killed. Anyone reading the evidence given to me by some of the natives would think that the police made it a regular practice to shoot the inhabitants of that compound.

10. Also, natives habitually speak of past conditions as if they were still continuing. For example, on one mine, practically the only complaint was that hammerboys were employed upon lashing work until noon, or thereabouts, so that they had no reasonable chance of drilling the 30 inches which is the *minimum* for which they get paid. In fact, it appears that this had been the case under the previous management; but it is quite clear that, for many months before my visit, they had no serious grievance upon this ground. The complaints which I received at that mine had been remedied long before they were made to me.

11. In consequence of this tendency, some of my recommendations may deal with abuses which have already ceased to exist. On the other hand, they may survive here and there, and it is, therefore, useful to bring the possibility to the notice of those responsible.

12. I have also found it quite impossible to rely upon native statements dealing with figures or hours.

13. This report, in consequence of the terms of reference, is necessarily occupied with a discussion of those points in the treatment of the native mine labourer which are or are said to be defective. It may, therefore, easily give to the reader the idea that the native's lot is entirely composed of hardships, and that his treatment is very bad indeed. I wish definitely to repudiate any such opinion. Since I entered upon this inquiry I have been astonished to learn how much care and thought is expended upon the native labourer's health and comfort; and all witnesses with any long experience of the mines—including every class and colour—are absolutely unanimous in the assertion that the improvement in the conditions of the native labourer on the Rand has been enormous and continuous.

14. A considerable number of the complaints made to me have been remedied during the sitting of the Commission as a result of their being brought to the notice of the managements concerned.

15. Generally speaking, the mines have given me every facility for conducting the inquiry; and most of them paid the natives who were delegated to bring the complaints of the compound, in spite of their day's absence from work.

16. I desire to thank the many persons who have supplied me with information, which must, in some cases, have cost a great deal of trouble to collect; and more especially to acknowledge the assistance received from Mr. H. S. Bell, of the Native Affairs Department, who, though not formally appointed, has in effect acted as Secretary to the Commission, and whose experience of native matters has been of great value to me.

PART II.

COMPLAINTS.

CHAPTER I.

COMPLAINTS AS TO WORKING CONDITIONS.

PART II.

ACCIDENTS.

17. There have been complaints from various mines that natives have been compelled to work in stopes which they considered dangerous, in spite of warnings given by them to the miner in charge; and there are authenticated cases where a subsequent accident has shown that the natives were right.

18. It is, of course, necessary, when there is a difference of opinion as to the safety of a working place, that someone on the spot should have the right to decide whether it is or is not safe; and clearly the decision of the superior must overrule that of the subordinate. I think, however, that it should be a rule that, where any dispute on the point arises, the miner should not decide it upon his own responsibility, but should send for the shift boss, if practicable, or at least for another European, so that no native should be compelled to work in a place about which he is doubtful, unless there are two opinions in favour of its safety. To omit this precaution should, in the event of an accident, be treated as negligence.

19. It is further necessary to impress on all concerned the serious responsibility incurred in giving and acting upon such an opinion; and this can best be done by ensuring adequate punishment in cases where accidents do actually happen after such warnings have been disregarded. Every accident involving death or serious injury is required by the Mining Regulations to be reported to the Mines Department and inquired into by an Inspector of Mines (Mining Regulations 268 and *seqq.*). Such reports, however, are not always made; there have been prosecutions for contravening the regulations; and, since these, of course, only occur when the omission is detected through other sources of information, it may safely be inferred that there are undetected cases. Naturally, this has not been stated in evidence; but, from what has been told me unofficially, I have no doubt of the fact. Mr. Kotze, the Government Mining Engineer, tells me, however, that, in his opinion, the fact that the accident rate has been increasing while the accident death rate has been decreasing, suggests that omissions to report are becoming less frequent.

20. In the course of holding an inquiry into the origin of a mining accident, the Inspectors of Mines have to take a good deal of native evidence. I find that they are often dependent upon the mine to supply an interpreter. This is not as it should be; they should have their own independent interpreters, or be in a position to borrow them from some other branch of the public service.

21. Where evidence establishing negligence is discovered, every endeavour should be made to obtain an exemplary sentence. In going through a large number of files dealing with accidents, I have come across several where the offence, if not actually amounting to culpable homicide, only escaped doing so by mere chance; yet the highest sentence I have met with was a fine of £25.

22. I am not suggesting that these sentences were wrong. In the present state of the law, there must, in every case of contravention of a Mining Regulation (unless death results), be an option of a fine (Act 12 of 1911, sections 16 and 17). Where this is so, the fine inflicted ought not to be so high that the accused cannot possibly pay it. Unless this rule be observed, the sentence virtually becomes one of imprisonment without the option of a fine, and so goes beyond the intention of the Legislature. No doubt, too, weight was very properly attached to the consideration that, in some cases, the Mines Department had cancelled or suspended the offender's certificate, without which he cannot pursue his trade.

23. I think, however, that there ought not to be this universal option of a fine. Quite 10 per cent.—and this is a low estimate—of the accidents which I have looked into were due to the negligence of some person other than the victim. When the lives of several persons habitually depend upon the care and skill of a superior, I do not think that imprisonment is at all too severe a penalty for serious negligence.

24. I notice that quite a considerable number of accidents arise from the breaking of " stulls," which are platforms erected in steep stopes partly to give standing places and partly to protect workers below from falling rock. I have some hesitation in offering an opinion on such a technical matter, but it seems to me that the evidence in these cases shows that more care might be taken in the examination of stulls. They are, from their position, difficult to examine closely; but there must be means of doing so if some additional trouble be taken.

25. There is no doubt that, in many cases, Mining Regulations 100 (11) and 106 (5), requiring the European miner to enter the working-place first and to assure himself that it is safe before allowing anyone else to enter, are habitually dis-

regarded; and, on some mines, no real attempt is made to enforce them. The natives are often anxious to get on with their work (many of them are on piece-work rates) at the earliest possible moment; and, as they are taken underground before the Europeans, they frequently begin clearing up before their white superior arrives. At the Crown Mines alone, in one week 21, and in the following 41, natives were convicted of this offence.

26. It seems to me that there are only two ways of enforcing this Regulation. Either the natives can be kept at the stations by the shaft where they are landed underground until the Europeans have passed them, or the Europeans can be sent down first. The latter method is nowhere practicable, owing to the long wait underground, which would be involved to the Europeans, since the number of natives to be sent down is something like 20 to every white man. The former is practicable in some places; in others, owing to the restricted station accommodation, it is not. Nor does it seem to work very satisfactorily: it is practised on the Crown Mines, and the numerous convictions referred to in paragraph 25 above show that it is often evaded. At this mine the enforcement of the rule is left to native police; probably, if a white man were sent first to each station, it would be more effective. The Nourse Mines have succeeded in retaining the boys at the stations by having a bossboy always there and a weekly visit from a shiftboss.

27. Where the stations are large enough, the natives can be kept there until the white men are down by having locked gates cutting off the stations from the drives, as is done on some mines.

28. There are two other solutions of the difficulty, which would, however, involve modification of the Regulation. At some mines, e.g., the Village Deep, the first people to go down the mine are a watering party, which goes through the whole mine before the natives are lowered. The examination might be made by the men in charge of this party, who are quite competent to do it effectively, and who must, in any case, do it for their own safety.

29. Again, if selected bossboys were allowed to make the examination, these could be sent down first, and there would be little or no delay in letting the natives get to work. There is general, though not universal, agreement among mining men that no difficulty would be found in getting experienced natives who could be trusted to do this properly.

30. The limitation of working hours (by section 9 of Act 12 of 1911) to eight a day makes it difficult to allow the natives to go to work at once as each of them gets down. On some mines it takes as much as two hours to lower all the natives, so that they would be starting work at very varying times, and would have to be stopped also at varying times, which may not always be practicable. Still, if, before any native enters the mine, the working-places have been examined and made safe, there is no longer any necessity to take precautions to keep labourers out of them, even though it may not be possible to make full use of the additional working time thus gained.

31. There were also complaints of cases of gassing. Under Mining Regulation 268, it is unnecessary to report such cases unless a person affected is likely to be disabled for 14 days. Even when no one is damaged to this extent, the circumstances may be such as to call for inquiry, either as to negligence or to acquire and disseminate information as to the directions in which danger may be looked for. It is difficult to require all cases of gassing to be reported, as gassing may be so slight as only to amount to a headache. I do not, however, see anything either impossible or unreasonable in requiring all cases where anyone has been rendered unconscious by gassing to be reported.

32. There is every probability that the mines will find the cost of any reasonable precautions against accidents well repaid by the increased popularity which will result from a reputation among the natives for scarcity of accidents. Mr. Lloyd, of the W.N.L.A., thinks that it will not make much difference in this respect, as the native is something of a fatalist. Mr. Lloyd's experience, however, is mainly of East Coast natives. I cannot help thinking that the more advanced Cape Colony native will consider such matters.

ASSAULTS.

33. A complaint which is all but universal throughout the mines is that natives are frequently assaulted by Europeans, generally underground. A certain number of such cases seem inevitable when the conditions of the work are considered. The mines consist of an enormous mileage of tunnels, in which a number of Europeans, many of them of no high standard of education or ethics, are each in practically unchecked control of several members of a servient race. As a rule, neither the master nor the servant understands the other's language, yet the

master has to give directions and the servant to obey them. Both parties are working under unhealthy and unnatural conditions. In these circumstances the temptation to and the opportunity for assaults on the servant by the master are constantly present; and these circumstances may perhaps be modified, but cannot be altogether removed.

34. Native Labour Regulation 16 requires every case of assault or alleged assault on a native to be reported to the Native Affairs Department. This regulation is not always obeyed. I think that it should be strictly and severely enforced.

35. On some mines it is the practice to discharge any European who assaults a native; and in some cases this policy has been successful in reducing such assaults to a minimum. On the other hand, it has been urged, with considerable reason, that a miner finds no difficulty in getting employment on another mine, and that it is better to keep him where his character is known, and, by repeated prosecutions, to secure an exemplary sentence against him.

36. Several managers have informed me that they find " a good talking to " more effective than immediate dismissal, at any rate in the case of a first offence.

37. It has sometimes been found difficult to secure convictions, the available evidence not being very strong. The corroboration of marks on the body is rarely obtainable in the case of habitual offenders, since these take care to strike the native where he is clothed. There is also considerable difficulty in identifying the offender, where he is not the man with whom the native assaulted habitually works. The complainant's evidence is, in the nature of things, exclusively native; and it is difficult to obtain the conviction of a white man on purely native evidence. Also, the European often manages to persuade some of the boys working under him to support his version. It has been suggested that a magistrate with special experience of native witnesses should be appointed to try such cases. Native evidence is, however, such an ordinary incident of all kinds of cases on the Reef that all magistrates who try criminal cases have such experience.

38. Some witnesses from the Native Affairs Department complain that, even where a conviction is obtained, the sentence is inadequate. As to this, the court which has heard the evidence is, of course, more likely to estimate the degree of the offence correctly than officials who are—very properly—biassed in favour of the native by the nature of their work.

39. It has been suggested that courts should have the power to suspend the offender's blasting certificate upon a second or subsequent conviction, thus depriving him for a time of his means of livelihood. This has proved a very efficient remedy in the case of offences by cabmen, and it would be quite justifiable to apply it, upon the ground that two or more convictions for serious assault upon natives show that the offender is not a person who can safely be trusted with the authority over natives necessarily confided to underground European workers, and that he ought not, therefore, to be allowed to earn his living in that particular way. This remedy would, however, be very partial in its operation, since many underground workers, e.g., Europeans in charge of tramming gangs, require no certificate of any kind; and many cases of assault come from this class.

40. On some mines the manager has obtained good results by compelling the offender to give pecuniary compensation to the injured native.

41. The appointment of underground inspectors who can investigate complaints on the spot has had a good effect on some mines; on others the system has not proved satisfactory. The position is a very difficult one, calling for both tact and strong character, as well as a knowledge of natives and of native languages.

42. As a matter of general principle, it seems to me a good thing that there should be some official of the company who goes underground, and whose principal function is to inquire into complaints by natives, and I think that such appointments might reasonably be required by regulation. It is essential that such an official should be a member of the compound staff, subordinate to the compound manager, not one of the underground men under the mine captain. His business would be to inquire into complaints, as far as possible immediately, and, in any case, at the actual spot where the dispute arose. Such a man obtains a knowledge of conditions underground which it is impossible for the compound manager to possess; so that he is in a position to appreciate the respective probabilities of conflicting stories. It is probably a good thing to leave the assigning of natives to the various gangs to this official, as is done at the Village Deep; and it is desirable that any natives employed on police duties underground should be under his orders. Such natives, if capable of interpreting, might save many misunderstandings.

43. It has been suggested that such underground supervisors should be Government officials, not servants of the mine. This would, however, involve much expense; and it would also relieve the employer of a responsibility which I think may fairly be placed upon him. But underground supervisors, like compound managers, should be required to hold a licence from the Native Affairs Department.

44. There seems to be, among the underground men on some mines, a lack of appreciation of the importance of the native labour supply. If it were pointed out to them that mishandling of natives renders the mine unpopular, and that such unpopularity must sooner or later result in the discharge of white miners, they might be more careful in their dealings with natives.

45. It seems to me that this is not a grievance that can be effectively dealt with by the adoption of any particular system; it is really a matter of the *personnel* of the mine; and that depends mainly upon the manager. Where it is known on any mine that the manager will not tolerate assaults upon natives, such assaults are soon reduced to a *minimum*. Every man has his own methods; and one method will probably be as effectual as another, provided the manager really intends it to be effectual. Where the number of cases of assault on a particular mine becomes and remains high, it is safe to conclude that the manager is not seriously attempting to put down assaults. In such a case there is no remedy, but the substitution of another manager.

46. Many boys stated that, after they had complained of being assaulted by a miner, they were sent back to work under him again. I do not think that this often occurs where the complaint is considered to be well founded; but, when it does occur, it certainly constitutes a grievance, as a miner has plenty of opportunities of " taking it out " of the boy in one way or another, and is, in these circumstances, likely to use them. Managers, on the other hand, say that they cannot undertake always to change the native's place of work on this ground, as they often find boys trumping up charges of assault expressly in order to get the change, because the rock is harder in one stope than in another, or for some similar reason. This contention is clearly sound. It seems to me, however, that, where a miner and one of his natives complain of one another—and there are usually, in such cases, charges and counter-charges—it is generally wise to separate them if there is any doubt as to who is in the wrong. For one thing, the way the parties get on with their new associates furnishes a useful test as to who was right in the original dispute; for another, no worker does his best for a master whom he wants to get away from.

47. I may mention, in passing, a complaint received from various natives that they were not allowed to attach themselves to any miner they liked, and to change masters whenever they wished to do so. Such a proposition is, of course, absurd; employees must necessarily work where their work is wanted, not where they would like to work.

48. I have received many complaints that when natives are being taken up in cages they are subjected to rough treatment, overcrowding and violence by the European skipmen and the native bossboys. The same considerations apply here as have been dealt with in connection with the general subject of assaults; but the special circumstances of such transport have to be allowed for.

49. At the end of the day there is a large number of boys waiting at the station to be hauled up. They are anxious to get up as quickly as possible, and, unless they are restrained in some way, they will simply rush each cage as it arrives, thus creating the very conditions of which they complain. In such circumstances, they will naturally be repelled by the skipman with more or less violence; nor is it easy to see how he can help himself.

50. Various contrivances are in use to avoid this. In some mines, compound police or bossboys are employed to make the natives line up and wait their turn. This seems to have improved matters somewhat; but it is alleged, with some probability, that a good deal of violence is used by the police. The Crown Mines have now detailed a European shiftboss for this duty; and the result seems satisfactory.

51. Another plan is to have the station fitted with double gates, the space between the gates containing the same number of boys as a cage does. Thus, when the gates next the shaft are opened, the others being closed, there is no opportunity for crowding. There is, I suppose, a rush to get into this reserved space, but it is at any rate not attended with the danger of falling down the shaft.

52. As to the overcrowding, the number of passengers to be carried in each cage is laid down by the Mining Inspector under Mining Regulation 34 (2); and it is an offence in the banksman or onsetter to allow a greater number to travel therein (Mining Regulation 32 (e)).

DELAYS IN HAULING.

53. Complaints have been made that natives are turned out of the compounds unnecessarily early in the morning, and are kept waiting a long time before being taken down below in the cages; in winter this is aggravated, on some mines, by having no shelter to wait in at the shafthead.

54. It must necessarily take a considerable time to drop some thousands of natives with limited hauling appliances; and the business has to be completed by a definite hour—usually about 6.45 a.m.—in order to leave time to drop the white men before the regular hour for starting work. All that can be done is to minimise the necessary inconvenience.

55. To a large extent this may be effected by increasing the size of the cages. Those now in use vary greatly; the largest of which I have heard takes 36 passengers every trip, the smallest six. It is evident that, if the former were substituted for the latter, the period occupied in hauling would be divided by six. Of course such large cages cannot be used everywhere; the *maximum* size possible depends upon various technical considerations; but some mines could use much larger cages than they have been doing.

56. The necessary delay can also be rendered much more tolerable by reasonable arrangements being made for the comfort of the waiting natives. These arrangements again vary almost infinitely at present. I have seen mines where there is a solid, covered passage from the compound to the shafthead, ending in a comfortable waiting room heated during winter with braziers, in which coffee or soup is served out before the natives go below. I have seen others where the natives have to make their way some distance over the open veld and wait at the shafthead without shelter of any kind until they can get taken down; and sometimes they are given no food at all before going down; though this is unusual, most mines providing them at any rate with some bread.

57. It is not possible to make the arrangements so comfortable in some places as they are in others; local circumstances, such as the space available, etc., have to be taken into consideration. There is, however, room for a good deal of levelling up in these respects; and Mining Regulation No. 143 (2), which requires shelters to be provided unless the Inspector of Mines grants a special exemption, supplies the means of compelling this. The regulation was not enforced for some time, but during the last few months several shelters have been started under instructions from the Mines Department.

58. When natives have reached the station, *i.e.*, the open space opening off the shaft where they are landed by the cage, they have to wait until all the other natives have been brought down and, after that, each gang has to wait until the European in charge of it arrives. This is necessitated by Mining Regulation No. 100 (11), which requires that no one shall enter a working place until the European in charge has examined it, and made sure that it is safe. The possibility of modifying this Regulation and thereby reducing this particular wait has been suggested in paragraph 28 and 29 above.

59. There are also complaints of delay in hauling natives up after the day's work is finished. As regards the general mass of day's pay natives, the same considerations as to the limitations of hauling gear, etc., apply as have been mentioned with respect to lowering in the morning. Many natives, however, are employed on piece-work; hammerboys, for example, when they have bored the standard number of inches required by their agreement, are at liberty to leave their work and return to the compound. At various mines these boys complain that they cannot get beyond the station until a late hour of the afternoon, because the cages are not running.

60. Some witnesses on behalf of the mine managements have stated that they do not want to give facilities to natives to come up early; they would rather get them to stay and drill further inches beyond the stipulated standard. I do not think this fair treatment; when they have agreed that the native shall be at liberty to leave after drilling his standard inches, they have no right to nullify their agreement by refusing him the opportunity to avail himself of his right.

61. This attitude is, however, not common; in most cases the management honestly intends to give the native reasonable facilities for leaving when he has

finished his task, and in many cases it succeeds in doing so. It is not possible to lay down in general terms what facilities a mine ought to give; in this matter, almost more than any other, everything depends upon the local circumstances. Some mines have such ample shaft room that they keep a pair of compartments for nothing but passenger traffic; in such a case, the management easily can—and generally does—arrange that natives can come up practically all the time. Others have only the compartments used for hauling rock; and this means the substitution of a cage for a skip whenever they have to haul passengers, a process which consumes a considerable amount of time. It is, however, usual to bring up shift-bosses for lunch, which means that a cage runs at noon and again at 1 p.m.; and it costs little time or trouble to allow this to make one or two extra journeys on each occasion in order to clear out any boys who are waiting. Casual parties of boys can also be brought up in a rockskip now and then without any interruption of the rockhauling beyond the loss of that particular load.

62. In short, I do not think it is difficult for any mine which really wishes to do so to arrange tolerably frequent opportunities for any native to get out of the mine from noon onwards.

63. I should add that the evidence as to the extent of this grievance is enormously exaggerated. The natives' statements of the hours to which they have to wait are, in many cases, palpably absurd.

64. It seems possible that such delays may have some bearing upon the death-rate. Drives and stations are draughty places; and, if a boy who has been doing hard work and is sweating violently, is compelled to remain in them for any serious time, his health is likely to suffer.

Lashing by Hammerboys.

65. A complaint which is found on a very high proportion of mines is that hammerboys are required to do lashing, *i.e.*, clearing the working-place of the broken rock produced by the last previous blast, before they can begin their own proper work of boring holes for the next blast. As a result of this, they are unable to drill so many inches as they would otherwise do. Since hammerboys are paid at piece-work rates, so much for every inch depth of the hole drilled, this is clearly a substantial grievance; and it is aggravated by a clause in the hammerboy's contract which provides that, unless he drills a certain *minimum* number of inches (usually 30 inches), he is not paid at all for that shift. It thus sometimes happens that a boy works at lashing for some hours and at drilling for several more, yet receives absolutely no equivalent in money.

66. I say "in money" because he does receive something, in the shape of board and lodging. On some mines, his food used to be docked if he had not completed his day's task; but I do not think this is done anywhere now.

67. A further aggravation of this complaint arises from the fact that most mineboys are engaged not for a period of time but for a certain number of shifts, usually 180 to 313. A shift in which the *minimum* is not drilled does not count as a shift at all, and it is thus theoretically possible for a native who has been engaged for 180 shifts, with the expectation of serving about seven months and earning in that time about £15—£30, to spend the rest of his life underground without earning a penny or making any progress towards the termination of his engagement. Of course, nothing even remotely resembling this ever occurs, nor would it pay the mine, as short holes are generally useless. I have, however, come across cases of several successive shifts being lost in this manner.

68. I think it is very doubtful whether the provision as to non-payment for holes of less than a certain depth is really necessary in order to keep up the average. The Durban Roodepoort has no *minimum*, but pays ½d. per inch up to 48 inches and 1d. per inch above 48 inches. In the last three months of 1913, their drilling average was 50·49 inches per shift, while the average over the Reef was only a little over 40 inches. The rock on that mine is, however, especially soft.

69. As to the extent to which this is, in actual practice, a grievance, I have received complaints of an excessive amount of lashing being demanded from nearly every mine, but I think that many of them are exaggerated and that many others refer to a bygone period. The proportion of shifts not paid for (commonly called "cancelled shifts") varies immensely. Over the six months ending 30th September, 1913, there were 20 mines where it was under 2 per cent. and 9 where it was over 10 per cent., one mine reaching 23·99 per cent. (Annexure 1). Of course the whole of these cancelled shifts are not due to lashing, but some of them are.

70. In most cases I am told by the management that the amount of lashing done by hammerboys is inconsiderable and does not seriously interfere with their work. On one mine, however, where a recently appointed manager has taken a personal interest in reducing the quantity, the average length of the holes drilled has increased by 4½ inches, and the percentage of cancelled shifts has fallen from 8 per cent. to 4 per cent. Clearly the amount of lashing formerly demanded made a material difference both to the hammerboys' earnings and to the period which it took them to work out their contracts.

71. I have come across a mine where 90 per cent. of the natives employed were hammerboys. There can be no doubt that, in that case at least, practically all the lashing must be done by the hammerboys.

72. It is to be observed that the employment of hammerboys to do lashing is, in a very large number of cases, a plain breach of contract. The form of contract used by the Native Recruiting Corporation, Limited (commonly called "the N.R.C."), which is the recruiting organisation supported by practically all the greater mines, except those controlled by Sir J. B. Robinson, and which supplies about 40 per cent. of the total number of recruited natives, runs as follows:—

"The term 'shift' . . . . when used with respect to hand drilling shall mean the drilling of a hole in hard rock of not less than 30 inches." (Annexure 2).

There is no stipulation that, in addition to this drilling, the hammerboy shall do any lashing whatever; in other words, the mines using hammerboys recruited under this form of contract have agreed to pay them a certain sum for drilling 30 inches and have no right to claim from them any work beyond this. In fact, the mines which require hammerboys under this contract to do any lashing whatever are compelling the latter to do work which they have not agreed to do and for which they are not paid anything.

73. It is, of course, said that they are in reality paid for the lashing, since, if a separate payment were made for this part of the work, the rate per inch for the drilling would be correspondingly reduced. This is not, however, an answer to the objection: whatever might be the case under another form of agreement, under this form the mine promises to pay the native his 1s. 6d. for drilling 30 inches and for nothing else. If the mine refuses to pay him unless he does some additional work and the native refuses to do that work, it is the mine, not the native, who is breaking the contract.

74. I may add that, even if the argument about indirect payment were sound, the native could not be expected to see it.

75. The omission from the N.R.C. contract of any clause requiring hammerboys to do a certain amount of lashing is not a mere oversight. Circular No. 55, issued by the N.R.C. to managers on 8th November, 1913, after stating that the Director of Native Labour had agreed to allow a *maximum* of two hours' lashing to be done by hammerboys, proceeds:—

"It has always been considered inadvisable to insert a clause in the native contract having reference to the shovelling work required of natives employed on hand drilling, as it is feared it may needlessly alarm them as to what they may be called upon to perform, and so adversely affect our recruiting operations."

76. I should think that requiring the employee to do something which he has not contracted to do would affect recruiting more adversely than setting out the bargain plainly and then adhering to it.

77. It is only fair to the N.R.C. to state that the omission to insert any allusion to lashing in their contract was made with the knowledge and sanction of the Director, who considered that it would be difficult to use any language which would not afford opportunities for abuse in the way of requiring excessive lashing. I agree that it is; but the omission does not prevent the abuse. Not to stipulate for any lashing and then to require some to be done is as much an abuse as to stipulate for two hours' and then to require three.

78. There is no doubt that most hammerboys, when engaging, are aware that it is customary on most mines to require them to do some lashing; but I cannot find that they have ever regarded it as other than a grievance.

79. Obviously, a hammerboy cannot get to work until the broken rock has been cleared away from the face; and, except in the usual case where there is a night shift for lashing only, this can be done more quickly by the hammerboy himself than by anyone else, since no time is wasted in sending in and withdrawing another gang. But the actual amount of clearing necessary to enable the hammerboy to get to work is very small; and I do not think that he would make any complaint if this was all that was required of him and if the lashing boys then came in behind him to do the rest of the work. This is the system at the Village Deep,

with the result that I received no complaints as to the lashing there. That mine comprises all kinds of stopes from 28 to 45 degrees, so that other mines ought to find it possible to work on the same system.

80. Some mines issue instructions that, whenever it is necessary to keep a hammerboy lashing for more than the *maximum* period, he shall be kept on lashing all day and paid accordingly. Others, again, require that he shall receive his *minimum* pay for a hole, even though he fail to drill the *minimum* number of inches. Elsewhere, an allowance, usually not defined but left to the discretion of the individual miner is made for the time spent on lashing, *i.e.*, a boy who has lashed for 3 hours and bored 36 inches may be credited with 42 inches.

81. On the New Unified any time in excess of two hours occupied in lashing is allowed in inches marked on the native's pay-ticket, at the rate of 6 inches for every hour.

82. On the Nourse Mine the same system is carried a little further, the boy not being allowed a fixed number of inches but a number in proportion to what he usually does. Of course, this vests a good deal of discretion in the individual miner; but I had no complaints as to lashing from this mine.

83. Again, at the City and Suburban, the lashing boys go down an hour before the hammerboys and clear out the stopes, so that the hammerboys do no lashing at all. This has been going on for the last four years and has given rise to no difficulty.

84. It may be worth noting that this mine succeeds in doing without recruited labour; it has no difficulty in filling up with voluntary boys. Of course it is an outcrop mine, and such are always popular; but few, if any, others discard recruited labour entirely. The rates paid to hammerboys on this mine are less than those provided by the N.R.C. contract.

85. In some contracts a certain amount of lashing is provided for. In that of Messrs. Marwick and Morris at the E.R.P.M. (Annexure 3), the labourer agrees "to do the necessary shovelling to clear the face of the rock before commencing to drill, but the time so occupied shall not exceed two hours." A native under such an agreement cannot complain of being required to do lashing, provided that the specified time is not exceeded and that no shovelling is required of him which is not necessary to clear the face of the rock. If, having done that amount, he is required to do some which is only necessary to reduce the number of lashing boys employed, he has a grievance.

86. Even where the contract stipulates for a certain amount of lashing, the method of payment for inches only, with nothing for lashing, does not tend to contentment. The hammerboy has two distinct pieces of work to do; yet he is paid at piece work rates calculated by reference to only one of those pieces. If the amount of lashing required of each native was the same, this would not matter so much; but it varies, not only from mine to mine and from stope to stope, but even from one boy to another in the same stope.

87. A great deal depends upon the shape of the stope. If it is narrower at the bottom than at the top, the rock pushed down by the highest boy accumulates upon the rock of the next boy and the latter has to pass on both lots, and so on all down the stope, until the whole mass has to be moved by the lowest boy, who really never gets a chance to drill his hole. If, on the other hand, the top of the stope is the narrowest part, the rock pushed away by each boy falls behind and clear of his next below.

88. It is possible, in stopes of the first pattern, to average the hardship on each boy by putting the boy who was at the bottom on Monday at the top on Tuesday; and this is frequently done. I was told, however, on some mines that this interchanging is not practicable, because the boys themselves will not have it. Each boy wants to stick to his own place—especially, I presume, those who have good places. But no such expedients will provide each boy with the same amount of lashing; and, until that is done, the objection to the method of payment remains.

89. This objection can be met by a rearrangement of rates, so that each boy should be paid so much for his lashing and so much for his hole. That is a fair method of payment, and the native could not say, as he now does—and with much force—"I may not have done my 30 inches, but I did do my lashing, and I ought to get something for it."

90. I think the best system is that of the City and Suburban. So long as the hammerboy does lashing at all, the amount done must, for the reasons given, be very variable, and it is not easy to adjust the pay accordingly, so that the abolition of lashing is the only way to get rid of complaints entirely. No one has been able to tell me of any exceptional circumstances which render it impossible for other mines to do what this one does successfully.

91. While I consider that the employment of hammerboys to do lashing without stipulating for this work in the agreement constitutes a distinct grievance, both as being wrong in principle and as being open to abuse, it is right to add that, taken as a class, the hammerboys get better pay and work shorter hours than any other native mine labourers, so that it does not appear that the practice is habitually abused or results in widespread hardship. It does, however, cause a great deal of discontent.

DRY HOLES.

92. Another complaint very commonly brought forward by hammerboys has reference to "dry holes," *i.e.*, holes which slope upwards and are therefore more difficult to drill, both because water cannot be used in them and on account of the difficulty of hammering upwards.

93. I should not myself have considered that this constituted a grievance, since it is obvious that all holes cannot be equally easy to drill; but it is clearly recognised as such among mining men and, in many cases, extra remuneration is allowed for such holes.

94. There is, however, great variety of practice as to the method of calculating this extra remuneration. In some cases as much as 100 per cent. is added for an upward hole and 50 per cent. for a horizontal one. In others only 6 inches is added, and that only if 30 inches is accomplished. These are about the extremes of the various rules officially recognised by the mines; but in many cases there is no rule, and the matter is either left entirely to the discretion of the miner concerned or (what comes to the same thing) no allowance is officially recognised, but an addition by the miner is winked at.

95. If it is possible for some mines to adopt a definite rule, it ought to be possible for the rest to do the same. Mr. Marwick thinks that want of consistency as to marking hammerboys is responsible for a great deal of the trouble. The miner may get into the habit of making certain allowances for an occasional short hole, having regard to local circumstances. Then a shiftboss comes along and insists on the rigid *minimum* being applied; or the reverse may happen. A universal rule would overcome this source of dispute.

96. An incident which sometimes prevents a hammerboy from finishing his hole is that the jumper jams or breaks. I understand, however, that this is usually due to his own carelessness.

INSUFFICIENT DRILLS.

97. On several mines the hammerboys complained that they were not allowed sufficient drills to accomplish their holes. In most cases I think this complaint was due to the lack of any organised system of dishing out the drills, so that the distribution degenerated into a scramble in which the devil took the hindmost, and the foremost took the drills. But some mines deliberately limit the number of drills below what the hammerboys want, in order to save steel. Natives do lose a lot of drills, either out of pure carelessness or to save the trouble of carrying them back, and some managers say that the fewer they have, the fewer they lose. The balance of opinion, however, among those managers whom I have questioned on the point is that it is not worth while to handicap the hammerboy in drilling his holes in order to economise the amount of steel thereby saved.

98. This difficulty does not arise where the hammerboys are systematically required to return their drills and get a receipt for them. Sometimes this takes the form of a metal token; sometimes only a note is taken of the number returned by each boy, and, next day, he is allowed to take a similar number.

99. A uniform scheme, devised by the N.R.C., is now under consideration.

100. Some natives also complained that the drills supplied to them were too short. Now and then there may be, of course, a temporary and accidental insufficiency of steel; but it is so plainly contrary to the interest of the mine to send down a hammerboy with inadequate tools that there is no fear of such a grievance occurring on any large scale.

SHORTAGE OF CANDLES.

101. From many mines there was a complaint that the supply of candles was insufficient and that work had in consequence to be completed in the dark or left incomplete; in the latter case with the result that no pay was earned for the day.

102. The system of issuing candles varies. In some cases it is left to the in-

dividual contractor to supply, at his own expense, candles to the natives under his charge; in others, a definite issue is made to each native. In the latter case, the remains of the candles are sometimes collected when the native returns to the surface; sometimes they are not.

103. It is, however, impossible to adhere to any system universally because in every mine some places are draughtier than others and will consequently use up more candles. It is therefore necessary to leave the issue largely to the discretion of the white man on the spot. No doubt occasional cases of hardship are bound to occur.

104. On one mine, where the candle issued was distinctly too small, a much larger one has now been substituted.

105. I do not think, however, that this complaint is usually well founded. At several mines where the natives asserted that they had to buy candles to supplement the supply, inquiries from neighbouring storekeepers failed to show any such purchases. I think the truth is that the boys had a sufficiency of candles but wanted to get more in order to sell the balance. Candles are a marketable commodity.

106. At the Knights Central, natives are allowed to buy lamps at cost price (7s. 3d.) and are supplied with carbide free, thus doing away with the necessity for candles in the case of those who care to get a lamp.

Long Hours.

107. Various complaints of excessive hours of work have been made to me, but native assertions as to time are so wild and undependable that I doubt very much whether there is much in them. It does appear, however, that fireboys do a twelve hour shift, which seems excessive.

108. Native clerks, also, are sometimes called upon to work overtime, at seasons of pressure, in which case they are usually paid overtime. There seems, however, some difficulty in ascertaining what overtime is, as the regular hours are often not clearly defined.

Sunday Work.

109. I have heard a good many complaints from natives who alleged that they were forced to work on Sundays. Such work is covered by their agreements; but Sunday work on the mines is so limited by law (section 6 of Act 12 of 1911) that comparatively few natives can be employed on that day.

110. On most mines, the Sunday work is largely, if not entirely, done by volunteers. It generally means rather a short day's work for a full day's pay, and many boys are glad to do it for that reason. At one mine, the natives even made it a grievance that they did not get paid for Sundays; they explained that they were quite willing to work and thought therefore that they should be paid.

Choice of Work.

111. Many natives complained that they could not get the class of work which they wanted. Recruited boys are all engaged to do any class of work which their employer requires of them. With voluntary boys different mines have different systems. All mines prefer, naturally, to engage them on the same terms as the recruited boys; their labour is thus available for any purpose for which it may at the moment be required. Some, however, will engage a labourer for a special class of work sooner than lose him; others refuse to accept natives on any but general contracts.

112. Similarly, when a recruited native who has completed his contract stays on, without a formal re-engagement, some mines will allow him to choose his work; others will not. This class can always leave at 7 days' notice (Native Labour Regulation 29); and even this short notice is not usually insisted upon.

113. It has been said that it is impossible to run a mine if you put each native on to the work he asks for. The Village Deep, however, manages to do so, and there do not seem to be any special circumstances which distinguish this mine from others. It is true that this course involves a certain falling off in tonnage. Mr. Whitehouse, the manager, was, however, very definite that the resulting contentment made it worth while.

114. It clearly does not constitute a grievance that an employee who has agreed to do all sorts of work is required to fulfil his agreement. But the complaint is so frequent that any means which can be adopted to minimise it will certainly make the mines more popular.

CHAPTER II.

COMPLAINTS AS TO COMPOUND CONDITIONS.

CHAPTER II.

Food.

115. There have been some complaints of insufficiency of food. As regards the meat ration, this was to be expected; a large number of natives will always want more meat, even though the amount supplied to them is far in excess of what a white man would eat. The ration to be supplied is laid down by regulation at 3 lbs. per week, and no European witness has suggested to me that it is insufficient. At the same time, Surgeon-General Gorgas' report has thrown doubts upon its adequacy, and I presume that the question will now be reconsidered by the medical authorities.

116. As to the porridge, which is the main staple of the native labourer's diet, some mines supply it in unlimited quantity, the native having only to come to the kitchen to be given as much as he wants without any question being raised as to whether he has already received his allowance. Elsewhere, the native has to produce his work ticket, which is stamped to indicate that he has received his portion. At the mines where the latter system obtains, the compound managers mostly assure me that any boy who wants another helping can get it for the asking. If so, there is no point in the production and stamping of the ticket; this can only be a precaution against the same boy coming twice. Even if, in fact, a native who asked would get some more, the system is manifestly likely to impress him with the contrary notion.

117. It seems quite clear that to give an unlimited supply costs no more than to give a limited ration; in fact, the evidence rather indicates that it costs less. There is nothing improbable in this; where a ration is given, its size must be conditioned by the largest appetite (within reason) of the class of persons rationed. As a result, those with smaller appetites waste a portion of what is given to them. If, however, anyone who wants more can get it, then the amount originally dished out can be reduced to the standard of the smallest appetite, or somewhere near it, and only a certain proportion of the persons fed will want more. Thus a lot of what was wasted under the other system is never served out at all.

118. The unlimited supply system has the further merit of simplifying the mechanism of issue both for the mine and for the boy, there being no production or stamping of tickets. It seems to me obviously the better method, and I have not been able to learn of any objection to it. It also provides an absolute and conclusive answer to any complaint of insufficiency of food.

119. There were several complaints that natives who had been detained underground exceptionally late came up to find the food all finished. It is, of course, easy to provide against this by seeing that, whenever a gang has to be detained to an unusual hour, a message is sent to the compound. Even without this precaution, the compound authorities always know the number to be provided for and the average per head required, so there should never be a shortage, however late some of the employees return.

120. I see reason to believe that there may be an occasional shortage here and there, not due to deliberate stinting of the food but to imperfect organisation. On one mine at least, there appeared to be no system for deciding the amount of mealie meal to be cooked every day; instead of taking the number of boys in the compound and sending so much a head to the kitchen, the issuer seemed to be roughly guessing what would be wanted. The result of this, over a period, was a considerable increase in the amount issued and probably a good deal of waste, but, obviously, such a happy-go-lucky method might easily cause a shortage on a particular day, if a lot of new boys had just arrived. Also, any omission to follow a strict system gives opportunities for theft.

121. I think that more attention might with advantage be paid to cleanliness in cooking and serving. Some of the compound kitchens are most unappetising places; and a good many of the meals which I have seen served must have contained, before they were eaten, a proportion of dust which might be much reduced

by sprinkling the compound with water at meal times on windy days. I have, however, received hardly any complaints on this point, so that I suppose the standard attained satisfies the natives generally.

122. I think, also, that on some mines more effort might be made to meet the individual tastes of special classes of natives, *e.g.*, letting Mozambiques have rice instead of porridge, etc. Even where there are only a few of the class, the expense and trouble involved would be very small.

123. I would suggest the amendment of the regulations on one point. There is a footnote to the ration scale running as follows:—

"The attention of employers is specially directed to the value of a hot ration given to boys about to go underground, for instance, a ration of bread and tea, coffee or cocoa, with sugar, or a ration of bread and soup."

124. Some employers ignore this polite intimation, and I think it might well be put in a more peremptory form. Any one who has had personal experience of doing heavy physical labour needs no medical knowledge to be aware of the value —I should be inclined to say the necessity—of a ration of this kind before starting.

125. A good many boys have asked that they should be given a food allowance and left to find themselves. It is perfectly certain that they would not feed themselves so wholesomely as the mines feed them; the present ration scales have been considered and reconsidered over and over again by a great variety of medical men. Also, a *minimum* scale is prescribed by law and enforced on the companies, which it could not be on the individual native. Many natives, especially after they have been here some time, have a taste for all manner of tinned abominations; and it would certainly not be good for them to live on such things.

126. Again, the cost of food to the mine is about 4d. to 6d. per head per day. This very cheap rate is due to the wholesale manner in which the feeding is dealt with, and, if the same amount of money were handed to the individual native, he could not feed himself properly upon it. To let the native feed himself therefore, means either an addition to the cost of labour or a reduction in the net earnings of the native.

127. At the Premier and other diamond mines, the natives do find themselves. The amount spent on foodstuffs in the compound stores at the Premier averages 11d. per head per day; but the average earnings per shift of the Premier natives are 3s., while those of the Reef native are 1s. 11d.

128. Generally speaking, I do not think there is much to complain of in the food supplied to native labourers on the mines. The prescribed scale appears to be generally adhered to, although strict adherence is not insisted upon; if the mine provides food of approximately the quantity and food value laid down, no objection is taken to minor variations in accordance with the view of the compound manager and medical officer concerned. I think this is a wise course; it allows for experiment and improvement.

129. There were not a great number of complaints as to the food provided.

WASHING ARRANGEMENTS.

130. In some few compounds there is no supply of hot water available for natives. I think there always should be.

FIRING.

131. On some mines natives complain of an insufficiency of coal and wood. The contracts provide for rations and quarters, but make no explicit reference to firing. It is, however, universally understood to be included; and, were natives are, as often happens, given their meat uncooked, it is only reasonable that they should be provided with means of cooking it. This is not always done; some natives who are given raw rations are regularly buying large quantities of firewood.

MARRIED QUARTERS.

132. Many mines have so-called married quarters, or locations, apart from the compound, for natives who have brought their wives with them. For these a rent varying from 6s. to 12s. 6d. per room per month is charged. More than one mine, in fact, where the natives in the location have to provide their own houses, charge up to 7s. 6d. a month as a species of ground rent. This, however, includes sanitary and other charges.

133. Several natives complained of having to pay this rent, claiming that the employer had to lodge the servant. The mines are quite ready to admit the boys to the compounds, and they have never undertaken to lodge the families of employees. At the same time, I think the rent is, in some cases, excessive for the accommodation provided.

134. Most mines would prefer to abolish these locations, finding them a source of liquor and other vice. I think these charges are, generally speaking, well grounded. While there are cases of reputable and respectable natives living in the locations, there is no doubt that many of the women there are not, in any sense, the wives of the men with whom they are living, but are mere temporary concubines, often locally picked up, who contribute to the household the proceeds of liquor selling and prostitution.

135. If it be considered desirable to provide for the permanent settlement of married natives upon the mines, the locations should be established at a substantial distance from the compounds, should offer a better class of building and, generally, should cater for the civilised and decent class of natives. The married quarters of the Dynamite Factory at Modderfontein show what can be done in this way.

136. The locations have been greatly improved of late years; but much still remains to be done. There is certainly some demand on the part of a few of the better class of natives for such accommodation, and I think that a good deal more trouble should be taken to see that the locations are reserved for respectable families. It is not, of course, practicable to demand the marriage certificate of every couple applying, but I imagine that there is no great difficulty in ascertaining from the alleged husband's compatriots whether the woman he wishes to introduce is really entitled, from the native point of view, to the *status* of a wife.

137. The result of this policy, if steadily pursued, would be to alter entirely the character of the location. At present they are responsible for a large proportion of the drink and disorder among natives; they are regarded with suspicion by the police and are constantly being raided. I think they might be made the reverse of this—a refuge for the quieter and more domesticated class of natives, which would lose all attraction for the livelier spirits.

138. I suggest that, where space is available, a location should be established, with huts and, if practicable, a bit of cultivable ground, and that this should be carefully superintended and reserved for reputable married natives. I see many reasons for doubting whether the native will take to the scheme or whether, even if he does, it will be good for him to settle permanently on the Rand; but, in view of Surgeon-General Gorgas' strong recommendations in favour of decentralisation on grounds of health, the experiment is worth trying. It has been attempted in Natal, without much success, but I do not know the details.

POLICE RAIDS.

139. There have been many complaints of the disturbance caused in compounds and locations by police raids in search of illicit liquor. I do not see how such searches can possibly be discontinued.

140. It is, however, desirable that, when the police have the compound surrounded, they should, before entering, send for the compound manager or his representative to accompany them. The intrusion of a number of strangers, especially if not in uniform, into a compound is liable to cause trouble with the natives, which would be less likely to arise if the party was accompanied by a familiar authority.

Delay in Discharge.

141. Complaint has been made that mines only pay once a week, so that a native who is employed on a mine which pays, *e.g.*, on Thursdays, is compelled, if he completes his contract on a Friday, to wait nearly a week before he can get money and go away.

142. This only applies to a few mines; the majority, while only paying the mass of natives on one particular day, have arrangements whereby a boy due for discharge can be paid and depart as soon as his contract is up. There is no reason why the remainder of the mines should not fall into line in this respect and thus remove a distinct grievance.

Compound Police.

143. In every compound the compound manager is assisted by a number of natives who are called police. They are not, of course, police at all, in the proper sense, but merely employees of the mine like the rest of the native labourers. They are, however, in fact invested with considerable, if rather vague, powers over the remainder of the natives; and the principal policeman, known as " the induna," is a person of very great consequence indeed in the compound.

144. The compound manager, having to control several thousand natives with the assistance of, at most, one or two other white men, must have some force of this kind. At the same time, such a force, armed with powers which depend entirely on the will of the particular compound manager and submitted to no discipline except what he chooses to enforce, may very easily become oppressive; and it is not surprising that many complaints have been received on this point.

145. A good many of these complaints may be put down to tribal jealousy; every tribe objects to being ordered about by a member of another tribe. This is generally met by choosing a policeman from each tribe which is represented in the compound in any considerable numbers; but the induna must belong to one tribe or another, and his appointment will usually give dissatisfaction to all tribes other than his own.

146. Allowing, however, for this feeling, I have no doubt that many complaints against these compound police are well founded. Allegations of habitual assaults are common; and, although most compound managers assert that they never allow their police to touch other natives, I notice that it is the ordinary practice of such police to carry sjamboks. Of course these may be, as I am assured, merely badges of office; but, when you put an offensive weapon into the hands of a savage, I doubt whether it is easy to convince him that he carries it solely for ornamental purposes. I have also seen natives—presumably police or bossboys—going underground similarly armed; and I have failed to learn what portion of their duties below requires to be performed with a sjambok.

147. The Director of Native Labour thinks that knobkerries would be better, on the ground that the native would have a greater feeling of responsibility in handling a weapon which may do serious injury. The W.N.L.A. substituted knobkerries for sjamboks three and a half years ago and have no single case of injury during that time. This is certainly strong evidence in support of the Director's suggestion: but I remain unconvinced that any weapon is necessary. If nothing but a badge of office is required, a brassard or armlet would suffice.

148. There were also many complaints that the compound police took too much upon themselves, interfering with natives who wished to speak to the compound manager, and generally usurping the latter's functions. This must always be the tendency of a body of this kind: and it is an abuse which needs constant watching by compound managers. Mr. B. G. Lloyd's experience with East Coast boys as police is that, after a couple of years or so, even the best of them degenerate and that frequent changes are desirable.

149. The method of selecting these police boys varies a great deal. Some compound managers allow each tribe to choose its own policeman, subject, of

course, to the compound manager's right of veto and discharge; and they assure me that they have found this system satisfactory. Other compound managers appoint the police themselves; others, again, take boys recommended by recruiters on account of their local influence or—what amounts to the same thing—boys who bring a large batch of recruits to the mine. At the mines which adopt the first system complaints of the conduct of the police were markedly below the average.

150. It should be remembered that the police boy is not solely a repressive force. He is largely used as an intermediary between the natives and the compound manager and has, in fact, a sort of representative position. Hence the complaints when any tribe has not a police boy of its own.

151. In this connection I may point out the desirability of having, as such intermediaries, natives who have had underground experience. In some cases boys who have never done underground work are virtually forced by recruiters upon compound managers, the object being to reward by a soft job a boy who has been useful in recruiting. This is hardly fair upon the compound manager, who is responsible for the control of the compound and should be free to choose his own assistants; nor can such a boy properly appreciate the troubles of the ordinary working native.

152. It has frequently been suggested that the policing of the compounds should be turned over to the South African Police and that compound police should be abolished. The only experiment of the kind which I know of was undertaken by the Transvaal Police when the Johannesburg Municipal Location at Klipspruit was created. From Major Douglas' evidence it appears that constant friction arose between the police and the compound authorities; and, about 1910, the police were withdrawn from patrolling the location, and now only come in when called upon by the compound manager.

153. I do not think that such a change would be desirable. To have the police directly interfering within the compound would tend to undermine the influence of the compound manager. That officer holds a very difficult and a very responsible position, and nothing should be done which might decrease his authority over his natives.

154. Also, a police boy's job is one of the plums of the mine service; if the police took it over, one of the labourer's none too plentiful chances of promotion would be stopped, and this might have a prejudicial effect on the labour supply.

REDRESS OF GRIEVANCES.

155. On a large number of mines the natives stated that they had no one to complain to, or that complaints produced no visible effect. I think that these assertions require a liberal discount and that many of them simply mean that the complaint, upon investigation, proved to be unfounded, a finding which naturally did not satisfy the complainant.

156. Apart from this. I think there are several matters which contribute to this grievance. For one thing, in cases where a complaint by a native against a miner has been found proved and the miner reprimanded or otherwise dealt with, that result has, in the supposed interests of discipline, been concealed from the native. I do not think this course wise: discipline is not maintained by maintaining a transparent fiction of infallibility on the part of superiors; and a grievance is not effectually redressed unless it is known to be redressed.

157. In a complicated organisation like a large mining company, a native may sometimes be in doubt as to the proper person to whom to prefer his particular complaint. I do not, however, think that this cause operates at all largely: on most mines the compound manager is willing to take up any kind of complaint by a native and forward it to the proper quarter, and most natives know this.

158. A more frequent cause of this complaint is that the compound manager has communicated to the underground staff a complaint concerning their depart-

ment, but has not been able to get any satisfaction. It is difficult to suggest any remedy for this; there is a natural tendency for the underground manager or mine captain to support his own subordinates, and sometimes also an inadequate appreciation on their part of the damaging effect of discontent in the compound upon the native labour supply and, in consequence, upon the output of the mine. In this matter a great deal depends upon the attitude of the manager. The compound manager, from the nature of his business, cannot have a detailed acquaintance with underground circumstances and will always be defeated by the underground men unless supported by the superior of both parties.

159. I think that, on some mines, the compound manager does not carry so much weight with the management as he should do. It has been suggested to me that an Association of Compound Managers, on the lines of the Mine Managers' Association, would tend to remedy this. I do not know enough about the working of such associations to express an opinion, but I am decidedly in favour of anything which tends to strengthen the compound manager's position.

160. Since the inquiry began, the Director has, under Regulation 17 (a), required a record to be kept of all complaints, showing how they are dealt with, for the information of the Native Affairs Inspector of the District. This should have a good effect, since the Inspector, if he is not satisfied with what is done, can exercise more pressure upon the management than the compound manager, as an employee of the mine, is in a position to do.

161. Another cause of this complaint is the natural disinclination of many natives, especially of certain tribes, to approach a white man with their troubles. This is largely met by the almost universal practice of appointing the compound police in accordance with the tribes inhabiting the compound, so that each section shall have its own representative, through whom complaints can be made. That such a representative is very necessary, appears from the many complaints received that such and such a tribe has no policeman. In most of these cases enquiry has shown that there were not enough of the tribe in that particular compound to warrant such an appointment. Where possible, it would certainly make for contentment to eliminate these small sections by collecting them on those mines where there are already a considerable number of their compatriots.

EDUCATIONAL FACILITIES.

162. A complaint has reached me that native labourers who are partially educated have no facilities for continuing their education or practising their religion in or near the compounds. This must always be largely left to the discretion of the compound manager: the latter cannot be expected to allow in his compound, under pretence of preaching or teaching, a native whom he believes to have a mischievous influence. But I think it would be quite reasonable to require that, in every compound, there should be set aside accommodation for educational and religious meetings.

163. I hardly think it necessary to add that educated and partly educated natives should have the opportunity of keeping together, apart from others. As a rule, the selection of each boy's room in a compound is largely left to himself, so they can settle their own company.

164. Special passes to attend school and church might, no doubt, be given more freely than is at present done in some compounds. I do not, however, see that any general rule can be laid down upon that point. But any employer who, for his own purposes, collects members of a less civilised race in large numbers lies under a very clear duty to give them the opportunity to get such advantages as they can from the contact with a more advanced civilisation. Unfortunately, the disadvantages to which they are exposed by that contact are many and easily attainable.

[U.G. 37—'14.]

165. The abolition of special passes has been asked for in this connection, but I do not think it practicable. The matter has been considered on several previous occasions, but the police have always been opposed to it in the interests of public order. Certainly, the last class who could safely be freed from such a check are the mine labourers; the prospect of several thousand natives who wanted to have a faction fight being at liberty to go out and have it in the open, or even in town, without asking anybody's leave, is too serious to be contemplated.

CHAPTER III.

COMPLAINTS AS TO HOSPITAL TREATMENT.

CHAPTER III.

Complaints as to Hospital Treatment.

166. Many complaints arising out of the treatment of natives when sick have been made to me. The grounds of some are, I think, removable; others are due to native ignorance, and do not, properly speaking, constitute grievances. It will be convenient to deal with the latter first.

Underfeeding.

167. On a very large number of mines there was a complaint that natives in hospitals are starved. This arises from the fact that, on most mines, natives coming into hospital on the medical side are put upon milk diet until it can be definitely determined from what disease they are suffering. It is matter of common knowledge that, for certain diseases, this is the only safe diet; and it cannot, in any case, do harm. The period that must elapse before the doctor can be certain of his diagnosis is probably longer in the case of a native than in that of a European, owing to the incapacity of doctor and patient to understand each other's language, and also, I suppose, to the deficiency in native languages of terms suited to the exact description of symptoms. In most cases, the only information which the doctor can get from the patient is an indication as to the part of the body which is giving trouble; for the rest, he has to rely mainly upon the thermometer and external symptoms. Even after the disease is diagnosed, it is very often—in the case of diseases involving a temperature, always—necessary to retain the patient upon a light diet.

168. The native does not understand these facts, and it seems to him gratuitous cruelty, or even a deliberate plot against his life, that he should be deprived of solid food and that his friends should be prevented from supplying him even at their private expense.

169. I do not see how this source of discontent can be entirely got over, in the present state of native intelligence and education. Clearly, the doctor cannot, out of deference to the patient's ignorant prejudices, treat the latter in a fashion which the doctor believes to be injurious: such a course of action would be a breach of trust. The trouble will continue until the native has arrived at understanding, if not the reason for all the doctor does, at least that the doctor is more likely to be right than the patient. This process can be accelerated in two ways—apart from the general elevation of the native—by doctors endeavouring to obtain the confidence of their native patients by sympathetic treatment and by explaining to them, as far as possible, the purpose of the restrictions imposed, and by persons of influence with the natives using every occasion to make it clear that European methods of medicine, though different from native methods, are unquestionably superior.

170. Meanwhile, it seems that the treatment can, in some cases at any rate, be modified so as partly to meet the natives' prejudice. At three hospitals where I received no complaint on these grounds, I found that, in addition to milk, either soup, thin mealie meal or beef tea was given; and rice added to the diet at an early stage.

171. As for food brought in by friends, there is no reason why patients suffering from surgical injuries, etc., should not be allowed to have such food. It is, however, difficult to keep it from reaching those cases which ought not to be allowed it; and for this reason some hospitals attempt to exclude imported food altogether. A better method, which is in use on some mines, is to have a special ward for those cases confined to milk diet. This is both more effective in itself and less inconvenient to visitors to and patients in the other wards.

Dressing of Wounds.

172. A constantly recurring complaint is that wounds have nothing put on them in the way of ointment, etc. This is of course absurd; it simply means that the native does not realise that all dressings are ready treated with antiseptics.

173. A somewhat similar complaint is that wounds are only dressed on the day of admission to hospital. Probably this refers to wounds caused by primary operations, in which case I understand that the modern practice is to leave the dressing on for a week or so.

COMPULSORY TREATMENT.

174. There have been many complaints that natives who feel sick are not allowed to stay in the compound but are compelled, if they do not go to work, to go to hospital. I do not think that this objection is reasonable: if any employee, whether European or native, is really sick, hospital is the best place for him. If he is not really sick, he ought to be at work or on leave. I have dealt elsewhere with the question of leave; and, putting that point on one side, I think that a native who says he is too sick to go to work should be confined to the hospital. If he is really ill, the hospital is the proper place for him: if he is malingering, the confinement is a reasonable punishment and deterrent.

NON-REPATRIATION.

175. Another very widespread complaint is that, while natives are engaged upon the understanding that they will be repatriated if they fall sick, they are not so repatriated. This is a difficult question. A native cannot reasonably expect to be released from his contract on account of sickness which is temporary and trifling; yet clearly many of them do so expect. It is still more out of the question that a native who cannot safely travel shall be sent home; yet his relatives often complain when this is not done.

176. I notice, however, that there appears to be great divergence among the medical officers as to when repatriation is necessary. The percentage of repatriation varies from less than 2 per cent. to more than 13 per cent. (Annexure 4). Some part of this variation is no doubt due to local circumstances; but part is also due to the different principles upon which medical officers act. When native A is repatriated from mine X on the ground of medical unfitness, and his brother B, suffering in precisely the same manner on mine Y, is detained, there may be sound reasons for each decision; but B will undoubtedly be discontented.

177. There is, I believe, a Mine Medical Officers' Association. If they could agree upon the general principles which should guide them in recommending repatriation, complaints of this class would probably be reduced. There is no uniformity of practice at present.

AMPUTATIONS.

178. Another point which gives rise to difficulty is that natives have a very strong dislike to amputations. Where the patient is unconscious and it is necessary to decide at once whether an amputation should or should not take place, the decision must be left to the medical man in charge, if there are no relatives on the spot. But, where the patient is conscious, it is quite clear that, as a matter of law, the decision must be left to the patient, whether he be European or native.

179. I always understood that professional ethics required the same course; and most mine medical officers follow it. I have, however, found cases where the surgeon takes upon himself to decide the matter, irrespective of, and sometimes in direct opposition to, the wishes of the patient. I think that, in every case, the patient, if conscious, or his relatives, where he is unconscious and there are relatives available, should be consulted. I do not believe that they will be found unreasonable if the matter is properly put to them: several doctors who follow the practice have told me that they find no difficulty in carrying it out.

180. There were various complaints of unnecessary amputations; but the complainants were not in a position to judge of the necessity. I do not think this complaint likely to be well founded: amputations cost the mine money and the doctor trouble.

DETECTION OF SICKNESS.

181. Many boys declare that their friends die in the mine hospitals of injuries and diseases which they could cure if they were allowed to take the patient home. Obviously, this is a matter upon which native opinion cannot weigh very heavily; but it seems to me capable of reasonable explanation. It is highly probable that, with regard to surgical injuries, they are right. The native at his kraal lives a very natural and, in the case of many tribes, a very cleanly life, so that cuts, etc., are likely to heal readily. The mines are, necessarily, full of all sorts of bacilli and are very dirty. It is easy to see that, under such circumstances, it needs the greatest care to prevent even small wounds from becoming septic; and natives take practically no care of small wounds. When allowance is made for this and also for the cheering effect upon a native's spirits of being sent home, it is easy to understand the underlying meaning of the complaint.

182. The only remedy that I can suggest is a closer scrutiny of those natives who do not report sick in order to discover, and treat as early as possible, minor injuries. The native is very chary of reporting sick. As a consequence, many cases do not reach the hospital until they have arrived at a stage much beyond that when medical advice should have been called in.

183. As long as a sick boy chooses to go to work, nothing can be done to discover him (short of a periodical examination of the whole compound) except to keep hospital attendants on the watch at the gate of the compound as the shifts are going down or coming up. This is adopted on several mines and results in the discovery of a considerable number of minor injuries which would otherwise not be reported until they had become serious. The amount of septicaemia has already been greatly reduced by this method.

184. In many cases, however, the sick native does not go to work, but hides himself either in the compound or outside. This can be detected by requiring an immediate report of any boy who is absent from his gang without explanation. Various systems with this object are in use on different mines, and I do not suppose that it much matters which is adopted. All that is required is that the compound manager should be advised at the earliest possible moment of the absence from work of any native, so that immediate search may be made for him and, if he is found to be sick, he may be sent to the hospital. It is especially necessary that thorough search should be made in the compound; a sick native there may be a centre of infection.

185. It is obvious that such a check is valuable for many other purposes than discovering sickness.

186. On a good many mines there is a periodical medical inspection. The whole compound, after taking off their coats, march past the doctors, who stop any boy who appears to them to be looking ill and subject him to a more detailed examination. I am informed that quite a number of cases are detected by this means, and I think that these inspections should be the rule on every mine.

187. All recruited boys are examined before distribution, and many of them are again examined on arrival at the mine. Voluntary boys, however, are not examined on arrival on some mines, as they dislike it, and it therefore tends to diminish the popularity of the compound. This objection could be got over if all mines agreed to insist upon it; and I think this should be done.

SCREENS.

188. I am informed that, in some mine hospitals, no provision is made for screening off the bed of a dying patient. If this is so, the matter should be remedied. Death is obnoxious to most people, especially to patients in a hospital, who feel themselves within measurable distance of it; and it is peculiarly obnoxious to many natives, whose tribal customs require the removal of the dying to a secluded spot.

Visiting Hours.

189. There were several complaints that natives were not allowed to visit their friends in hospital. At some hospitals the facilities for visits were somewhat inadequate; but I think that, in most cases, this has now been altered. The isolation of the sick native from his ordinary companions is one of the causes of the unpopularity of hospitals. It is worth while to mitigate this, as far as possible, by liberal visiting regulations.

Castor Oil.

190. A frequent complaint, in one form or another, is that all patients are treated alike—"always castor oil" is the way the native generally puts it. The foundation for this appears to be that, in some mine hospitals, all patients on the medical side are given a purgative as a matter of course on admission. Several doctors have told me that this is perfectly right and the usual practice: several others, when I asked them if they did it, scoffed at the idea. It is not done in the Johannesburg General Hospital.

191. Similarly, some medical officers habitually use castor oil for this purpose; others hardly ever, substituting other purgatives to which natives do not have the same dislike.

192. In matters of this kind, which divergency of practice proves to be indifferent from the medical point of view, I do not see why the tastes of the patient should not be studied.

Malingering.

193. Another frequent complaint is that natives who report sick are accused of malingering and ordered to go to work. It is tolerably obvious that an English doctor who speaks no native language, while he may be able to declare with certainty that a native is ill, cannot be equally positive that he is not ill. The inducements to a native to malinger are very small. He gets no pay—and pay is what has induced him to come to the Rand at all—and where the rule is (as I think it should always be) that a native must be either at work, on leave or in hospital, he spends the day under conditions that he very much dislikes. It seems to me that there is very little prospect of much malingering on a properly administered mine: and I would suggest that, whenever a native professes to be ill, he should be taken into hospital without question and, if the doctor cannot detect any malady, be put to bed on milk diet. Such treatment cannot harm any native: it will greatly displease the genuine malingerer; and it will eliminate any chance of a native who is really ill being sent to work. I do not believe that it will materially diminish the efficiency factor of any mine.

194. I see reason to believe that, in some cases, too much is left to the hospital superintendent. There seems to me often no sufficient security that he may not reject natives reporting sick, without consulting the medical officer. The difficulties of diagnosis which I have already pointed out are, of course, even greater to the superintendent than to the doctor; and I do not consider any system satisfactory under which the superintendent weeds out the sick parade and under which only those natives who pass this test ever see the doctor at all.

195. I think more caution should be exercised in rejecting patients on the ground that they are malingering. Dr. Adam, of Randfontein, told me that he would not venture to reject a boy on that ground except after careful observation for several days. When such an opinion is seriously held by an experienced mine medical officer, it cannot be right that there should be any opportunity for unqualified hospital superintendents to reject a patient off hand. Cases have occurred where natives brought before a court upon a charge of loafing have proved to be seriously ill.

196. Malingering would certainly be checked by a more frequent grant of leave. If a boy knows that he can stay away from work for a day or two by simply asking, he will be under no temptation to feign sickness. Many mines are already fairly generous in this respect, others less so. I think that, seeing the native's disinclination for continuous labour, it would be worth the while of

every mine to let it be known among their boys that any native who wants a day off can have it for the asking—subject, of course, to the exigencies of the work. Where this system is in practice, it does not seem to be abused or to cause inconvenience in working. The absence of pay for such days is an automatic check on excess.

Work in Hospital.

197. In the case of several mines it has been shown that convalescent patients are compelled to work. In most cases the work is trifling; in some, it seems to me substantial. But, in either case, there is no difficulty in adjusting the matter. As long as a native is in hospital, he should not be compelled to do any sort or kind of work whatever. Natives do not love hospital so much that they will stay there—earning nothing—in order to avoid going to work.

198. Some medical officers state that, during convalescence, it is good for the patient to do some work, as a matter of exercise. There are, however, mine hospitals where no work at all is done by any patient, so that the desirability of insisting on light work for convalescents would seem to be simply the opinion of individual medical officers, not a settled practice of the profession.

199. In any case, work done should be paid for—of course on a scale proportioned to its value. This is already done on some mines, 6d. a day being the scale. I am sure that the native dislike to hospital, which is very marked and, in my opinion, very regrettable, since it induces him to avoid treatment in the earlier stages, would be mitigated by the abolition of work or by payment for whatever was done.

Change Houses.

200. It seems to me that change houses ought to be provided for all natives, not merely for tropicals. The native, like the European, often comes up from his underground work with his skin and his clothes—such as they are—soaking in sweat or in water. Under these conditions, the proper course for everyone— white or black—is to change into dry things before facing the outer air. This would seem even more necessary for Africans than for Europeans: among the latter the homeborn, at any rate, have been considerably hardened in youth by the eccentricities of what we are pleased to call our climate.

201. Under the present conditions, on some mines, the opportunity for changing is simply what the native can arrange in his corner of a compound room; and he has sometimes to go half a mile or more through the open air before he can reach it. The provision for drying wet clothes is simply the sun and the veld.

202. Of course precautions must be taken to maintain discipline in the change houses and see that natives do not do foolish things like going from a hot bath into the open air in wet clothes. Annexure 5 shows the conditions on which the W.N.L.A. insisted in the case of tropical natives; and they seem to me excellent.

Medical Attendance.

203. An important question in connection with native mine hospitals is whether they receive an adequate amount of medical attention. After hearing a great deal of evidence on this point and studying a large number of statistical returns, I have come to the conclusion that it is impossible to give a definite answer to this question, because with regard to many hospitals no information exists as to the amount of attention really given. It is easy enough to ascertain the number of medical officers attached to each mine and the proportion which they bear to the daily average of patients; but the factor which baffles all inquiry is that a large number of them have other duties and that it is impossible to ascertain what proportion of their time and energy they devote to the hospital or hospitals under their charge. In most cases no records are kept even of the hours at which medical officers have attended native hospitals.

204. It is evident that a doctor with one small mine hospital may easily do it full justice and yet have time for private practice: it is equally evident that a doctor with a private practice sufficient to absorb all his energies cannot properly attend to that and also to, say, a couple of large mine hospitals. That he must neglect or scamp some part of his business is certain; and there is considerable probability, based on obvious considerations, that the private practice will get the best of the practitioner's energies.

205. It is, of course, impossible to say, without a careful inquiry into the particular case, that a particular practitioner is undertaking too much work: the amount that a man can do satisfactorily depends on innumerable individual considerations, such as his own power of work, the local situation of his private patients, etc., etc. To make such an inquiry would necessitate constant observation, preferably by a medical man, of each hospital during a long period.

206. But, though I cannot possibly decide whether individual medical officers or any particular proportion of the total number are neglecting their native mine hospitals, there is no difficulty in asserting that the part time system places them under strong temptation to do so; and doctors are not exempt from the universal law of human nature that the stronger a temptation the higher percentage of men will succumb to it. That this view is shared by, at any rate, some portion of medical opinion is shown by an article in the *South African Medical Journal* of 10th January, 1914, which points out the "almost impossible moral strain" upon a medical man whose attention is competed for by Europeans who can enforce it and by natives who cannot. I entirely agree with this view.

207. Medical men who support the part time system have alleged that exclusive attendance upon native patients leads to insufficient work and is a peculiarly monotonous form of practice, which will tend to deter good men from undertaking it. I do not think good men ever have any difficulty in filling up their spare time; the article above quoted specially mentions the opportunities for research work which specialising in native hospital practice on the mines would offer, and such opportunities must be peculiarly attractive to many able practitioners.

208. One other argument used by the *Medical Journal* is that the part time system results in too much being left to the hospital superintendents. As I have pointed out above, I think that this defect already exists on the mines.

209. In those hospitals where whole time medical officers are employed, it is possible to ascertain how many patients the medical officer is actually attending; and the various figures reveal an extraordinary divergency of opinion as to the number of patients whom one doctor can adequately attend. Annexure 6 shows the average daily number of patients in those hospitals where there are whole time medical officers; and the number of patients per doctor varies from 84 to 265.

210. Annexure 7 shows that part time medical officers are, in addition to their other duties, in charge of native hospitals where the average daily number of patients per doctor varies from 19 to 352.

211. Even a layman may safely assert that either the doctor who devotes his whole time to 84 patients has an extremely soft job or that the 352 natives who get such time as their medical officer does not devote to his other duties are inadequately attended. In view of the number of less extreme figures given, it seems probable that there is some truth in both assertions.

212. I am informed by the medical men who appeared before me on behalf of the Witwatersrand Branch of the British Medical Association that they are not aware of any standard adoption in general hospitals as to the proportion of medical officers to average daily patients; nor could I get this information from any of the other doctors whom I questioned on the subject. I learn, however, that the Johannesburg Hospital, with a daily average of 446 patients, employs the exclusive services of 6 medical officers, showing a proportion of 75 patients to each, without allowing anything for the assistance of the staff of Honorary Visiting Physicians and Surgeons.

213. This comparison must be modified by the consideration that mine hospitals serve as convalescent homes and also contain a number of patients suffering

from trifling injuries, for which they would not be detained in the Johannesburg Hospital; so that the average patient in a mine hospital needs less attention than the average patient in the General Hospital. I do not, however, see how this difference can be reduced to figures; but even after making large allowance for its effect, if the number of medical officers at the Johannesburg Hospital is at all reasonable, that of some of the mine native hospitals must be insufficient.

214. Another test which may be applied is the total population under the care of each medical officer. Annexure 6 shows this with regard to whole time officers and Annexure 7 with regard to part time officers. These show that whole time officers are in charge of populations varying from 4,266 to 12,359 natives; while doctors, a part of whose time and energy are devoted to other duties, attend native populations varying from 307 to 8,614.

215. In January, 1914, the Public Service Commission advertised for a whole time medical officer for the Pretoria Central Prison. A correspondent signing himself "Medicus," who wrote to the *South African Medical Journal* of January, 1914, attacking the terms offered, stated the population concerned as 1,500 convicts, two-thirds white, and 500 staff, including women and children. He subjoined a list showing that, in Great Britain, the number of prisoners assigned to a medical officer varies from 120 at Perth to 583 at Dartmoor.

216. The February number of the *Journal* reported that a joint meeting representing the Pretoria and Witwatersrand Branches of the British Medical Association had decided to circularise members of these branches advising them not to apply for the appointment. The *Journal* supported this action, and, after giving other reasons for its view, added "But there is a third and even more important aspect to this problem. It may well be questioned whether any one medical officer, however, capable and energetic he may be, can satisfactorily discharge the duties of such an appointment."

217. The conditions of prison life, whether for convicts or warders, can hardly be less healthy than those of the native mine labourer. It is true that the native mine labourer has passed a medical examination before he gets to work at all, so that a large number of diseases which are at present in a general population have been eliminated from this particular class of patient; but the same is the case with prison officers. It follows that, in the opinion of, at any rate, a portion of the medical profession, the provision of a single medical officer for populations of mine labourers ranging up to 12,000 must be inadequate.

218. It has been pointed out that the average of native patients to every medical man on the mines is very much smaller than in Basutoland, the Transvaal, etc. I do not think that it is practicable to compare such very different propositions. In his own kraal the native is living his natural life, which happens also to be a singularly healthy one. At the mines he is living a highly unnatural and exceptionally unhealthy life. Besides, there is no reason to suppose that the supply of doctors in the native districts is adequate to the needs of the population; in most rural areas it certainly is not. The unfortunate fact that a remote farmer has, in any emergency, to send 40 miles for a doctor does not seem to me a reason for trying to reproduce that state of things in a large industrial community.

219. I think there is no room for doubt that, in most cases, the provision for medical attendance upon native mine labourers is inadequate.

220. Since writing the above paragraphs, a case has come to my notice where a native was injured by a fall of rock about 9 a.m., his leg being badly broken and great loss of blood occurring. He reached the mine hospital about 11 a.m. No attempt to get a doctor was made until 1.45 p.m., after the hospital superintendent had dressed the injury. A note was then sent to the mine medical officer (there being no telephone at the hospital) to which he replied that he could not come until 5 p.m., as he could not get an anæsthetist. The patient died, of shock and hæmorrhage, at 4.50 p.m., no doctor having seen him.

221. I wrote to the medical officer concerned, drawing his attention to the above facts and inquiring whether he wished to give evidence on the matter. I have received no reply, and therefore do not know the explanation, which may, of course, be quite satisfactory. As to the facts, there is, however, no doubt; that native, from whatever cause, did not receive adequate medical attention.

222. In June, 1913, the Director of Native Labour, in a report (called for by the Minister) to the Secretary for Native Affairs, expressed the opinion that " the attention given to-day to native labourers by most Mine Medical Officers is shockingly inadequate." The Minister read this passage in the House of Assembly. The Council of the Witwatersrand Branch of the British Medical Association has sent me a statement in which they pass several strictures upon the Director of Native Labour, and in which they say, *inter alia* :—

" We ask that you will kindly take all steps to ascertain the actual condition of affairs, to which we attach the request that you will express a definite opinion in your report whether the result of your investigations has led you to justify the above criticism as applied to Mine Medical Officers for natives on the Witwatersrand as a body."

223. I regret that I am unable to comply with this request. Even if my reference required it, which it does not—I was instructed to investigate the grievances of native labourers, not of Mine Medical Officers—I could not possibly do so. As pointed out in paragraphs 203-205 above, the question of whether the amount of attendance given by an individual medical officer is adequate can only be resolved by a close and prolonged inquiry into the nature and amount of his other work as well as into his ability, industry and conscientiousness. Clearly, I cannot do this in respect of every mine medical officer along the Reef; and without doing so, I cannot say whether or not the attendance by "most Mine Medical Officers " is adequate.

224. (In spite of what I said at the beginning of the last paragraph, I cannot, in the interests of my class, resist going outside my reference to point out that, in any case, the Association is in error in turning its guns upon the Director of Native Labour. A permanent official who, in the course of his duty, makes statements or offers opinions to his superiors is answerable for them to his superiors and to no one else. If an outside person or body questions him as to his communications with the Minister at the head of his Department, he is not only entitled but bound to tell the inquirer, of course in the most polite language possible, " to go—elsewhere." If the Minister chooses to publish the permanent official's opinions, that is a matter over which the official has no control, and for which he has therefore no responsibility; the Minister thereby adopts the opinion, and it is for the Minister to defend it.)

225. I think that the appointment of whole time medical officers for native mine labourers should be made compulsory. Any mine whose hospital contains an average number of natives sufficient to occupy a reasonable proportion of a medical man's time should be required to engage the exclusive services of such an officer.

226. In small hospitals it would not be reasonable to require this. Small mines lying adjacent to each other might, however, be required to maintain a joint hospital with a whole time medical officer. The extent to which this policy can be carried out is conditioned by the necessity of having the hospital tolerably close to the place where accidents happen, and to the residence of the probable patients. Where necessary, the Director, after consultation with a Government Medical Officer, might grant exemptions.

227. Although I have not been able to obtain from the medical witnesses any statement as to the number of patients that a single doctor can properly attend, I have no doubt that, with all the experience on the point which exists upon these fields, many doctors must know quite well how many native hospital patients can fairly be dealt with by one man. A proportion between medical officers and patients should be established by regulation.

228. It is an accepted principle that the mine native labourer needs a great deal of protection if he is to be properly treated; there is a large sub-division of the Native Affairs Department, under the charge of the Director of Native Labour, which is mainly occupied in providing this protection. When the labourer is sick, he certainly needs more protection than when he is well; and I do not think that this can be sufficiently provided by the Native Affairs Inspectors, who are

laymen and, however zealous, may easily overlook matters which a trained medical man would at once notice.

229. The Government does provide a certain amount of medical supervision to native hospitals. The Mines Medical Inspector and Medical Officer to the Native Affairs Department has certain powers of entry and examination under the Transvaal Native Labour Regulations, and, upon the report of this Officer, the Director of Native Labour can require certain defects to be remedied. The Medical Inspector, however, has a very extensive range of duties. He is required to supervise, from a health point of view, all the mines in the Transvaal, besides making occasional excursions to mines in the other Provinces. He inspects every compound (except those within Johannesburg Municipality) and every mine hospital. The amount of time and labour consumed in every such inspection may be judged from the forms which he fills in (Annexures 8 and 9). He is also concerned with the conditions underground.

230. Under these circumstances, only a limited portion of his time can be devoted to mine hospitals. As there are 94 native hospitals in the Transvaal, scattered from Randfontein to Springs on the Reef, and some of them as far away as Nigel, Witbank, Vereeniging and the Premier, it is manifestly impossible for this officer to know them all intimately. I think that the Native Affairs Department should be given more medical assistance to supervise native hospitals.

Nursing Staff.

231. The nursing in native mine hospitals is done by male natives, under the supervision of European superintendents. In some cases there is no separate superintendent, the compound manager undertaking this in addition to his other duties.

232. There is no provision requiring that hospital superintendents should have any qualifications whatever. In a European hospital, it is a matter of course that anyone holding such a position shall be a trained and qualified person. As a matter of fact, many of the existing superintendents do hold qualifications of one kind or another; but they need not.

233. There is no existing test which might reasonably be utilised for this purpose, and no training school for male nurses in this country. The Transvaal Medical Council holds an examination for female nurses, but not for male nurses. I think there should be a regulation establishing a test which should be required in all future appointments.

234. There were many complaints of assault by the attendants in the mine hospitals. I think that these were greatly exaggerated, but had some foundation. The large majority of the attendants are male natives, mostly recruited from among the mineboys and practically all without any training except what they have picked up in the course of their duties. Seeing that there is a normal hospital population along the mines of over 5,000, and that about 500 native attendants are employed in nursing them, it seems to me that it would be well worth while to make some provision for training natives in these duties.

235. The Johannesburg General Hospital employs trained native orderlies in the native male wards under the supervision of European sisters. This seems to afford an opportunity for creating a body of trained native male nurses for use in mine hospitals.

236. The experiment has been tried of sending partially trained mine hospital attendants to Johannesburg Hospital to be further trained; but it failed because they would not stand the discipline. It seems to follow that, in the important matter of discipline, the standard of the mine hospital was below that required in the General Hospital.

237. The native mine hospitals deal with a comparatively limited range of disease, so that it would not be necessary to have such an elaborate training as nurses in general hospitals undergo; but some training is certainly desirable.

238. An obstacle in the way of obtaining skilled attendants is the small rate of pay. The N.R.C. Schedule B limited the maximum payment for hospital atten-

dants to 2s. a shift. This has now been increased to 2s. 6d.; but even the latter figure is not adequate remuneration for trained work.

239. I think that facilities should be provided for training native male nurses, that rates of pay should be offered which would induce natives to avail themselves of those facilities and that, when a sufficient supply of trained attendants is available, the employment of untrained ones (except as probationers) should be prohibited.

240. In the Johannesburg Hospital, with a daily average of 446 patients, the nursing staff consists of 174 persons, an average of one to every $2\frac{1}{2}$ patients. Over the whole of the native mine hospitals there is an average of one white man for every 51 patients, and one native for every 10·5 patients; taking Europeans and natives together, this gives one attendant to 8·7 patients (Annexure 10). Nor can all of those attendants be considered as nursing staff; in many cases the return includes every member of the staff of the mine hospital, including cooks, cleaners, etc.

241. This average is widely departed from on individual mines; a white man may have as many as 129 or as few as four patients to look after on the average; and sometimes one native is provided for every two patients, sometimes for every 22 patients (Annexure 10).

242. On the night of the 27/28th June, 1913, the Native Affairs Inspectors paid a surprise visit to the native mine hospitals. The reports leave no doubt that some hospitals are insufficiently staffed or supervised. The variation in the proportion of attendants to patients leads to the same conclusion. While local conditions may, here and there, justify some variation, it is, broadly speaking, certain that a given number of patients, drawn from one class and working under similar conditions needs a corresponding number of attendants.

243. I think a standard relation between the number of attendants and the number of patients should be compulsory. Understaffing must lead to hurry and loss of temper, and thus contribute to the danger of roughness with patients.

Hospital Charges.

244. There have been, in the past, some cases where a charge has been made to natives for certain services, such as drawing teeth, etc. If that exists anywhere now, it should be stopped; under the labourer's contract he is entitled to free medical attendance.

Burials.

245. A certain number of complaints arise out of matters connected with the burial of the dead. The most frequent of these is that no coffins are provided unless paid for by the friends of the deceased. I gather, however, from witnesses acquainted with native customs, that it is only among a minority of natives of the class from which mine labourers are drawn that coffins are used for the burial of those who die at their kraals. In these circumstances and in the absence of any stipulation on the subject in the contracts, I do not consider that this constitutes a grievance. All that can be expected of the mines is that the dead should be buried, as far as possible, in the manner in which the majority of them would have been buried if they had died at home.

246. There were some complaints about the native cemeteries on mines. In one case it was said that the graves were too shallow; but this has now been corrected. In some cases old cemeteries have been covered with mining debris; and even those in use are not always properly fenced and cared for. The common law of South Africa, no less than considerations of ordinary decency, demands that any burial place be treated as *res religiosa* and exempted from commerce. All such cemeteries should be properly fenced off and preserved from other uses.

247. Some boys said that they were not allowed to bury their dead themselves; others that they were compelled to bury strangers. Some mines are subject to municipal by-laws which prescribe methods of burial. On those, however, which have their own cemeteries, there seems no reason why the practice, which already obtains on most of them, of leaving the friends of the deceased to conduct the interment in accordance with their own customs (subject, of course, to supervision as to health and decency) should not be universally adopted.

248. Where the burial is conducted by the Municipality, certain fees are charged, which are deducted from the deceased's estate. Some boys put this forward as a grievance. I do not consider it as such; all estates are subject to such deductions.

CHAPTER IV.

COMPLAINTS AS TO PAY.

CHAPTER IV

COMPLAINTS AS TO PAY

WAGES GENERALLY.

249. The demand for higher pay is universal, as it would be from any body of wage-earners who were asked to state their grievances. The only mine where this claim was not put forward was one where, a month before my visit, the natives had actually gone on strike for an increase.

250. In a good many cases the complaint took the form of a reference to "the good old times" before the war; and I heard wonderful tales of the money that used to be earned. How far these were correct cannot be ascertained with accuracy, since detailed records of the pay for different classes of work have not been kept until recently. Also, it is not possible to ascertain whether free railway fares should be added to some of the figures, since, until 1912, there was no uniformity in this matter, some mines giving them and some not doing so. It is also not always clear whether the earlier figures refer to a calendar month or to a period of 30 shifts. Subject to these considerations, the figures supplied by the Chamber of Mines are as follows. The average pay of all natives for 30 shifts was:—

1890	...	...	...	...	43/- or 49/7½
1898	...	...	...	...	49/9 or 57/5
1902	...	...	...	...	34/8
1906	...	...	...	...	56/-
1910	...	...	...	...	54/1

251. Since 1910, records are available showing surface and underground **wages** separately. The figures are:—

				Underground.	*Surface.*
1910	...	...	...	56/7	47/7
1913	...	...	...	58/9	53/3

252. Since 1st July, 1910, hammerboys' wages have been similarly distinguished, and show:—

| 1910 (last 6 months) | ... | ... | ... | ... | 61/11 |
| 1913 | ... | ... | ... | ... | 68/6 |

253. In May, 1897, the Chamber agreed upon a uniform schedule of wages (Annexure 11). This, compared with the present schedule (Annexures 12 and 13) so far as the different classification allows, shows that the rates underground are, in nearly all cases, higher now than they were 17 years ago. On the surface, some rates have risen, others fallen, while some are practically the same. Without knowing the proportion of each class now and formerly employed, it is not possible to say whether surface rates, as a whole, are higher or lower. Taking surface and underground together, they are certainly higher.

254. On the other hand, I am told that the schedule of 1897 represented a reduction of approximately one-third on the scale previously in force; if so, wages were higher in 1896 than they are now.

255. The most recent revision, which took effect at the end of 1912, is that expressed in Schedule B. of the N.R.C. The mines concerned—and these employ 80 per cent. of the total native mine labourers—have agreed to pay these rates and no others. Those rates (which are set out in Annexures 12 and 13) have resulted in a slight decrease of the previous rates paid to the natives as a whole, the average per shift for 1912 being 1s. 11·58d., and for 1913 1s 11·075d. The hammerboys, however, have profited by the change, their average for 1912 being 2s. 2·75d. while, in 1913, it was 2s. 3·175d.

256. A change which is in effect a reduction of wages is that several mines, which formerly used to pay the railway fares of natives recruited to work on them, have, since the N.R.C. started, ceased to do so, and now deduct the amount of the fare from each native's wages.

257. There is at present a decided tendency, which, as far as I can judge, is likely to increase, to substitute machines for hammers. This means a reduction in the native's average wage; hammerboys average 2s. 4d. per shift, and machine boys only 2s. 0·5d. Also, since two machine boys break as much ground as 12 hammerboys, many of the natives taken off hammers will be put on to lashing and tramming, at which work the average pay is only about 1s. 8d. per shift.

258. The existing rates of pay average about £2 12s. 6d. per calendar month (allowing for 26 working days). As will be seen from Annexure 14, this does not differ greatly from the amount paid for similar work in other parts of South Africa.

259. Probably the mines could increase their average wages without cost to themselves by increasing the proportion of piecework. On the Reef generally only 33·7 per cent. of the native labourers are on piecework; on individual mines the proportion varies from 66 per cent. to 13·8 per cent. (Annexure 15).

260. At the Village Deep, all the boys are on piecework, with the result that the average rate for July, 1913, though affected by the strike, was 2s. for both machine and lashing boys, while the average over the Reef was something under 1s. 10d. The management are satisfied that they are getting value for their money.

261. At the Brakpan Mines a recent substitution of piecework for day's pay among lashers and trammers has resulted in the average earnings going up to 2s. 2d., whereas the day's pay rate is from 1s. 6d. to 2s. In this case also the mine considers that it has gained by the change.

262. At the Modder B., a change of the lashing boys from day's pay to piecework resulted in sending up the average earnings to 1s. 9d. per shift, the previous *maximum* rate being 1s. 8d. per shift.

263. The principal obstacle to the piecework system being extended is the " *maximum* average clause " of the N.R.C. schedule of rates. That schedule provided that certain classes of natives working on contract or on bonus *plus* day's pay, were to be paid such rates that the average pay of that class of native on any mine should not exceed 2s. 3d. a shift (Annexure 12). This has been modified from time to time (details appear in Annexure 13), but the principle is still retained for natives employed on tramming and shovelling piecework. I do not think that this is a fair stipulation. There are cases where mines have cut piecework rates solely in order to keep within this clause, of which the natives are, of course, ignorant; and, even if they knew of it, they could not understand its bearing on their pay. Such a limitation is inconsistent with the theory of piecework.

264. This *maximum* average clause causes a good deal of inconvenience to the mines themselves in some cases. On the Crown Mines, for example, comparatively few hammerboys are employed; and, as hammerboys are exempt from the operation of this clause, the result is a lower average wage all round than is paid on other mines, where the proportion of hammerboys is higher.

265. At the Nourse Mines there was a system of piecework lashing and tramming under which the natives engaged were earning up to 8s. per shift. This was crushed by the *maximum* average clause, and lashing and tramming boys on those mines now average only 1s. 9·2d. per shift. Yet the manager is of opinion that the former arrangement was more satisfactory to the mine, as it certainly must have been to the native. Naturally, that set of natives have been lost to the mines; and they were highly efficient workers.

266. The Crown Mine were, in October, 1912, paying 1s. per truck for piecework lashing and tramming. As a result of the *maximum* average clause, the Crown Mines have had to cut their rates for piecework tramming again and again in order to keep their wages bill within this clause; and they were in October, 1913, paying only 5d. per truck. (I should add that they have recently thrown in free food, whereas formerly piecework boys found their own food.) As a result of this cutting, they lost 600 boys within a few days, and another 400 shortly after. Seeing that the average earnings of this class of native fell from 4s. a day to 2s. 1d., this is not to be wondered at.

267. It is quite evident that, when a mine is driven, as in this instance, to cut rates, not because the management think that they are not getting value for their money, but merely to comply with an arbitrary clause of this kind, the work must suffer.

268. The effect of this clause is that, whenever the general run of natives on this work becomes more efficient, the management is compelled to reduce the rate, thus actually penalising efficient work. This does not seem to me the way to get the best out of a labourer.

269. The purpose of the clause is, of course, to prevent the mine outbidding each other for piecework labour, just as the prescribed rates prevent them with respect to day's pay labour. It seems to me, for the reasons given above, to be unsound in principle, and it has certainly caused dissatisfaction, which is to nobody's interest.

[U.G. 37—'14.]

270. It has been suggested that, in place of the *maximum* average clause, there should be an agreed *maximum* per ton, i.e., that each mine should be free to pay its boys whatever it liked, provided that it did not thereby increase its present cost per ton (which is by this time well known) for each class of work.

271. This would have the advantage that the only limit on the native's earnings would be his own efficiency; if he shifted 8 tons instead of four, the mine would be allowed to pay him double; and at the same time the cost to the industry would be no greater. The whole idea of piecework is that, the more the labourer does, the more he is paid. The *maximum* average clause, as at present existing, is in conflict with this idea; a *maximum* per ton would not be.

272. By Articles 16 and 17 of the W.N.L.A. Articles of Association, any mine which engages a native coming from another employer within a Labour District has to pay £2. Some mines pay this amount out of their own funds; others have, in the past, transferred the charge to the native, by deducting it from his pay at the rate of so much a month during his contract with them. The effect of the latter course (which is, by the way, a contravention of section 15 of Act 15 of 1911, since the Director has not authorised such a deduction) is that the boy gets lower wages after the change than he would have done had he stayed on his old mine. For a native to find that he must either stay on a mine which he wishes to leave or submit to a substantial reduction of pay can hardly tend to contentment.

273. It has been stated that this is no longer done on any of the mines. I am under the impression that more than one compound manager has told me that he is actually doing it, though I cannot now trace the statement in the evidence. I may have learned it—as I have learned many things—in unrecorded conversation. In any case, there is no harm in mentioning the matter, in case any examples may chance to survive.

Lack of Promotion.

274. A common complaint was that there was no increase of pay for long service, with its accompanying increased efficiency. As regards day's pay for boys, this is to a great extent the case; but it is the ordinary position of the unskilled worker everywhere. He soon reaches the ordinary rate of pay for the work which he does, and then he remains stationary.

275. There are provisions in the schedule of pay at present in use for increasing day's pay to some small extent—from 1s. 6d. to 1s. 8d. in some classes, from 1s. 8d. to 2s. in others, and so on. There seems, however, to be no uniformity in the method of adjusting these increases. On some mines it is the underground manager, on some the compound manager, on some the manager who settles, within the limits of the schedule, what each native is to get. Also, there is great variety in practice; some mines seem to promote natives as much as they can, others to keep down their pay as much as possible.

276. Possibly an arrangement under which any boy not proving inefficient obtained his rises at definite periods after enlistment might promote contentment and encourage natives to remain longer.

277. A curious experience was related by the manager of the Knights Central. He had piecework tramming boys at rates varying from 8d. to 11d. a truck, according to the distance trammed. At their own request, all the rates were made the same, irrespective of distance, the new arrivals being put on to the harder places and being moved to the easier ones as their seniors left.

278. This provides for promotion to some extent, but the system could hardly be applied except where the variations in rate are comparatively small. At the Nourse Mines the rates varied from 2d. to 10d.; and it is hardly likely that a uniform rate would give satisfaction there. But the difficulty as to promotion does not really arise in connection with piecework; in such work pay increases automatically with efficiency.

279. A good many boys complained that, every time they returned to a mine, they had to begin at bottom rates, even though they had worked there, on and off, for years and had been getting top pay before they went on their holiday. I understand that such a boy is not, in fact, worth so much after his holiday as before, since he returns out of condition. I suppose, however, that he gets over this in a month or so.

280. The real grievance of the native on this point is the colour bar, which blocks practically all his opportunities of promotion. He argues—and I see no flaw in the reasoning—that if he can do the same work as white men, there is

no reason why he should not receive the same remuneration. That in many instances he can do it and in some instances is actually doing it, admits of no doubt.

281. Under the present Mining Regulations (Chapter I.), certain positions of responsibility must be filled, in the Cape and Natal, by a "competent" man, whether white or coloured. In the Transvaal and Free State, they must be filled by a "white" man, whether competent or incompetent. If my life ever depends upon these people's care and skill, as many lives do to-day, I hope that it will be in one of the former Provinces.

282. In the course of this inquiry I have met educated natives, employed on the mines, who have brought forward grievances peculiar to their class. These all resolve themselves into one—absence of opportunity to do the work for which their education has fitted them, and thereby to earn sufficient to maintain them in the state of civilisation which they have attained.

283. Some of these natives were extremely sensible, well-mannered and well-reasoning people; and they complained bitterly that they were, for all practical purposes, classified by everyone with raw savages. One cannot but sympathise with their situation; but there is no use in offering recommendations upon a grievance of this kind.

284. The concrete points which they have raised are that compound police should be selected from educated natives, and that native clerks are underpaid. They have urged that police boys have occasionally to scrutinise passes, special or otherwise, and that they ought to be able to read them. I do not think this case very often arises; most of the police boy's duties lie within the precincts of the mine, where passes are not often asked for (it is the native police attached to the South African Police who habitually examine passes); and a capacity to read and write, or even a more advanced education, does not necessarily carry with it the qualities required to maintain order among a mass of generally un-educated natives.

285. There is no limitation placed by the N.R.C. schedule upon the wages of native clerks. They are usually paid from £3 15s. to £5 a month. As all the natives on a Select Committee of the Transkei General Council agreed to recommend a *minimum* rate of £4 a month, the existing rates can hardly be unreasonable.

286. There is some scope for improvement in wages and opportunity of promotion without actual removal of the colour bar. Native hospital attendants who were properly trained and native clerks who could be relied upon as intelligence officers to keep the compound manager informed as to the state of feeling in the compound (see paragraph 504 below) would be economically worth a good deal more than the present rate paid to the natives doing these classes of work; and thus an avenue of promotion would be opened.

NON-MARKING OF TICKETS.

287. A perpetual source of complaint is the non-marking of tickets. Every native labourer is furnished, at the beginning of each period of 30 shifts, with a book of 30 tickets with counterfoils. At the end of each day's work, the miner under whom the native is employed marks upon both ticket and counterfoil the date, the class of work upon which the labourer has been employed during that day and, if the labourer is a hammer boy, the number of inches drilled by him; and signs the ticket and counterfoil. He then tears out the ticket and puts all tickets so torn out into an envelope, which he forwards to the time office. The native retains the book containing the counterfoil.

288. Each book of tickets has (on most mines) a number of additional tickets, of a different colour to the worktickets, at the end of the book. If the native does not do his day's work, no workticket is marked or taken out, but one of these "loafer tickets" is torn out and sent to the time office. For a day so recorded, the native gets no pay, nor does the day's work count as a shift towards the completion of his contract.

289. Whether the native is or is not paid for his day's work is thus largely in the discretion of the miner (using that word to cover all Europeans engaged in mining work); and, obviously, that discretion may be exercised in an arbitrary or unfair manner. During the six months ending 30th September, 1913, the average of hammershifts unpaid for throughout the mines was something like 5 per cent. Among classes other than hammerboys, the percentage was only about 0·4 per cent. (Annexure 1).

290. The position of hammerboys in relation to this matter must be considered separately from that of other boys. Hammerboys, under their contract, are not entitled to a ticket unless they do a specified task. Other boys are engaged on day's pay, not piecework (I am speaking broadly; there are some other boys engaged on piecework, but I do not refer to these); and there is no justification for requiring them to do a specific task on penalty of forfeiting their pay.

291. Of course, if an employee fails to do what he has undertaken, he is not entitled to his pay; but what most boys have undertaken to do is to put in a reasonable day's work, not to accomplish a definite task. Nevertheless, it is certainly the practice on some mines to require from these boys a standard task and to refuse payment if it is not attained. This if often done in the case of machine boys, who are very generally required to drill 4 holes on pain of not getting their tickets marked, or in the case of a small machine 6 holes. Incidentally, it may be pointed out that machine boys are subject to accidents over which they have no control, such as the failure of the compressed air supply which drives the machine, or a breakdown in the machine itself.

292. Similarly, tramboys complain that their tickets are not marked merely because they have happened to upset one of the trucks; and shovellers that they are refused tickets if they have not completed a particular task.

293. As I have said above, the cancelled shifts among boys other than hammerboys only average 0·4 per cent. This is not, however, a fair measure of the extent of the grievance, because there is a great deal of variation in the figures of the different mines, eight of them running above 1 per cent. while one reaches 3·3 per cent. It is no satisfaction to a native thus deprived of his earnings that, on another mine, natives are paid in full.

294. Various attempts have been made to reduce this grievance. On one mine, where complaints of non-marking were few, no miner is allowed to give a loafer ticket without at once reporting his action to the shiftboss and satisfying him that there were good reasons therefor.

295. The Knights Central have what seems to me a very good system. Whenever a native's ticket is not marked for two consecutive days, the time office puts his name on a "loafers' list"; and, whether any complaint is received or not, every such case is automatically investigated.

296. On the Simmer and Jack the same principle is carried further. A daily list of all natives who were not marked on the previous day is sent by the time office to the compound, and each case is investigated.

297. At the Van Ryn Deep, the rule is that, if a boy loafs, he is to be sent out of the mine before noon at latest; only under those conditions may he be given a loafer ticket. If he is allowed to remain, nominally at work, until a later hour, his ticket must be marked in any event.

298. I cannot, however, see any necessity for these merely palliative measures. It is quite easy to destroy the root of the grievance by simply applying an universally accepted principle. When a dispute arises between the parties to a contract, what each party is entitled to is the decision of an independent tribunal as to its respective rights. Where the dispute is whether a native mine labourer has done a fair day's work, it is exceptionally easy to procure such a decision, since, by Pass Regulation 32 (5) and by Regulation 19 (2) (a) under Act 1511, it has been made a criminal offence for such a labourer to loaf. When a native is convicted under the regulation, he is clearly not entitled to his pay and it may safely and properly be withheld. But I think it should be an absolute rule that a day's pay native who has attended at his working-place should either be so convicted or receive his wage.

299. It is, of course, said that the trouble and expense involved in prosecuting every native for loafing is practically prohibitive. As a matter of fact, it is no more trouble and much less expense than the civil litigation which would follow as a matter of course if any employer took upon himself to pronounce that his white servant had not worked hard enough and therefore refused to pay him. To refuse a ticket to a day's pay native on such grounds really amounts to settling a claim to a special privilege as against native servants which no other employer has and which a mine would certainly never attempt to claim against white employees. I think that such a claim is quite unjustifiable and ought not to be tolerated.

300. It may be said that every employer who considers that his employee has not done the work which he undertook to do can refuse to pay and that the employee has then, as his only remedy, the right to sue. But the distinction between the position of most employees and that of a native mine labourer is that the former can, practically always, sue the employer; at the worst, he can, if

he has a *prima facie* case, get leave to sue *in forma pauperis*. I do not think that I need waste words in pointing out why this remedy is not available to the ordinary native mine labourer: the fact that, out of the thousands of hammerboys who have been recruited under the N.R.C. contract and have, at least, a *prima facie* case for breach of contract (*vide* paragraph 72), not one has sued a mine, speaks for itself.

301. The hammerboy is, of course, in a different position. He has undertaken to do a *minimum* task, and has agreed that he shall get no pay if he fails to accomplish it. There would be nothing further to be said if he had absolute freedom to set about his work in his own way; but that is not the case so long as hammerboys have to do lashing before they get to their holes. In the case of the N.R.C. native this is, as I have pointed out above, an additional task imposed at the will of the employer and absolutely unwarranted by the contract. Even where two hours' lashing has been stipulated for, it is quite possible that more may be imposed; and, when the servant has thus been prevented from carrying out his part of the contract by the wrongful action of the employer, the forfeiture of his wages is neither legally nor morally justifiable.

302. Besides this, the hammerboy, in many cases, is placed at a quite peculiar disadvantage. If the miner is working under contract, it is he who ultimately pays the native's wages, since he is credited by the mine with the amount of rock broken and debited with all the expenses incurred in breaking it, including the wages of the boys employed under him. Thus the miner has a direct pecuniary interest in depriving the native of his wage, since the saving thus effected goes straight into the miner's own pocket. Such a system seems to me absolutely indefensible.

303. It has been argued that the contract miner is so anxious to get long holes that he will do everything to encourage his boys to drill their best, and is more likely to overmark them than to undermark them. That may be so in some cases; there must certainly be others where the temptation to an immediate saving outweighs the prospect of ultimate gain. A case has been quoted to me by a mine manager where a miner was found habitually marking on the counterfoils retained by his natives a greater number of inches than he marked on the ticket which he sent to the pay office and upon which he was charged. Another manager told me that, when the miner is put on day's pay, the inches immediately go up; which seems to indicate that the contractor is inclined to keep them down.

304. The inducement to the contractor to undermark his hammerboys varies considerably. On some mines he is charged $\frac{1}{2}$d. for every inch bored, irrespective of whether the *minimum* is or is not reached. In such a case, if the boy has drilled 30 inches, the miner will only gain 1d. by marking him 28 inches. In other cases, the miner pays nothing for any hole under the *minimum* so that, on a mine where the *minimum* is 36 inches, he would save himself 1s. 6d. by refusing, on any excuse, to mark the ticket of a boy who had drilled that amount.

305. Whether the inducement is great or little, it is always there. The only system I have heard of which does away with this inducement entirely is said to be in use on some of the outlying collieries. There the miner is always charged with a full shift for every native who goes down in his gang, so that he has no personal interest in the question of whether a boy is or is not paid; his only concern is to get a day's work out of the native.

306. Unless there is some check on the miner (as I explain later, many mines have established a check in one form or another) the usual contract system really amounts to this, that, if the miner chooses to pay the native, he does so; if not, he simply pockets a part of the whole of the native's wages. Certainly no contract on these terms has ever been agreed to by any servant; I should doubt whether any employer has ever had the face to propose it.

307. Of course, the native who disputes the miner's decision may, theoretically, sue the mine for his day's pay. I have already pointed out why, in the circumstances of the native mine labourer, this remedy is practically valueless.

308. The only course which is really open to a native who has been deprived of his day's pay is to appeal to the compound manager. This he has not, as a rule, an opportunity of doing until the hole has been blasted and the evidence destroyed.

309. It must also be remembered that, even where the hole is undoubtedly less than the *minimum*, this may be due to circumstances which are no fault of the native. Holes are sometimes required in places where it is impossible to put in 30 inches in the course of a shift. I believe that allowance is usually made for

this; but it is unfair to the native to leave the exercise of this discretion to a person whose interest is antagonistic to his own.

310. The hammerboy feels very keenly that someone gets the benefit of the short hole which he has drilled without pay. Over and over again it has been said to me, " I drilled a hole, even if it was only 24 inches; I get no pay. But my master charges and blasts the hole all the same; and he gets paid for the rock broken by it."

311. Many mines have established some check upon the miner. On the E.R.P.M., for example, every miner sends a daily report to the mine captain, showing how many inches each of his boys has drilled that day. This enables the mine captain to keep an eye on each gang; and he would presumably make inquiries if any miner's report habitually showed an unusually high percentage of cancelled shifts.

312. Some mines leave the incomplete hole unblasted and let the native complete it on the following day. Some witnesses tell me that a hole cannot be left unblasted without seriously interfering with the shape of the stope, but many others entirely deny this; and the rule is actually in force upon the Aurora West and in one section of the Princess Estate.

313. I think that there should be a definite and universal rule that no contractor may refuse to mark a hammerboy's ticket on his own sole authority. If he considers that the boy has not accomplished his task, he should, where practicable, get a shiftboss or other superior to confirm his action then and there; where this is not practicable, as it often may not be, the hole should be left unblasted until a superior has seen it.

314. The same rule should be applied when there is any dispute between the miner and the native as to the length of a hole. On general principles, a party to a dispute who destroys evidence may usually be taken to be in the wrong: *omnia praesumuntur contra spoliatorem*. If the miner, with knowledge of the native's claim, blasts the hole before the shiftboss sees it, the native's estimate of its length should be accepted.

315. The rule should also be applied when a miner refuses to mark a boy's ticket for a hole on the ground that it has not been bored in the direction ordered. The shiftboss cannot, of course, know what instructions the miner gave; but I understand that any skilled man can, after inspecting the ground, make a very fair guess at what those instructions are likely to have been.

316. Besides, a miner who is looking after his boys properly ought to be able to detect an error of this kind before it has gone very far, and restart the boy in the right direction.

317. There are a certain number of grievances connected with tickets which seem to me to be due to misunderstandings.

318. Some mines either have no loafer tickets at all or supply the miner with a separate book of them. In the former case always, in the latter when the miner has forgotten or mislaid his separate book, he marks the short day's work on the ordinary work ticket. Every boy reckons the progress of his period of contract by the completion of these books; he knows, for example, that a contract of 180 shifts means that he must finish six books. But, where lost shifts are recorded on work tickets, this calculation is thrown out; and, at the end of the sixth book, the boy finds that he has still several shifts to work.

319. Often, no doubt, he knows perfectly well what the explanation is; but sometimes he does not; and the system certainly causes avoidable discontent.

320. In some few mines the miner, instead of simply marking on the tickets the class of work which the boy is doing, marks the rate of pay to which he is entitled. Often, the miner is wrong about this and overmarks or undermarks the rate. This is corrected in the time office and makes no difference to the boy in the long run, but it causes discontent if a 2s. boy sees 1s. 6d. on his ticket every day, he is discontented during the month; if a 1s. 6d. boy sees 2s. being marked on each of his 30 tickets, he is highly discontented at receiving £2 5s. instead of £3 at the end of the month.

321. A weak point of the ticket system is that the miner not infrequently contrives to lose a ticket or two, which he should send to the time office. This can, of course, be corrected if the native produces his counterfoil; but he also frequently loses this. This, however, seems to me an inevitable imperfection, and I do not think it occurs often enough to constitute a grievance. After all, it is generally the boy's own fault if he loses his ticket.

Time in Hospital.

322. It is a frequent complaint that days spent in hospital do not count towards the period of contract. As the contract is not for a period of time, but for a definite number of shifts to be worked, there is clearly no agreement that such days shall be counted. Native Labour Regulation 23, however, provides:—

> " Every day on which such native labourer has been incapacitated through accident occasioned by no fault of his own . . . . shall be counted as part of the period of such contract."

323. I think that this provision is usually carried out; but certainly many natives are under the impression that it is not. This is largely due to the fact that, in most cases, the allowance is made in the time office and the native knows nothing of it. Somes mines have, however, adopted a system under which the ticket of a native sent to hospital under these circumstances is taken charge of by the compound manager, who tears out a slip every day, which goes to the time office, and marks the counterfoil " accident." Thus the patient, when discharged, can see for himself that his contract has been going on during his detention in hospital.

324. Some mines do not notify the natives that these days count against their contract and only inform him of the credit when specially asked by him about it. I think that some system under which the native can see the exact state of his contract should be compulsory.

325. Some natives asked that their contracts should run all the time they were in hospital, even though they were not there through any accident. This is clearly inconsistent with the express terms of the contract, which stipulates that the employee shall work a certain number of shifts, not during a certain period. Also, it would encourage malingering.

326. It may, however, be pointed out that the regulation above quoted deprives the native of any benefit from it if the accident is due to any fault of his own, however trivial. The phrase of the Workmen's Compensation Act—" wilful and serious misconduct "—might fairly be substituted.

327. There does not seem to be any established system for deciding whether the accident is or is not due to the patient's own fault. Unless the mine is able to show that it was his fault, I think it should be presumed that it was not. Negligence as a rule, has to be proved and is not presumed against anyone.

328. Several natives asked for pay while in hospital, and asserted that white miners' pay continued while they were sick. This, of course, is not the case. Many white miners get allowances while sick; but these are paid by their own benefit societies out of their own contributions, i.e., they are savings. The native makes no such provision for sickness; if he is disabled by an accident, the claim thence arising is not a claim for wages but for compensation, and is dealt with under that head.

329. In some cases natives complained that, if they began a day's work, but were incapacitated from finishing it by an accident and were taken to hospital, their tickets were not marked for that day. On most mines it is usual to pay in these circumstances, and I think the practice should be universal.

Administration of Estates.

330. On some mines I was told that, when a native dies, his relatives never get the wages or compensation due to him. Every native who dies has to be reported to the Native Affairs Department (Regulation 33), and that Department immediately takes charge of his estate and communicates with his relatives. Under these circumstances, the mine can only annex the property either by omitting to report the death or by falsifying the deceased's credit balance. They cannot remain entirely silent about his death, because the Native Affairs Department has a record of every boy in the compound, and, if one is missing in the monthly payment of pass fees, the mine has to account for him somehow. They may return him as having deserted; but, if he is really dead, the chances are that the facts would get to the knowledge of the Native Affairs Department through his brothers on the mine.

331. Nor is it easy to falsify the credit balance. As a rule, the individual who records the amount due does not handle the money, so that his fraud would not enable him to annex the amount. Altogether the risk would be so great and the profit so dubious that there is little probability of such frauds being perpetrated.

332. Once the money is handed over to the Native Affairs Department, it can only be retained by any officer by his producing a forged voucher. This may possibly occur in individual cases—it is a risk against which it is impossible to guard entirely—but the chances of its being done on any scale are negligible.

333. The last way in which the estate may fail to reach the dependents is that the Native Affairs Department may be unable to trace them. The extent to which this happens is easily ascertained. During the year 1912 the total amount paid to the Native Affairs Department on account of estates of natives other than Portuguese was £4,767 15s. 7d. Of this £4,285 13s. 2d. was duly distributed, while £382 5s. 1d. (or 8·2 per cent. of the total), has been paid to revenue as unclaimed. Inquiries are still pending in respect of £99 17s. 4d., which may or may not ultimately be handed to the heirs.

334. As regards Portuguese natives, the whole amount received is paid over to the Portuguese authorities. I understand that they are not very successful in tracing the relatives; but that is a matter which no one in the Union can remedy, unless arrangements can be come to by which the duty is transferred to the W.N.L.A.

335. As far as Union natives are concerned, there seems to be little ground for this complaint. I think the real fact is that the " brothers "—a very vague term, used to denote all manner of kinship, affinity or mere neighbourhood—on the spot consider themselves entitled, or at any rate would like, to divide the estate then and there among themselves. Its proper division among the heirs naturally causes them to complain; but they certainly have no grievance.

336. There is also the possibility of theft, either underground or in hospital, from the person of a native killed or fatally injured in an accident. Mr. Marwick tells me that he has so often heard of cases where no money could be found on the body of a native who was believed to have been in possession of a good deal that he thinks such thefts not uncommon.

337. One can easily understand that, in the confusion following an accident, opportunities for such theft may well occur, as natives commonly carry their money on their person. It would perhaps be well to draw the attention of responsible persons to the desirability of searching for and safeguarding any valuables in the possession of injured natives.

Charge for Losses.

338. There were several complaints that, when a native loses his ticket, or the wristlet bearing his mine number, he is charged for a new one. The practice in this respect is very divergent on different mines, many of them making a charge of from 3d. to 2s. 6d. in these circumstances. As the Director has never sanctioned this deduction, it is a contravention of section 15 of Act 15 of 1911.

339. Several mines make no charge at all; and compound managers, who have had experience of both systems, state that they do not find any additional carelessness as a result of the abolition of the charge. In these circumstances I do not see why the deduction should be permitted, especially as the loss may occur without negligence on the part of the native. In any case, some of the charges are excessive.

Limitation of Length Drilled.

340. On a few mines hammerboys have complained that they were not allowed to go on drilling beyond a certain *maximum*. This is a real grievance; the employer of a piece-worker certainly ought to find him in work enough to fill up the usual working hours.

341. The complaint seems to arise chiefly in cases where the native has finished one hole of standard length and has not time enough left to enable him to finish another. He could drill, say, 12 inches, but the miner does not want a 12 in. hole, and so refuses to point him out a new place. There seems no reason why this should be done; many managers have assured me that it would cause no inconvenience to let the boy drill his 12 inches, leave that hole unblasted, and continue it on the following day.

342. In one instance a manager told me that he had limited the hammerboys for a while, because the mine could not afford the extra payment. This has, however, now been remedied.

CHANGE TO LOWER-PAID WORK.

343. A great grievance with the hammerboy is that he is, every now and then, taken off hammers and put to do lashing work for a few days. Since hammerboys earn considerably more per shift than lashing boys, this is a serious diminution of the labourer's income.

344. In cases where the native has been especially engaged for hammer work, this treatment is, of course, a definite breach of contract. Such breaches are very rare, and I do not doubt that they arise only from overlooking the terms of the engagement, and would immediately be remedied when discovered. The widespread complaint comes from the recruited native, who has been engaged to do any kind of mine work at the option of his employer for the rate of pay attached to that particular class of work. When such a boy has been kept on hammerwork for some time, he ignores the terms of his engagement and considers that he has a prescriptive right to be kept at hammers

345. Clearly this is not a real grievance; all that is required of the native is that he shall abide by the terms of his agreement. At the same time, to put hammerboys on to lashing does, however unreasonably, cause discontent. Most mines recognise this and only have recourse to this expedient when absolutely compelled to do so by the emergencies of mining. When so compelled, many mines continue to pay the hammerboys employed on lashing at the *minimum* rate for hammerwork instead of at lashing rates. This is, under the ordinary contract, purely an act of grace; but so many mines follow the system that presumably the resulting content is found to be worth the extra money. Other mines might advantageously consider whether it would not be worth their while to follow this example.

346. This, of course, only applies to natives usually employed on hammers and taken off for purely temporary reasons. Many natives are tried at hammerwork and, being found inefficient at that, are permanently transferred to other classes of labour. Such boys are paid by every mine at the rate attached to the class of work which they are actually doing.

HALF SHIFTS.

347. A complaint peculiar to the coal mines is that, for a great deal of time, some of the natives are on half shift, so that it takes them double the usual period to work out their contracts.

348. It seems to me that this does not amount to a grievance if the native is not allowed to leave and go to a mine where he can get full time work; but the case is already provided for by Regulation 26 (c), under which the Director may cancel the contract of any native whose employer cannot find him in work. As a matter of fact, a large number of these boys are time-expired, and stay on their own free will because they like the job. In such cases there is no grievance.

349. There is an apparent grievance in the system of payment for these half-shifts. A full day's work is from 6 a.m. to noon, and from 1 p.m. to 5 p.m.— 10 hours. A half-shift is from 6 a.m. to noon—6 hours—yet, for two half shifts, the native gets paid only as much as for one full day, *i.e.*, he gives 12 hours' work instead of 10 hours, yet he is paid no more.

350. Against this must be set the fact that the mine has to feed him for two days instead of one, so that there is no saving to them, in fact, rather the contrary. The comparison is as follows:—

	Works	Is paid	Is fed for
Working 30 shifts on full time, a native	300 hours	£3	6 weeks, *i.e.*, about £1
Working 30 shifts on half time, he ...	360 hours	£3	12 weeks, *i.e.*, £2

351. Thus, on full time the native receives, in money and food, 1s. for $3\frac{3}{4}$ hours' work; on half time, 1s. for 3 3-5 hours' work. The real difference is therefore slightly in favour of the half shift system. Of course, the native takes longer to complete his contract.

DEFERRED PAY.

352. A certain number of natives are engaged by the W.N.L.A. on what is known as the deferred pay system. The present contract in such cases provides that, in respect of Portuguese natives from south of latitude 22 S., 9d. per shift in respect of any period of re-engagement after they have completed their 12 months' contract (except for the last month before leaving) shall be paid on their return to Portuguese Territory. In respect of natives from north of latitude 22 S. (who are, however, no longer being recruited), half their wages are paid in Portuguese Territory.

353. Under a new arangement to take effect on the 1st July, 1914, all Portuguese natives will be paid on their return to Portuguese Territory 9d. per shift for the first 12 months and the same for any period after 18 months (except for the last month before leaving). The wages for the six months between one year and 18 months will be paid in full in the Transvaal.

354. It is, however, at present doubtful whether this new arrangement will take effect; the matter is now under consideration.

355. There were a few complaints against this system, due, I think, to the human desire to spend rather than to save. I do not, however, consider that there is any grievance in a system which is directed to assisting the native to save money. His main purpose in coming to the mines is to get home with some money in his pocket; and, seeing how prone he is to succumb to the temptation of spending all his earnings on the spot—the Portuguese native is especially liable to this—I think the principle of deferred pay sound.

DEDUCTIONS.

356. There have been some complaints as to the deductions made from natives' wages. With the exception of one or two matters, to which I have drawn attention elsewhere, I do not see any reason to suppose that illegal deductions are made to any great extent. I think, however, that the reason for deductions is not always sufficiently explained; if all the mines would adopt the system already in use on some of them of having an officer present on pay day whose sole duty it is to make clear to each native the ground of any deduction shown on his pay ticket, complaints on this point would probably diminish.

BREACHES OF CONTRACT.

357. I do not think that actual breach of contract by underpayment is common. In such a case the native has already the remedy of complaining to the nearest Inspector of the Native Affairs Department, which is always ready to take up any such case.

DESTRUCTION OF RECORDS.

358. Most mines periodically destroy old pay tickets and other records. There can be no objection to this after a time; but I do not think that, during the pendency of a contract, any document bearing on that contract ought to be destroyed.

CHAPTER V.

COMPLAINTS AS TO COMPENSATION.

CHAPTER V.
COMPLAINTS AS TO COMPENSATION.
AMOUNT OF COMPENSATION.

359. There is a considerable dissatisfaction as to the compensation granted for incapacitation or death by accident or from phthisis. It is not easy to say whether this is due to ignorance that any compensation at all is granted or to discontent with the amount awarded; a native so often says: "There is no compensation," when he knows perfectly well that there is, and is merely trying to express his opinion that its amount is inadequate.

360. At present, the compensation money is paid to the native by the Native Affairs Department after he has left the mine, so that his comrades of the compound do not know that it has been paid. This ignorance might be dissipated by an official announcement at the compound of the fact of the award and its amount. I presume every compound contains enough natives who can read to make sure that the contents of any notice posted on a board at the office would become common knowledge in the compound before very long.

361. The compensation payable to natives is regulated by Act 15 of 1911, section 22, which runs as follows:—

"22. (1) There shall be payable by the employer of any native labourer compensation in respect of any personal injury caused by accident arising out of or in course of his employment whereby such native labourer has become permanently, totally or partially incapacitated or has met his death.

"(2) Whenever such accident occurs the Director shall proceed to assess the amount of compensation upon the following scale:—

(a) In the event of partial incapacitation (which shall mean inability owing to the injury to resume work similar to that at which he was employed at the time of the injury or for which he was fitted by trade or calling), a sum being not less than one pound, and not more than twenty pounds;

(b) In the event of permanent total incapacitation for work, a sum being not less than thirty pounds and not more than fifty pounds;

(c) In the event of death, a sum of ten pounds.

"Provided that no compensation shall be payable under this Act in respect of an injury to a native labourer which was due to his own serious and wilful misconduct, which shall include drunkenness, wilful contravention of any law or statutory regulation made for the purpose of ensuring the safety of, or preventing accidents to, workmen, or any other act or omission which the Director, or board hereinafter mentioned, having regard to all circumstances of an accident causing injury, may declare to be serious and wilful misconduct.

"(3) If any employer dispute that compensation is payable to a native labourer or fail to pay any amount assessed under this section, the matter shall be determined by a board which shall consist of the magistrate of the district as chairman, a nominee of the employer concerned and a medical practitioner nominated by the other two members of the board or, failing agreement as to such nomination, a medical practitioner appointed by the Minister for the purpose. The board shall have all the powers possessed by a court of resident magistrate as to the summoning and examination of witnesses, the hearing of arguments and the enforcement of orders. The decision of such board shall be final.

"(4) The Director shall pay any sum received as compensation in the case of permanent or partial incapacitation to the native concerned, and in the case of death to any wife, child, parent or other person who shall be proved to the satisfaction of the Director to be dependent on such native labourer: Provided that the manner and form in which payment shall in each case be made shall be in the discretion of the Director, and provided further that no sum payable to any dependent shall be liable to attachment for any debt by the deceased native labourer, nor shall the amount of any compensation recovered or recoverable on behalf of the dependent form part of the deceased labourer's estate for the purpose of any law for the time being relating to the administration of, or the duty on, estates of deceased persons.

"(5) Nothing in this section shall be taken to debar any native labourer from claiming compensation under his rights at common law or under any law relating to the payment of workmen's compensation in force within the Union or any part thereof: Provided that if compensation has been recovered by a native labourer or dependent under this section no action shall lie against the employer for the recovery of damages or compensation in respect of the same accident."

362. Summarised, this means that the native gets:—

For the permanent loss of his trade, if he can still do other work (partial incapacitation) ... ... £1—£20

For the permanent loss of all earning power whatever (total incapacitation) ... ... £30—£50

For death, if he leaves dependents £10

while, for temporary incapacitation, he gets food, nursing and medical attendance for so long as he is detained in the mine hospital and also, if the mine medical officer considers him unfit for further work for the present, the cost of sending him to his home.

363. This provision is complained of as insufficient. It seems to me that three tests may be applied:—

(1) How far is this provision really an equivalent for the financial loss which the labourer has suffered?

(2) How does it compare with the provision made for the European in similar circumstances?

(3) In cases of total incapacitation or death, does it supply reasonable livelihood for the labourer and those dependent upon him?

Financial Loss Suffered.

364. In order to reply to the first question, it is necessary to ascertain the present value, at the date of the accident, of the labourer's probable future earnings if the accident had not occurred. The average earnings per shift of a native labourer on these fields during the six months ending 31st December, 1913, were 1s. 11·2d. The compensation for total incapacitation therefore amounts to paying the labourer the value of his labour during from 311 to 517 shifts. By continuous working, a native can score 313 shifts a year; in fact, however, he does not often approach this, and, on an average, he only does about 283 shifts during a calendar year even if he stays on the mine all the time. This again, he does not usually do; a native labourer from within the Union who may be said to be working regularly (as native regularity goes), will stay on the mine only about half his time, spending the other half at home.

365. Allowing for all these things, the compensation granted for total incapacitation is the equivalent of what the labourer would, but for the accident, probably have earned in a period of from 2 to $3\frac{1}{2}$ years.

366. There are no means of ascertaining how much working life is left to the average native who is totally incapacitated, but, when allowance is made for the comparative youth of the ordinary native labourer and for the fact that, even after he gives up working at the mines, he can still earn money or money's worth for a number of years at his native place, it seems tolerably safe to say that this payment is not a real equivalent for the financial loss which he has suffered by his total incapacitation.

367. The same reasoning applies still more strongly to the compensation for death. The £10 paid in this event is the probable average earnings of only eight months; and it cannot be supposed that this is anything like the probable working life of the deceased.

368. In cases of partial incapacitation the loss is more difficult to calculate. The mine native's trade is, mainly, that of an unskilled labourer. A hammerboy is, of course, skilled to some extent; and an injury which renders him unable to continue that work may leave him capable of lashing or tramming. In such a case, the *maximum* compensation payable amounts to his probable loss for the next $7\frac{1}{2}$ years, since the difference between the average hammerboy's wage and that of the average lashing boy is about 4d. per shift. As I said above, there is no means of calculating the probable average duration of the working life of a native to whom an accident happens; but this period does not, like the periods assigned to total incapacitation or death, seem obviously inadequate.

369. This, however, only applies to a limited class of native mine labourer. The remainder, having no trade but that of unskilled labourer, cannot lose their trade without at the same time losing all power of earning at all. A lashing boy who has lost his leg must not only give up lashing, but must also give up any hope of getting any employment except in those light jobs which are too rare to constitute a real market for his labour.

370. Such cases are now treated as cases of partial incapacitation. Under the present law, I think they must be so treated; but they seem to me to be, in fact, cases of total incapacitation. Looked at from this point of view, the £20 which is the *maximum* compensation payable is the equivalent of the native's average earnings during only eighteen months. His probable loss must greatly exceed this.

371. It must also be remembered that the native may receive as little as a twentieth part of this amount. Compensation for partial incapacitation is, between £1 and £20, in the discretion of the Director. I suppose that the Director

naturally leans towards the native's side; but he seems to me to be placed in a difficult position by the absence of any indication in the statute as to what is to guide his discretion. The corresponding provision for Europeans lays down the probable loss of earnings during the next three years as the measure of compensation; there is nothing like this in the section dealing with natives.

372. I have attempted, but without success, to discover what amount individual natives who have been compensated for partial incapacitation have actually earned afterwards. Practically all of them leave the mines and disappear within a short period after receiving compensation.

373. **With regard** to temporary incapacitation, the native gets hospital treatment and, in some cases, repatriation. The cost of hospital treatment for a native is about 1s. 6d. per day, *i.e.*, £2 5s. per calendar month. The cost of repatriating such temporary incapacitated natives as are repatriated (Annexure 16) would not, if spread over the total number of temporarily incapacitated natives, materially add to this figure and so may be ignored. In a calendar month the native would receive, if working, the equivalent of about £3 (allowance being made for the cost of his food, etc.), so that his net loss is about 15s. a month.

COMPARISON WITH COMPENSATION TO EUROPEANS.

374. To apply the second test, a European labourer's compensation is prescribed by Act 36 of 1907 of the Transvaal. The main lines of that Act provide that he shall receive:—

For the permanent loss of his trade, if he can still do other work (partial incapacitation). } His probable loss in the 3 years after the accident, not exceeding £375.

For the permanent loss of all earning power whatever (total incapacitation). } 3 years' wages, not exceeding £750.

For death, if he leaves dependents. } 2 years' wages, not exceeding £500.

For temporary incapacitation. Halfpay, so long as the incapacitation lasts, up to 6 months.

375. As explained in paragraph 364, the totally incapacitated native receives wages from 311 to 517 shifts, *i.e.*, for one year to one year and eight months' continuous work. The European receives wages for three years continuous work. The native gets also the cost of his repatriation, about £1 5s., and of his hospital treatment. If we suppose the latter to last, on the average, for a month—figures are not available—these extras are the equivalent of about 7 weeks' continuous work; so that, on the whole, the native's compensation covers about half the period of that allowed to the European.

376. The native's *maximum* is £50; adding the extras mentioned above, £54 5s. 0d., the European's £750. The maximum which a European workman can earn is £500 a year (if he can earn more he is not entitled to compensation); and he varies from that down to (dealing with casual labour, and allowing for periods of unemployment) perhaps £50 a year. His *maximum* compensation is therefore from 18 months' to 15 years' pay; or, taking the mean to be about £250 a year, 3 years' pay.

377. The native mine labourer's *maximum* wage is probably (including food, etc.) about £70 a year, his *minimum* about £25; so that his *maximum* compensation is from 9 months' to 2¼ years' pay; or, taking his mean earnings at £36 (the average on the mines, allowance being made for food, etc.), about 18 months' pay. Thus the *maximum* compensation which he can obtain, when expressed in terms of the produce of his labour, is again about half of that provided for the European.

378. In the matter of partial incapacitation, the native who has a trade to lose and another to fall back upon gets his probable loss over a period varying from 4½ months to 7½ years; the European gets his probable loss for 3 years. The unskilled native is in much the same position as the unskilled European, except that he can only get a *maximum* of £20, while the European can get £375. The lower ranks of native mine labourers average about 1s. 8d. per shift, so that the compensation is equivalent to payment for 240 working days; the European gets payment for three or four times as long, even putting the pay for unskilled European labour at 10s. a day, which is certainly above the ruling rates.

379. The European's compensation for death is two thirds of that for total incapacitation; the native's is from one third down to one fifth.

380. In respect of temporary incapacitation, the native is better off than the European. The latter gets half pay, and that for six months only; the former gets more than two thirds of his ordinary pay, without limitation.

SUFFICIENCY FOR MAINTENANCE.

381. Turning to the third test, it may be said with confidence that a payment of £10 to the dependents of a native from within the Union who is killed does not, in most cases, supply a reasonable livelihood to those dependents during the period that their dependency is likely to continue. There is, of course, great variation both in the number of dependents and in the scale of living to which they are accustomed; but to a family consisting of a wife and three children £10 represents, as far as I have been able to gather from witnesses familiar with native territories, only about eight months' subsistence on the lowest scale of the blanket Kaffir. To a comparatively civilised native family, it represents subsistence for less than half that period. Taking the average, it may perhaps mean six months' keep; and it is certainly not to be expected that the family will become self-supporting in that time.

382. These figures are based upon the Cape Colony expenses; on the East Coast, the money goes a good deal further. Probably £10 there represents a full years keep at least; and Mr. Lloyd tells me that, on the East Coast, there really are no dependents. Women and children being valuable assets, there is always some heir who is willing to take them over and maintain them.

383. The provision for a totally incapacitated native compares favourably with that for dependents. It varies from three times to five times as much, and, since the addition of one more mouth to feed does not make anything like that difference, it follows that the family are better off than if the native had been killed. Under the present arrangements, whenever a native is totally incapacitated by an accident, it would pay the mine to let him die. None of the natives appear to have discovered this; when they do, it will not be surprising if it breeds suspicion among them.

384. To summarise, the compensation for injury given to the native labourer is not an equivalent for his probable loss: it is, except in the case of temporary sickness, markedly less than that provided for the European, regard being had to their respective earning power; and it is not, in the case of Cape Colony natives, sufficient to support the dependents of a native killed at his work. In these circumstances, the complaint as to its inadequacy seems to me well founded. I do not see why natives should not be compensated upon the same basis as Europeans, *i.e.*, probable loss of earning power.

385. It is probable that, in most cases, an annuity would benefit the incapacitated native more than a lump sum. On the East Coast, however, there is no machinery for distributing annuities.

COMPENSATION FOR MINERS' PHTHISIS.

386. The compensation paid to natives for miners' phthisis (or silicosis) follows the same lines as their compensation for injuries. Where the native's capacity for underground work is not seriously or permanently impaired, he is considered to be partially incapaciated; where it is, he is considered to be totally incapacitated (Act 19 of 1912, section 30).

387. Whether the native gets this compensation depends, however, largely upon the mine medical officer. Until recently, there was no check upon the latter's diagnosis, and it was quite possible that a native suffering from Phthisis might be repatriated as being medically unfit upon some other ground. It is quite possible to make mistakes in this matter: there are cases where one doctor might diagnose silicosis and another only consumption. Also, it is possible that a native suffering from some totally different disease might be repatriated on that account, without the fact that he had also contracted silicosis being discovered.

388. In any case, it is obviously an unbusinesslike arrangement to leave the decision as to whether the mine is to pay compensation virtually in the hands of a nominee of the mine.

389. A recent circular from the Director has instructed Inspectors to call in the Mines Medical Inspector whenever they see reason to suspect phthisis in a repatriated native. This, however, does not seem to me to go far enough; the Native Affairs Inspector is a layman and may well be no judge of such matters. I think that, in every case of repatriation, the mine doctor's diagnosis should be confirmed by a Government medical officer.

390. As I understand that, already, such an officer does inspect every such patient in order to satisfy himself that the patient is fit to travel, it should be possible to arrange that he should also look for symptoms of silicosis.

391. If a native is not repatriated but simply leaves at the end of his contract, he is not medically examined at all and may go away with silicosis without the fact being detected.

392. Seeing the native's dislike to reporting sick, it seems probable that there are a considerable number of undetected cases; as Dr. Loeser told me: " A native

never reports with a chronic illness. He goes on working until he collapses. He has not got the sense to say that he is losing flesh or his breathing is not so good as it used to be, or anything of that sort."

393. The great variation in the percentage of cases detected suggests the same. There are mines where these cases represent more than 1 per cent.—in some small mines 2 per cent. and even more—of the average native population; there are others which have not reported a single case (Annexure 17). This may, however, be accounted for, at any rate to some extent, by the fact that on some mines the native population averages much longer service than on others, and is thus more likely to contract the disease.

394. Some mines have periodical inspections of their natives. Such inspections result in a good many finds; but their value must vary a good deal with the degree of care used. When, as sometimes happens, 1,000 boys an hour are inspected, there must be a considerable risk of missing cases.

395. Mine doctors have not invariably shown themselves efficient guardians of the native's interest. By section 30 (4) of Act 19 of 1912 (the Miners' Phthisis Act), whenever a case of silicosis in a native employed on a mine comes to the notice of a mine doctor, the latter is required forthwith to report it to the mine manager and the mine manager to the Department. When a native is discovered to be in a stage of silicosis which is regarded by the Act as equivalent to total incapacitation, he is usually very near death. If the compensation is assessed and recovered during his life, he obtains from £30 to £50 from the mine; if he dies before this is done, his claim dies with him, and all that the mine is liable for is £10, and that only if the native leaves dependents. (This, at least, is the interpretation put upon the Act by the Law Advisers, and their opinion is being acted upon.)

396. It is thus to the interest of the native that the word " forthwith " in the sub-section should be strictly obeyed; the interest of the mine is the other way.

397. During the first year that this provision was in force, the total number of cases reported by mine medical officers was 117. Of these 26 were not reported until after the native's death. I do not lay much stress on this, as I understand that it may not be possible to detect silicosis in every case except by means of a *post-mortem* examination. It so happens, however, that the original form of report (afterwards discarded), provided for the medical officer stating the date upon which he first detected the disease. There were 19 reports sent in upon these forms; and, according to the written statements of the medical officers concerned, the average interval between discovery and report was 12·47 days. In one case 58 days elapsed.

398. The interest of the native clearly demands some further protection; but it is not easy to see how this can be given, short of having every mine labourer examined on discharge by an independent medical man. Such an examination would, I dare say, have a value of its own apart from the mere discovery of cases entitled to be compensated for miners' phthisis. It would, however, mean the employment of several full-time medical men; and this seems disproportionate to the end to be gained.

399. The appointment, elsewhere recommended, of resident whole-time medical officers with a limited number of patients would probably lead to the detection of more cases of phthisis, as such officers would have more time for examinations.

400. Of course, the best remedy of all is that the native should be taught his own rights in the matter, so that, as soon as he felt that there was something the matter with his chest, he should go to the Native Affairs Department and put in his claim. The Department could then send him to its own or to some independent medical officer to be examined, and, if there was any doubt as to the nature of his disease, it could be referred to a suitable tribunal.

401. At present, comparatively few mine labourers comprehend their position in this respect; to teach them must be a matter of time. A circular has, however, recently been sent to Inspectors instructing them to disseminate informaiton on the point among the natives; and I am informed that the number of applications has more than doubled since then. When I was making enquiries in the compounds, it was clear that the very existence of this form of compensation was unknown to a large number of the boys.

402. With reference to the state of the law mentioned at the end of paragraph 395 above, it seems to me that the ambiguity should be cleared up and that, if there is to be any difference between the amount paid for total incapacitation and the amount paid for death, the amount payable should not depend upon the promptitude with which the mine pays up; more especially since promptitude is contrary to its interest.

403. It may also be noted that, in many cases of total incapacitaiton, the labourer is within a few days or weeks of death when he obtains his compensation; yet any part of it which he does not spend goes, under the present law, to his heir, not to his dependents.

CHAPTER VI.

COMPLAINTS AS TO CONDITIONS OF CONTRACT.

CHAPTER VI.

COMPLAINTS AS TO CONDITIONS OF CONTRACT.

Choice of Mine.

404. A complaint has been made against the **W.N.L.A.** that, in allotting natives to the different mines, no account is taken of their own wishes; that friends coming up together are sent to work on mines far apart, or that a native coming with the intention of joining friends already at work on one mine is, against his will, sent off to another.

405. The basis of the **W.N.L.A.** agreement is that each mine or group of mines belonging to the Association is allotted a certain "complement" of native labourers; and the recruits are divided in such proportions as to give each group the same percentage of its complement. Thus, if the complement of group A. is 10,000 and of group B. 20,000, and if A. has 8,000 boys and B. 16,000 the next batch arriving will be equally divided between A. and B. If however, A. drops to 7,000, while B. still retains 16,000, the next 1,000 boys arriving will all be sent to A.

406. As a general rule, the **W.N.L.A.** engages natives for work upon the Reef generally not for any particular mine. A certain number of their recruits, however, are engaged for named mines. These, who are known as "specials," are boys who have worked on that mine before; they sign the usual form of agreement, undertaking to go anywhere on the Reef, but, if they state, when first taken on that they wish to go back to their old mine, and if they prove by production of their passports or otherwise that they have actually worked there in the past, they are given green tickets (Annexure 18), entitling them to be allotted to their old mine.

407. On the arrival of a party at Johannesburg these "green ticket" boys are first called for, and they, together with any "brothers" whom they have brought with them and have had recorded on the ticket, are allotted to their old mines.

408. Article 11 of the Articles of Association of the **W.N.L.A.** limits the number of boys who may be so dealt with to $32\frac{1}{2}$ per cent. of the total number engaged. The number producing green tickets very closely approximates to that figure; and, for a year or so after the formation of the N.R.C., the remainder of the natives were allotted, irrespective of their own wishes, to such mines as were in need of labour.

409. This caused so much discontent that, some months ago, it was given up; and now, after the "green ticket" boys have been sent out, any of the remainder who desire to go back to their old mines and can produce evidence that they have previously served there are given an opportunity of doing so. Those who succeed in this, together with their "brothers," are then allotted to their old mines. These are termed "document" boys.

410. The remainder are then informed of the mines at which they are required, *i.e.*, if there are 100 of them, they are told "30 of you will have to go to A., 25 to B., 20 to C., 15 to D. and 10 to E." After an interval during which the boys can discuss their wishes, 5 volunteers for E. are called for and the first 5 natives stepping up are taken. Volunteers for the other mines are called for in succession; and then any boys remaining are distributed according to the numerical requirements of the mines which still have vacancies.

411. The percentages of the various classes are:—

Green tickets and brothers ...	...	...	...	31·72 per cent.
Documents and brothers ...	...	...	...	18·7 per cent.
Remainder ...	...	...	...	49·58 per cent.

412. It is interesting to observe that Article 11 has thus been, *de facto*, modified by the pressure of native opinion so as to admit the document boys to

the same privileges as the others and thereby to extend the limit of $32\frac{1}{2}$ per cent. to more than 50 per cent.

413. Some natives have alleged that, in spite of their having been engaged as "specials," they have, in fact, not been allotted to their old mines, but sent elsewhere. There may, of course, have been isolated errors, but I do not think that these can occur in many cases; a "special" is so described on the way-bill which accompanies him throughout the various stages of his journey from the first moment when he receives his green ticket.

414. Nor do I think that there is any intentional evasion of the under-taking given to the native. The fact that the document boys are allowed to go to their old mines shows that there is no longer any pressure upon the Association to adhere to its $32\frac{1}{2}$ per cent. limit, so that there is really no motive for such a breach of contract. It is to be observed that the Association are under no con-tract with the document boys to return them to their old mines, so that doing so is merely an act of grace. It is unlikely that, while doing this, they would at the same time fail to do as much for natives to whom they are under contract.

415. It should be observed that the native may very well not want to return to his old mine and may deliberately abstain from producing his green ticket or his documents on the chance of getting to some other mine for which he has a fancy. If this scheme fails and he finds himself on a mine where none of his friends are or which he dislikes for any other reason, he often claims to have been a green ticket or a document boy in order to get a change. In such a case he has no grievance; he had his chance and deliberately refused to avail himself of it.

416. Where natives have not been engaged as "specials" they have, of course, no grievance at being allotted to which ever mine they are wanted for; that is what they have agreed to. It has, however, been suggested that, if each native were recruited for a named mine, there would be a more prompt remedy applied to any grievances, as an unpopular mine would soon run short of labour.

417. This reservoir of unappropriated labour does, undoubtedly, render it pos-sible to supply a complement to mines which, on their own merits would fail to get their share. There are, however, two considerations to set against this. In the first place, some mines are less popular than others on account of circumstances which they have no power to remove or modify. Outcrop mines are, generally speaking, more popular than deep levels; and mines close to the attractions of a town are better liked by the natives than those away in the country. Secondly, the Association itself has a strong motive for checking any avoidable causes of unpopularity, as tending to damage their recruiting; and the Association can bring a good deal of pressure to bear upon individual mines to alter their methods, where these do not satisfy the Association.

418. It seems to me highly probable that this unappropriated reservoir of labour is the only real preventative of touting by individual mines. The de-mand for labour is greater than the supply; and the employers, despite their close organisation, are not really loyal to their agreements with each other. For ex-ample, all mines comprised in the N.R.C. have agreed upon a uniform rate of wages; but it is very generally believed (and I have no doubt that the belief is well founded) that there are many evasions of this agreement. In these circum-stances I think that the system of allotment is, at any rate, the lesser of two evils.

419. I cannot suggest any additional methods, compatible with the system of allotment, of trying to meet the wishes of the individual native.

PERIOD OF CONTRACT.

420. A good many natives have complained of the restrictions imposed upon them by having to enter into a contract for a long period. No recruited native is engaged for less than 90 shifts, *i.e.*, between three and four months, and the con-tracts extend from this period up to a year. This leads to a good deal of desertion. Mr. Graham Cross, Assistant Resident Magistrate, who had a long, but not very recent, experience of dealing with cases of native desertion, tells me that he can-not recollect any case of a native who was on a monthly contract being charged

with that offence. These cases have of late been dealt with by the Resident Justice of the Peace at the Pass Office; and the experience of the officers who have taken that duty is that 85 to 90 per cent. of the natives charged with desertion are on long contracts.

421. Voluntary boys are engaged for periods varying with the different mines. The practice of each mine is shown on Annexure 19.

422. The general opinion is that, if natives were recruited on weekly or monthly contracts, the average number of shifts worked by each boy would fall off considerably, thus reducing the total quantity of labour available.

423. It appears that the boys who have overstayed their period of contract and are therefore at liberty to go at a week's notice do, on an average, remain, in the case of East Coast boys, for 80 or 90 shifts, and in the case of N.R.C. boys, for 25 shifts. As they have, before coming on to the weekly contract, done a period of from 3 to 12 months' work, it may fairly be inferred that, if they had not done this, they would continue longer on their weekly contract.

424. On the Durban Roodepoort, East Coast boys remain without a break for an average of 620 days and other natives for an average of 465 days; but this is an especially popular mine.

425. On the Van Ryn Estate, boys engaged on a monthly contract stay, on the average, 5 months; but this also enjoys more popularity than many other mines, being an outcrop.

426. It is very doubtful, to say the least, whether the general run of mines, more especially the deep levels, could maintain their labour supply without the system of contracts.

427. Also, the contract is a great and, I am inclined to think, a necessary protection against natives leaving in panic. In July, 1913, for example, there would probably have been very few natives left if they had all been free to leave on a week's notice. Of the boys who were so free, a very large proportion did leave and were lost to the industry.

428. All piecework natives who contract for three months or more are allowed a probationary period during which they are paid whether they accomplish their task or not; and I am told that some old hands, whose utmost efforts during that period have only enabled them to bore six inches or so a day, from the moment it expires, become, by some miracle, capable of accomplishing their regular 36 inches. This probationary period is, in the case of natives who come straight from home, very desirable, if not absolutely necessary, as their hands are soft and their muscles out of condition; and this concession clearly could not be made to natives engaged for one month only. The temptation to go from mine to mine doing a probationary period upon each would be irresistible.

429. A method, which appears to me to be sound, of meeting the native's desire for a shorter contract has been suggested. The varying popularity of different mines naturally results in a deficiency of labour to the less popular. If mines falling below a certain percentage of their full strength were to take recruited natives on shorter contracts than the other mines, this would tend to attract labour to the former and thus maintain the balance which is the object of the N.R.C. and W.N.L.A., while, at the same time, giving the native more freedom in selecting his period of work. The unpopularity of a mine would perhaps be automatically compensated by this additional attraction. It seems to me that this experiment might be worth trying; if it proved unsuccessful, there would be no difficulty in dropping it.

Release from Contract.

430. At present, the question of the terms upon which a native is released from his contract is left to the individual mine. A good many mines are fairly generous in cancelling a native's contract or allowing him to go home on leave when they have satisfactory evidence that some real emergency requiring his presence at home has arisen. That this is not more generally done is largely the native's own fault. He often tells some cock and bull story of trouble at home when his real

object is to get away and work on some other mine to which he has taken a fancy; and a high proportion of natives who have been allowed to go home on a promise to return later and work out the remainder of their contract do not redeem their promises.

431. I think it would be a reasonable thing to insert in the contract a stipulation enabling the native to determine it on payment of a sum by way of liquidated damages proportionate to the unexpired period. I do not suppose it would be much used, but it could do the mine no harm (if the damages were properly calculated) and it would give the employee a method of escape in the event of a real unanticipated emergency.

432. Another method is that, when native A, whose contract has still two months to run, desires to go home, he is allowed to do so provided that he can arrange with native B to agree to an extension of two months in the latter's period of contract.

433. Both these methods are already in actual use on some mines, so they cannot involve anything impracticable. The embodiment of one or both in the contract would place the matter upon a definite footing.

Uncertainty of Terms.

434. There has been some criticism as to the vagueness of the N.R.C. contract with reference to the amount of wages to be paid. With regard to several classes of work it does not set out a definite wage, but states that payment will be " at the usual mine rates " or " at the ruling current rates " (Annexure 2). This would appear to leave it open to the mine to reduce the wage whenever it can engage a few boys locally on cheaper terms and thus establish a new " current rate." It will be observed that the native, being bound to the mine, has not the corresponding opportunity to raise the current rate by getting another mine to engage him on better terms.

435. I do not see how this is to be avoided as long as natives are engaged wholesale, and for general work. To set out all the rates of pay for different classes of work on different mines would complicate the contract to such an extent that there would be less chance than ever of the native understanding it.

436. The W.N.L.A. gets round the difficulty by engaging all natives at a *minimum* rate of 1s. 6d. a shift. This is not entirely satisfactory, because it does not set out the true contract between the parties; in the case of a hammerboy, for instance, neither employer nor employee contemplates that the latter shall receive only 1s. 6d. a shift.

437. While I am not aware of any other case in which an employee binds himself to work for a long period without stipulating for a fixed wage. I think that the importance of the omission may easily be over-estimated. I have no doubt that, by this time, the rates of pay for the different classes of work are perfectly well known to the natives generally; and I think that, with the existing difficulty of getting labour, there is not much chance of any unfair alteration of rates.

Breach of Conditions.

438. There was a complaint from a W.N.L.A. boy that he had been engaged at his home only for a six months' contract, but that, on arrival here, he was told it was for 12 months. Since the W.N.L.A., invariably recruit for a uniform period of 12 months, I think that the fact must be perfectly well-known in the districts where the Association operates.

439. The N.R.C. recruit for certain mines on which the rates payable under the general N.R.C. contract do not prevail.

440. At the Durban-Roodepoort the contract is varied in the presence of the Native Affairs Department. I do not see any objection to this. An employer and employee are always entitled to vary their contract by mutual consent; and the Native Affairs Department can make sure that the native really does consent and understands what he is consenting to. If he prefers to adhere to the terms of

his original contract, the Department can secure that the mine pays him on those terms. As a matter of fact, he never does; boys who engage for the Durban-Roodepoort know and like its peculiar terms.

441. There are cases, however, where the terms of the contract are varied without reference to the Natives Affairs Department. I see no reason to suppose that any unfairness results from this, but I think that it is a sound general principle that the Department should be a party to such a variation. The assumption involved in all the protection afforded to the native labourer is that he is a minor under tutelage. No minor can, by general principles of law, vary a contract without the assistance of his guardian; and the native's guardian in this respect is the Director of Native Labour.

CHAPTER VII.

MISCELLANEOUS COMPLAINTS.

CHAPTER VII.

MISCELLANEOUS COMPLAINTS.

TAXATION.

442. Some natives complained that they were subject to double taxation, paying both at their kraals in the Cape Province and also at the mines in the Transvaal.

443. The Transvaal tax of £2 per annum is not chargeable upon natives resident in the Cape Province who have paid their tax there. In order to prove that they have so paid, they must produce to the Transvaal collector their Cape Province receipt. This receipt is, however, needed by their family in the Cape Province in order to show that the local levy has been paid; and the difficulties of transmission to and fro are often serious to a native.

444. It seems to me that, where a native claims to have paid his Cape Province tax, the Native Affairs Department might well take upon itself the burden of verifying the allegation by reference to its representative in the district whence the native comes. The payment must be recorded in their books; and it is easier and more certain for two public officers to communicate than for two natives to do so.

445. I understand that there is at present some difficulty in identifying the native; but it is evident that this difficulty has to be got over, under any system, if the native is to be secured against paying twice over.

446. Almost everywhere, the natives from Portuguese East Africa complained of the Portuguese tax deducted from their pay. It appears that recently Portuguese officials claimed and received from the mines a sum of £1 for every Portuguese native staying more than a year on the mines, which tax was deducted by the mines from the pay of the native. When this came to the notice of the Director, he objected, and the money has been refunded to the natives. I understand that the matter is still pending as between the mines and the Portuguese Government; but, whatever may be the ultimate arrangement, the grievance of the native has been removed.

NATIVE AFFAIRS DEPARTMENT.

447. At one time the Native Affairs Department had two classes of officers looking after natives on the mines—Inspectors and Protectors—the former having certain judicial powers, while the latter were administrative officers, intended to act specially in the interest of the native.

448. Latterly, the two offices have been amalgamated, or rather are now held by the same man, and various natives have complained to me that the man appointed to protect them inflicts penalties upon them instead. I do not entirely understand this complaint; natives must be accustomed to a patriarchal form of government, and I suppose that both their own chiefs and the magistrates in the Native Territories hold that sort of double position.

449. At the same time, I do not think such a primitive method of administration good in itself. It is necessary in thinly populated territories because you can only afford one man to the district, and he must do whatever there is to be done. As soon as it becomes possible, with due regard to economy, to subdivide such functions, they should, as a rule, be subdivided. The impartial frame of mind which is desirable in a judicial officer is largely a matter of training and habit; and this quality is not cultivated by performing the functions of a Protector, who must often be frankly anxious to secure the native's success in his dispute with a white man.

450. I think that both classes of work would probably be more efficiently performed by officers specializing in each, and I recommend that the old arrangement be reverted to.

451. I also think that some, at any rate, of the Inspectors or Protectors should have a certain amount of civil jurisdiction. Native labourers on the mines have a good many disputes among themselves over civil matters, questions of debt, etc. Until the Native Labour Regulation Act, 1911, came into operation, the Inspectors of the Native Affairs Department had jurisdiction to decide such disputes and to execute their judgments by means of orders upon the pay of the native against whom judgment was given. This jurisdiction, conferred by section 5 (1) (c) of Transvaal Proclamation 37 of 1901, has been repealed by Act 15 of 1911, and no other provision has been substituted.

452. Practically everyone with experience in the matter agrees that the former provisions were very useful. It is apparent that the native mine labourer suffers under special disabilities in recovering his debts, etc., by ordinary process of law.

He cannot afford to employ a solicitor; his lack of language and education prevents his issuing summons and conducting his case in person; and (in many cases) his distance from the court and (in all cases) the necessity under which he lies of obtaining a special pass to visit it are further obstructions to his obtaining the ordinary remedies. For practical purposes he is debarred access to the courts; and this constitutes a very strong case for providing him with some substitute.

453. I understand that the former provisions were re-enacted in the original draft of Act 15 of 1911, but were cut out in Select Committee. If the purpose of this was, as I have been told, to protect the interests of legal practitioners, experience has shown the uselessness of the precaution. I doubt whether a single civil case has been brought in the Johannesburg courts by a native mine labourer during the two years that Act 15 of 1911 has been in force; certainly the total number of such cases is absolutely negligible. The change has brought no perceptible advantage to the legal profession; its only effect has been to deprive the labourer of any legal means of enforcing his rights.

454. A small but curious complaint concerning the Native Affairs Department was that, at some pass offices, every native is compelled to have a native name. Some natives, Christians of a generation or two's standing, have no such name; and apparently, some of them have run across a clerk, or clerks, who, being unaware of the possibility of this, have insisted on the native's producing, or inventing something with which they can fill up the blank on the passport marked "Name (native)." I mentioned the matter to the Director, and I do not suppose that it will recur.

TRAVELLING.

455. There were several complaints in connection with railway travelling, especially as to overcrowding. In ordinary circumstances, the number of natives in a carriage is such that they have room to sit but not to lie down, and, in the commonest type of carriage, there is a long bench down the middle which is filled with natives sitting back to back, with nothing but each other to lean against. It seems to me that, on a journey which involves two nights in the train, this must be extremely fatiguing.

456. At the same time, it must be remembered that the native from the Transkei (which is the longest journey) pays his own railway fare, and that these "batch" trains give him a much reduced fare. He is, in fact, simply in the position of everyone who chooses to take a cheap excursion ticket; he puts up with increased crowding in order to save money. There are other trains, with better native accommodation, for those who choose to spend their money upon them. Years ago, when I cared less about comfort and more about shillings than I do now, I have made night journeys—though never, I admit, more than one night at a time—in England in just as cramped conditions; and the postcart in which 20 years ago every one in South Africa travelled day and night, sometimes for a week or more on end, was often quite as uncomfortable.

457. The East Coast native does not pay his own fare; but he has only one night in the train.

458. I am informed, that there is a good deal of overcrowding at certain seasons. This should not be permitted; the ordinary number of passengers is quite the largest compatible with tolerable comfort.

459. I am afraid I am unable to support the ingenious argument of one native, who supported his request for a free pass to the Rand in the following terms:—"I am always given to understand that the trains belong to the Government, and I think that, if the Government wants me to come up here and work, then the Government should pay for my train fare." I may add, in passing, that the belief that the Government owns the mines is all but universal among native mine labourers.

460. There were several complaints that natives had been charged various sums up to 10s. for food provided for them on the train and that they had received no notice of this deduction. I think there may be ground for this complaint. On the attestation sheet (Annexure 2) there is a column reserved for food deductions. If this column is filled in, its contents will be notified to the native by the attesting officer: but, if it is blank when handed to that officer, nothing will be said to the native on this subject. These sheets are in triplicate; one goes to the recruiter, one to the Government compound at Driehoek and the third is retained by the attesting officer. The Driehoek copy is not posted direct to Driehoek, but sent up with the batch of natives concerned; if it were posted, the natives would sometimes arrive before their papers. It is thus possible for the recruiter to make entries upon this after the attestation is complete, even without any intention of fraud; he may not have ascertained how much the native wants for food until just before the latter entrains.

461. The attestation sheet is again read to the native on arrival at Drie-hoek; and, if he then takes any objection to the deductions, reference is made to the copy kept by the attesting officer, and any alterations would be discovered. If, however, the boy does not pay attention to what is told him—and he is quite likely to be getting rather bored with the subject by this time—he may not notice the matter until he finds this money deducted from his wages, a month or two later.

462. The only remedy which I can suggest is that attesting officers should leave no blank spaces on the forms but, where there is no entry, should fill up with a "Nil" rubber stamp; where the whole column is blank, a single line down the middle would serve the purpose and save labour.

463. I have been told that natives are unduly hustled by the railway staff, and sometimes left behind, on the short journeys round the Rand. In the last few months I have been on the look out during my railway trips on the Springs-Randfontein line and have also taken journeys along it on Sunday for the express purpose of watching the treatment of natives thereon. I have seen nothing to ground any serious complaint; most of the hustling was done by the natives themselves.

464. From the mines round Germiston came a complaint that the native booking-office was unreasonably far from the station. It is, in fact, more than 200 yards from the principal entrance to the station. About 15,400 natives a month use it. I do not know whether this arrangement is only temporary, during the rebuilding of the station.

465. The railway carries natives at a different rate from coloured people. As a rule, this distinction is a benefit to the native, since his rate is the cheaper; but, I have come across cases where undoubted natives, being light in colour, have been charged the higher rate. To distinguish between a native and a coloured man often puzzles persons of more experience than a casual railway servant.

466. The railway fare from Port Shepstone to Germiston is, for a Zulu from Natal, £1 16s. 6d.; for a Pondo from Cape Colony, £1 2s. 7d.

467. From the correspondence on this subject between the Railway Adminis-tration and the Native Affairs Department it appears that this distinction arose from the desire of Natal, when a separate Colony, to compete with the Cape railways for the traffic from Cape Colony to the mines; and also from a desire to restrain Natal labour from going to the Rand. These considerations appear to have lost their force since Union: and the arrangement appears to the natives —as, indeed, it does to me—inequitable.

Local Credit.

468. Many native labourers buy tin boxes from the local stores and leave them with the storekeeper, buying from time to time things which are put in these boxes and left at the store partly for safe custody but largely by way of pledge, the articles, or some of them, having been bought on credit.

469. This practice leads to disputes with the storekeepers and also to natives buying on credit things which they do not need. Some tribes can be induced to buy anything if they have not to pay for it immediately.

470. Some natives also suffer losses under this box system. If the store-keeper goes insolvent, the boxes with their contents are sold in the estate and the native gets nothing. Of course a native mine labourer has no chance to see the statutory advertisements or to protect his interest otherwise.

471. I do not see that the native mine labourer has any legitimate use for local credit. He is provided with all necessaries in addition to his pay; he gets paid monthly; and, during the period that he is at work, he should be saving money, not getting into debt. I think that, on the Rand, debts from native labourers to Europeans should be irrecoverable and any pledge for such debts invalid.

472. It may be objected that this is inconsistent with my recommendation in paragraphs 452 and 453 of additional facilities for the recovery of debts from natives. I do not think so; in that case the question was of debts between natives themselves, where Europeans were not involved. The native can pre-sumably look after himself in dealing with his own kind; he certainly cannot always hold his own with the Reef storekeepers. Mine labourers will, in any event, lend money, or deposit it for safe keeping, among themselves; so it is necessary to provide them with a remedy. But they will not get credit from European traders if the debt is irrecoverable; the trader will see to that.

473. The mines might each provide a store-room for their boys' boxes and other personal property, as is already done at the Angelo.

PART III

CONTROL.

PART III.

CONTROL.

474. There are normally about 200,000 native mine labourers on the Reef. They are all male, practically all adults and the large majority in the prime of life. They are scattered over 50 miles of country in blocks of from 1,000 to 5,000 in each compound. They can mobilise themselves in a few minutes, armed with such weapons as assegais, jumpers, axes, etc. A good many of them consider, whether rightly or wrongly, that they have grievances against the Europeans, and most of them are savages, whose only idea of reform is violence. All of them want more pay, and most of them are under the impression that the employment of force by European miners during the riots of last July resulted in the latter obtaining their demands. It is not necessary to emphasise the possibilities of mischief which are latent in such a condition of affairs.

475. Hitherto these great masses of natives have been controlled by moral force only. They have shown themselves remarkbly amenable to authority and very disinclined to make any attack upon Europeans, their occasional riots having been mostly inter-tribal fights. The question is whether it will long be safe to rely upon the continuance of these conditions or whether it is necessary to make provision for a possible outbreak.

476. The three safeguards which have hitherto existed have been—
(1) The personal influence of the compound managers.
(2) The native respect for European authority as personified in the police.
(3) The inter-tribal jealousies which have always rendered it possible, in the last resort, to protect Europeans by utilising one tribe against another.

477. There are unmistakable signs that all these three safeguards are tending to break down.

478. During the riots of July—or, rather, by great good luck, not until the riots were over—the natives in the compounds of the Village Main, Village Deep, City and Suburban and Meyer and Charlton refused to go to work without increase of pay. They entirely disregarded the orders and exhortations of their compound managers—at the City and Suburban they hunted the compound manager out of the compound with stones, inflicting serious injuries—of the Director of Native Labour, of Mr. Graham Cross, A.R.M., and of Mr. Taberer, of the N.R.C., who has been long and widely known, at any rate to Cape Colony and Basutoland natives.

479. Mounted police were called in, but this produced no affect at all. The natives were quite prepared for a stand-up fight with these police, and at one mine they actually stoned them.

480. The resistance was only quelled by calling in a company of soldiers, whose fixed bayonets appeared to cow the natives and who succeeded in arresting the leaders in each compound, after which the remainder went quietly to their work.

481. It is noteworthy that, in each of these compounds, there were Zulus, Basutos, Cape Colony natives of various tribes, Shangaans and other East Coast natives, and also Tropicals. They acted absolutely together. There is, however, a good deal of reason to believe that intimidation played a considerable part in this unanimity, and that a good many natives who had no desire to join were driven to do so by threats from the others. The strongest tribe dominated the compound, for the moment at any rate.

482. There is no doubt that, on this occasion, we were within an ace of a native outbreak on a serious scale. That it did not occur was due solely to the fortunate accident that the natives delayed their action until the morning of Tuesday, 8th July. Had they come out on the Saturday or Sunday, there would have been neither police or troops available; they were both fully occupied with the white rioters. There were several thousand natives in the four compounds affected, and if they had broken out, there would have been great danger of the infection spreading all along the Reef.

483. Again, it is certain that, during the last dozen years, tribal faction fights have markedly decreased. I cannot, however, say with certainty that this is due to the lessening of tribal jealousies, because there is no doubt that supervision has increased during the same period.

484. There is an increasing class known as "Reef boys" who have lost all tribal bonds and who never go home, but live on the Rand year in and year out. They are generally of bad character and are either criminals themselves or associates of criminals. These boys are likely to give trouble in the event of industrial disturbances.

485. There is wide difference of opinion among persons in touch with the mine natives as to how far these tendencies have proceeded. Upon the whole, the more general view seems to be that, for the present, the natives will continue to be, as of old, susceptible to moral restraint. But there is practical unanimity that the three safeguards mentioned above are giving way, though there is much diversity as to the degree of the change.

486. I am inclined to the view that a great change has already taken place, in spite of the testimony to the contrary of a considerable majority of persons who, I quite admit, know a great deal more about the native than I do. My reason is that this testimony necessarily consist almost entirely of mere expressions of opinion, however expert, as to what would happen in hypothetical circumstances. On the other hand there are a good many actual and unmistakeable facts. In the four compounds mentioned above, the natives did entirely disregard their compound managers, they did actually attack the police, and they did stand together solidly against the forces of the white man. At the Premier, in November last, a faction fight between Moshesh Basutos and Shangaans developed into an attack by the Basutos upon the white compound guards and police and was followed by the looting of the compound store, and order was not restored until firearms had been resorted to and three natives killed and sixteen wounded.

487. Then again, education is advancing among the natives and this advance is, as usual, bringing in its train agitation and organisation. There is no doubt that deliberate attempts are being made among the natives to get rid of tribal distinctions and to unite the Bantu races for the purpose of obtaining better conditions from the Europeans. There is no necessity to call evidence of this; a study of the native press, the proceedings of native political unions, etc., will make it clear to anyone that there is a movement—a perfectly legitimate movement—in this direction.

488. It is also certain that this movement has made some progress. I know nothing except that I have read in the papers of the strikes of native women at Bloemfontein and Winburg, but the mere fact that there could be such strikes at all shows that the native with whom we have now to deal is a very different person from the native of a generation back.

489. I see no necessity to take an alarmist view. With ordinary care and good government, no question of hostilities between natives and Europeans should ever arise. But that is not a sufficient reason for neglecting to provide against them. It seems to me that house insurance is a fair parallel; the risk of an ordinary well-built residence being burned down is very small indeed; but every prudent householder insures, all the same. The results of even a partial and temporary outbreak of compound natives, if it were not checked at once, would be so grave that it is only common prudence to make serious provision for the possibility of such an occurrence.

490. The suggestions that have been made to me as to precautions against a general outbreak among native mine labourers may be grouped as follows:—

(1) A dormant military organisation among the whites on every mine.

(2) A permanent European guard on each mine.

(3) The closed compound system.

(4) That compounds should be so designed that, while habitually open, they should be closable upon an emergency.

(5) An intelligence department or secret service in the compounds to keep in touch with native feeling.

(6) A mobile force of police available to strike in any direction.

(7) The limitation of the number of natives in the compounds to a definite proportion to the number of Europeans.

(8) Closer supervision of the compounds at night.

(9) Searches for arms at regular intervals.

(10) The more complete separation of tribes in the compounds as while at work.

491. (1) It is very necessary that any riot should be checked at once; therefore the force must be on the spot, and this is a consideration which seems to me to point strongly to the first of these suggestions as the most effective measure.

492. On every mine there should exist some scheme under which the available European force could be instantly mobilised in the event of native trouble. This country has an unusually high proportion of civilians accustomed to the use of arms, and most mines could turn out a very respectable force if the necessary preparations were made beforehand. All that is necessary is to ascertain which members of the staff are capable of bearing arms, arrange that each of them shall know where he can immediately obtain a supply of arms and ammunition—shotguns are quite effective, and a good many men keep them for sporting purposes—and appoint a spot where they are to fall in upon the arranged signal. Officers having been appointed beforehand and plans arranged as to the method of action, a serviceable force ought to be collected on any mine in a very short time indeed.

493. The numbers of such a force would, however, be their weak point. If the outbreak came at a time of industrial disturbance—and at such a time it is at once most probable and most dangerous—only the staff could be depended upon. I need not point out the urgent necessity of limiting the organisation to those men who can, in all circumstances, be depended upon to take the side of law and order. There is no doubt that, during the recent disturbances, some at least of the miners urged the natives to join in the strike. To arm and include among the defenders any persons holding those views would be fatal.

494. But, even taking the numbers available at the lowest estimate, there would probably be sufficient, in combination with the further precautions which I suggest later on, to check the rioters until additional force arrived. There is no doubt that such additional force would soon mobilise itself. In such circumstances as those supposed, the large majority of Europeans would turn out before long. All that is needed is to provide for the first rush.

495. (2) I doubt the wisdom of establishing permanent armed guards on each mine with a view to native outbreaks. The creation of a number of private armies in the middle of a peaceful population smacks of the middle ages. For the greater part of the time these men would be idle, and it is doubtful whether private commercial companies could keep up that strict discipline without which an army is always more of a danger than a protection. Further, the rank and file would be drawn from the same class as the European miner; they are unlikely to acquire much *esprit de corps*, and there is the grave danger that, in the event of industrial disturbances, they might prove undependable. Also, they would be a source of serious and, as it seems to me, unnecessary expense.

496. (3) Various witnesses have advocated the closed compound system, *i.e.*, that each mine should be surrounded with a wire fence and no native allowed outside this during his term of service, nor would any stranger be allowed within the fence without a permit. This system is in use upon the diamond mines.

497. I do not know that this system would in the actual event of an outbreak be much superior to that of "closable compounds" discussed under the next head. If the outbreak took place inside the compound, it could under the latter system be turned into a closed compound in two minutes; if on the mine, the wire fence would offer little resistance.

498. It does, however, seem to me that the system would, by preventing communication from compound to compound, put difficulties in the way of any organised and simultaneous outbreak along the Reef. I think also that the system would discourage the class of native who comes chiefly to enjoy the delights of urban life, and the mines would be well rid of them.

499. There can be no doubt that many incidental advantages, not directly connected with the present subject, arise from closed compounds. Theft of gold is rendered more difficult; the natives are better and more cheaply supplied by the compound stores than by outside storekeepers; desertion is reduced; the curse of the illicit liquor trade is completely done away with, so far as the mine native is concerned, and he is protected from many other sources of temptation. In fact, at the Premier and at De Beers there is practically no crime.

500. These considerations are not, however, pertinent to the present subject, and I think that, for purposes of control, the closed compound system has no great

advantages over the system of "closable compounds," while to establish it would cause many difficulties. On some mines, owing to want of space, it is simply impracticable.

501. (4) I think that steps ought certainly to be taken to render the compounds more easily convertible into places of detention. Where the compound has strong, steelcased gates which can be locked from the outside (as at the Premier Diamond Mine), only one entrance, and high walls with no outer windows, a comparatively few armed men can prevent exit from it and thus isolate a disturbance which might otherwise spread with alarming consequences. The obvious defects of the present compounds are unnecessary entrances, external windows, and walls scarcely above the level of the lean-to roofs of the rooms built against them, over which it would be easy to scramble and then to drop outside the wall.

502. Of course, the exact nature of the alterations required is a matter upon which expert military or police opinion would have to be taken. Here I only wish to urge that compounds should be, for the future, constructed with a view to the possible necessity of detaining their inmates by armed force.

503. The weak point of this precaution is that, on their way to and from shift, the natives are in the open, and that they may choose that moment to break out. It is not, however, likely that outbreaks would be simultaneous along the whole Reef and it would be an immense gain if, upon receipt of the news of such an outbreak at one point, the natives elsewhere could be confined to barracks, so to speak. Even at the actual scene of the outbreak, there would be considerable advantage in having adjacent a closable compound where those natives who could be driven into it would be controlled with comparative ease.

504. (5) An intelligence department is an essential accessory of any scheme of defence. It is very necessary that the Government should be constantly informed of the movements of native opinion, especially upon such a subject as that now under discussion. The native is, however, very secretive towards Europeans as regards his own affairs, and, as far as I can gather, not many compound managers are in a position to anticipate the next move of the natives under their charge. The N.A.D. has certain sources of information, which might be developed. This is a subject upon which it is obviously undesirable to go into details, nor am I competent to do so, but I would urge that the importance of the matter should be constantly kept in view.

505. (6) A grave drawback to relying upon any force of police, mobile or otherwise, is that if, as is most probable, a native outbreak takes place as a result of disturbances among the Europeans, this force is almost certain to have been diverted to deal with the latter. In case of serious riots among whites, it may easily be impossible to keep in reserve for a further contingency any part of the force available. In any case, there will certainly be tremendous temptation to the authorities, if pressed for men, to utilise the services of a large and efficient force, already on the spot, to repel the immediate danger, taking the chance that the situation may not be complicated by an additional danger which has not at the moment, actually arisen.

506. (7) As to limiting the number of natives in proportion to those of white men, the logical course would be to limit them in proportion to the number of white men who could be counted on to bear arms against them in the event of an outbreak; other white men might as well not be there. This proposal therefore resolves itself into requiring a guard, actual or potential, of so many Europeans to every thousand natives, to be kept up by any importer of native labour on a large scale. This has been discussed in paragraphs 491—495 above.

507. (8) At most compounds there is no white man on duty at night; in many, there is virtually no supervision at all. This is obviously an unsafe position; a planned rising would, by choosing its time, get a long start before anyone heard of it. I do not think that a compound of any size should ever be left without a white man on duty.

508. (9) Most compounds are already searched for weapons at intervals. The practice is a good one, as far as it goes; but its main result has been to show that native mine labourers can supply themselves with such weapons as assegais and mining tools at very short notice. There is, at present, no reason to fear that they will obtain firearms.

509. (10) It has been suggested that the tribes should be separated both in the compounds and while at work, in order to check the growing unity amongst the natives. As a matter of fact, they are already separated in the compounds, so far as this can conveniently be done, not with the intention set out above but in order to check their ancient habit of faction fights. Underground, there is no organised

attempt to keep them apart, but, in fact, the different tribes are to some extent separated by their inclination for different kinds of work. To carry this any farther is not practicable.

510. Besides the above considerations, I do not think that any attempt to prevent the natives from amalgamating is justifiable upon moral grounds. *"Divide et impera"* may be a good policy, but if the natives are inclined to substitute internal peace and mutual help for their practice of tribal quarrels, that is a movement towards civilisation, which we ought to encourage, not to frustrate.

511. In an outbreak the compound manager will probably know—he certainly ought to know—who are likely to be the ringleaders. A prompt seizure of these will often avert further trouble. This, however, is not a matter for which preparation can be made beforehand further than by the compound manager acquainting himself with the natives under his charge, and that is so obviously a part of his everyday work that it is hardly necessary to call attention to it. I only mention the matter because so many compound managers have told me, in reply to questions as to what they would do in the event of trouble, that they would call the police, not in the least realising that, if there is ever serious trouble, it will probably come just when no police can be spared. I think that all compound managers—and also mine managers—ought to be thoroughly awake to the fact that, among the possibilities for which they have to make provision is that of having to control their compounds solely with local resources and without prospect of immediate help from outside.

512. It is, I take it, unnecessary to urge the importance of having ready a plan, prepared beforehand, for handling the natives in the case of further disturbances. No doubt all concerned have compared their experiences during the troubles of last July and have decided how to act in the event of a similar emergency arising.

513. In considering the possibility of disturbances in the compounds, it is impossible to overlook the part played by intoxicating liquor in provoking such disturbances. All experience shows that most compound rows begin with some natives who have been drinking, and that, when exceptional circumstances, such as existed in January 1914, allow of the almost complete cutting off of illicit liquor, there is always unusual peace in the compounds.

514. I need not go into this subject at any length, since in the Report of the Transvaal Liquor Commission, 1908-1910 the whole subject of prohibition in relation to the mine natives was fully dealt with, and I have seen no reason to change the views there expressed. The only point which I wish to bring forward at present is that compound managers have in their hands the power of almost completely suppressing the consumption of liquor in their compounds; my recent enquiries have convinced me that many of them do not exercise that power to nearly the extent that they might do.

515. Perhaps the commonest drink in the compound is " Khali," a fermented liquor in which golden syrup and a local root, powdered, are the active agents. It can be very quickly made—much more quickly than kaffir beer—and it causes a great deal of drunkenness.

516. I do not understand why it should have so much effect, since the samples that have been analysed show a very low alcoholic strength, hardly as much as ordinary malt liquor. It may be that, apart from its alcohol, the root has some action as a drug. For the present purpose, however, it is unnecessary to inquire into its precise action; the undoubted fact is that it does cause much drunkenness.

517. A compound manager who, personally and by his compound police, exercises proper supervision over his compound, can almost entirely prevent the use of this stuff within its walls, and many of them do so. The difficulty is that this action is necessarily taken at the expense of a certain amount of popularity among the natives, and that is a point upon which compound managers are naturally very sensitive, since their living largely depends upon the number of natives whom they can attract to their compounds. As a result there is undoubtedly a certain amount of underhand competition going on to make certain compounds attractive by winking at the manufacture and consumption of liquor.

518. This can be, and ought to be, stopped; what is wanted is uniform action. Many compound managers would be only too delighted to suppress liquor in their compounds with a firm hand if they could be assured that their neighbours would do the same. Each of them desires his compound to be orderly, and they all know that liquor is the greatest foe to order; but each of them is naturally disinclined to take action which will result in driving his supply of labour into the arms of a slacker neighbour. If that slacker neighbour were squeezed out, that very undesirable form of competition would cease.

519. Captain Kirkpatrick, Inspector of Police in charge of the East Rand, informed me that, as a result of pressure put by him upon compound managers, a local storekeeper who sold 84 cases—a case is four dozen tins—of golden syrup in October, 1913, sold only two cases in November.

520. This is a matter in which everyone's interest points in the same direction. The mines, the police, the N.A.D., and everyone who has the welfare of the native at heart must all, for various reasons, desire to see the secret consumption in the compounds of injurious forms of alcohol stamped out, and they ought to work together to that end. If they do work together loyally, without private reservations which may for the moment advantage a particular mine but must injure the common aim in the long run, the evil can be stamped out.

521. I recommend that it be made an offence in a compound manager that more than a negligible quantity of liquor should be found in his compound. Of course, it is too much to expect that he should absolutely prevent the manufacture or importation of small amounts; but when it comes—as it sometimes does come —to the police, in the course of a raid, finding hundreds of thousands of gallons of liquor in one compound, then it may be said without hesitation that the compound manager is either conniving or incompetent.

522. I do not think it is necessary that the penalty should be severe. The Minister, by section 11 of Act 15 of 1911, already has the power to cancel a compound manager's licence if the latter be convicted of any offence and thus to prevent his carrying on the business by which he earns his living. This tremendously drastic power clearly ought to be used with caution. But one or more convictions for the offence suggested would certainly justify the cancellation of the licence.

523. A great deal could be done by arranging to have a white man at the compound gate with instructions to prevent the importation of alcohol and to note where the materials for its manufacture, such as golden syrup, were mostly going to.

524. I see no objection to making it an offence to be in possession of the root from which " khali " is made; it does not appear to have any legitimate use.

PART IV.

RECUITING.

PART IV.

RECRUITING.

PRESENT SOURCES OF LABOUR.

525. A great many complaints and suggestions have been received in connection with the system under which the mines obtain their native labour. At present such labour is obtained from four sources:—

(1) The Witwatersrand Native Labour Association, Ltd.
(2) The Native Recruiting Corporation, Ltd.
(3) Private Recruiters.
(4) Voluntary natives.

526. During the year 1913, 244,343 natives were engaged for service on the mines. Of these 42,680 were brought by the W.N.L.A., 57,109 by the N.R.C., and 49,414 by private recruiters; while 95,140 were voluntary natives i.e., natives who presented themselves at the mines for employment, and who were not enlisted through any agent.

527. The W.N.L.A. and the N.R.C. are organisations composed of practically all the mining companies, with the exception, in the case of the N.R.C., of the Robinson Group. The W.N.L.A. operates in Portuguese East Africa and also in British Central Africa, though the latter has now ceased to be available, owing to the action of the Union Government in prohibiting the recruiting of natives north of latitude 22. The N.R.C. recruits within the Union.

528. Natives recruited by the W.N.L.A. are brought to a compound at Johannesburg and are thence allotted to the various mines composing the Association in definite proportions agreed upon among themselves. Most of such natives enlist for service on the mines generally, not for any particular mine (subject to the arrangement as to " specials " and " documents " which was described in paragraphs 406—409 above). Their period of contract is one year, which is generally interpreted as 313 shifts. They are engaged to do any kind of mine work at the option of the employer.

529. The method of the W.N.L.A. is to establish in their recruiting areas scattered stations consisting of a couple of huts in charge of a native, with a supply of food. Any native who wishes to go to work will be received at any of these stations, fed and, twice a week, sent off with other recruits in charge of a conductor. These parties walk from station to station, gathering up additions on the way, until they reach a divisional camp, whence they are forwarded, by road, steamer or rail, to Ressano Garcia.

530. There are about 75 stations; and the Association employs about 30 Europeans and about 250 natives within Portuguese Territory. Besides these, there are about 200 native runners, who are supplied with gaudy jerseys and get a capitation fee of 10d. for every recruit they bring in. If the recruit comes to a station direct, without the intervention of a runner, he himself gets the 10d., with the result that now only 2 per cent. are brought by runners; the others present themselves for enlistment.

531. The Association provides the recruit with free passage and food to Johannesburg. It gives no advances, but provides an outfit, the cost whereof is deducted from the native's wages. At the end of his service it repatriates him at a charge not exceeding £1.

532. All recruits are engaged at a minimum wage of 1s. 6d. a shift; in fact nearly all of them receive more. The form of contract and a translation is attached (Annexures 20 and 21).

533. The recruiters of the W.N.L.A. are not paid capitation fees, with the exception of the almost obsolete native runner. They receive salaries and a commission calculated, not upon the number of recruits collected by each, but upon the total number collected by all. About two-thirds of their earnings arise from salary, about one-third from commission.

534. Natives recruited by the N.R.C. are brought to the Government Compound at Driehoek, Germiston, and thence dispatched to the various mines for which they have enlisted. Each native is engaged for service on a particular mine. The period of contract varies from three months upwards, the average being 171 shifts. The engagement is for any kind of mine work at the option of the employer.

535. The N.R.C. depends for its recruiting principally upon traders in the Native Territories, more especially within the Cape Province. A native wishing to go to work comes to one of these traders, who advances him money up to, until recently, £5 (at present £2) and turns him over to the agent of the Corporation, who supplies him with a railway ticket and food for the journey to Johannesburg. The cost of the fare and the food are deducted from the recruit's wages.

536. The recruits are engaged at a wage varying with the class of work they may be set to do when they arrive on the mine. For form of contract see Annexure 2.

537. There are about 1,000 licensed labour agents working for the N.R.C., though most of them have their own businesses as well. The agents employ perhaps twice as many runners. Payment is made by capitation fees varying in amount according to the period for which the recruit contracts. Each recruiter is thus in active competition with every other recruiter, though working for the same principal.

538. Private recruiters generally work upon the lines of the N.R.C. The largest of them, Mr. A. M. Mostert, is a contractor, i.e., he himself employs, pays and feeds the natives whom he recruits subletting their labour to a mine and being paid an agreed sum for each shift worked. The others are mostly labour agents pure and simple i.e., natives engaged through them contract direct with the mine, the recruiter's only interest being a capitation fee proportioned to the period for which the native agrees to serve.

539. The voluntary portion of the labour supply is divided into local volunteers and new arrivals. The latter are natives who have come to the Rand at their own expense, and who make their own agreements with the mine on the spot. The local volunteer is a native who, having completed a previous job, either with a mine or with a private employer, engages himself to a mine.

540. A large number of natives who have been originally brought up under contract for a definite period, continue working for the same mine after that period has expired. In the absence of special arrangements (which are in practice never made) the position of these natives is governed by Native Labour Regulation No. 29, by which they are declared to be weekly labourers, i.e., they can leave after giving seven days' notice. In many cases this notice is not insisted upon, and the native will, in fact, be allowed to go at a day's notice if he has any adequate reason for desiring it.

THE PRINCIPLE OF RECRUITING.

541. Various witnesses have advocated the abolition of recruiting. There is perhaps some confusion in the minds of some of them as to what constitutes recruiting. If A desires a servant and pays B to persuade C to take service with A, the essence of recruiting is present. That agreement certainly cannot be abolished by any external pressure. You cannot enforce a law forbidding B to persuade C, even if it were reasonable to enact it: nor can you prevent A from giving money to B if C enters A's service.

542. Nor do I see why recruiting, in this essential form, ought to be abolished. It is desirable from every point of view that the native should work; and there is therefore nothing improper in persuading him to do so. It is true that there are many reasons, physical and moral, for doubting whether the mines of the Rand are a good place for him to work; but the necessary conclusion from that line of reasoning, if accepted, is that natives ought to be altogether prohibited from working on those mines. You cannot logically say that 50,000 people should be allowed to put themselves in the way of physical and moral degeneration, but that 200,000 should not.

543. I think there is tolerably general agreement that, while much might be done to improve the conditions under which natives work on the mines, it is, even under existing conditions, better for them to work there than not to work at all; and there is certainly no labour market in South Africa which could utilise all the native labour available if the mines were closed.

544. Since, then, it is proper for B to persuade the native to work on the mines, it cannot be wrong for A to pay B for his services in doing so.

OBJECTIONS TO EXISTING METHODS.

545. But, though I see no harm in the principle of recruiting, there may be many objectionable features in its incidents. The objections taken to the existing system may be summarised as follows:—

(1) It involves enormous expense.

(2) It necessitates engaging natives on long contracts.

(3) The recruited labourer is not as efficient a worker as the voluntary labourer.

(4) Recruiters induce natives to contract by false representations or by promises which are not fulfilled;

(5) Many of the recruiters are traders; and the prospect of obtaining capitation fees for natives sent to the mines induces them virtually to enslave natives by extending to them excessive credit.

(6) The system of giving advances of money to natives on engagement is undesirable;

(7) The touting of recruiters lowers the prestige of the white man.

(8) The recruiting business is now a vast monopoly of the mines, so that other industries, notably agriculture, have not a fair opportunity to compete for labour.

(9) Chiefs virtually compel their subjects to join, being bribed to do so by recruiters.

(10) Recruiters send up natives who are not physically fit for the work. These boys are rejected by the mines, but not repatriated, and so are left without friends or employment loose on the Rand.

(11) Many mines, if convinced that a native under contract is really needed at home, allow him to go on leave upon his promising to return later and complete his contract. In many cases such natives do not keep their promise. This has been attributed, in some instances, to the action of recruiters. The latter would get no fee on such a returning boy and so (it is alleged) they induce him to take service with some mine other than that which he left, and send him up as a new boy.

546. (1) The cost of recruiting is certainly a very large item in the expenditure of the mines. Although exact figures are not available, the total annual cost cannot be far from £600,000, and some estimates put it much higher. In addition to the administration expenses and the capitation fees paid to recruiters, which latter item approximates to £200,000 a year, there is a very large sum always outstanding by way of advances to natives. A percentage of this is actually lost, owing to the native, from one cause or another, failing to supply the labour on account of which he has received his money, or owing to the default of the recruiter. One witness, who was certainly in a position to know, put these losses at 20 per cent. of the total money advanced.

547. (2) The long term of contract which, as explained in paragraph 420 above, the native dislikes so much, is largely a result of the cost of recruiting. A boy engaged for six months has cost the mines something like £4 10s. before he does any work at all. In these circumstances, they are naturally loth to let him go before his time is up, as such a transaction may involve them in a direct loss. With the voluntary native no such consideration arises, and he is, in fact, much more readily allowed to cut short the period of his contract.

548. (3) The voluntary boy appears, on the whole, to be a more efficient and contented labourer than the recruited boy. It must, however, be remembered that voluntaries, as a class, have longer experience of the work than recruited boys, so that their superior efficiency is not necessarily the result of the method of enlistment. Also the voluntary boy's spell of consecutive work is, on an average, shorter than that of a recruited boy.

549 (4) There can be no doubt that a considerable number of false representations and unfulfilled promises are practically certain incidents of the recruiting system. The recruiter is paid by a capitation fee on each native whom he enlists; many recruiters are not men of high stamp; and in these circumstances

they are not likely to be too scrupulous as to the means which they employ to induce the boy to sign on. The large number of complaints which I have received on this point leaves me in no doubt that a good deal of misrepresentation is used.

550. Every native recruited within the Union has to be attested by an officer of the Native Affairs Department, who, before allowing the attestation, is supposed to make the terms quite clear to the boy and to satisfy himself that the native accepts them. No doubt, in the majority of cases, he does his best, but, apart from the occasional negligence which will always arise where a large number of men are constantly going through a piece of routine business, it may be doubted whether a civil servant who has always been stationed in a native district himself sufficiently understands the effect of all the conditions of a mining contract to be able to make it clear to a raw native.

551. Also, there seems to be no doubt that the native himself frequently regards the attestation as a tiresome formality to which he need pay no attention, having already settled his bargain verbally with the recruiter. Indeed, several natives have told me that the recruiter impressed this view upon them, as one can quite understand might well be the case.

552. At the Government Compound at Driehoek, every boy has his attestation form again read over to him, and, if he denies that he made the agreement therein set out, the matter is inquired into. If misrepresentation is established, the native is either repatriated at the recruiter's expense or he is released from his contract and sent out to look for work as a voluntary boy, in which case the recruiter of course loses his capitation fee, and also any disbursements which he has made on account of the native.

553. In the case of those natives who are recruited in Portuguese Territory by the W.N.L.A., the contract is read over to them for the first time at Ressano Garcia, and not repeated at Johannesburg. It is, however, comparatively simple (see Annexure 21) all natives being engaged for the same period and at the same wage, and there being no deductions for food, railway fare, advances, etc.

554. I do not attach much importance to the process of attestation. The native's real safeguard against misrepresentation is that, by this time, the principal terms of the contract offered by the mines must be common knowledge throughout the recruiting areas. Still, there certainly continue to be cases where the recruiter or runner contrives to mislead the recruit as to his prospects.

555. It is only fair to say that the amount of misrepresentation appears to have diminished since the formation of the N.R.C. That body, being really a branch of the mines, is interested in the ultimate, as well as in the proximate, result of its action, and takes longer views than the individual recruiter. The interests of its agents do not, however, always agree in this respect with those of their principal.

556. (5) There is no doubt that recruiters who are also traders do extend to natives an amount of credit which they would not do but for the prospect of inducing them to go to the mines and thereby to earn a capitation fee for the trader. Since debt is an habitual vice with most natives, anything which tends to encourage them in the habit is an evil.

557. (6) It has for a long time been the practice of recruiters to stimulate the willingness of natives to come to the mines by giving them an advance upon their wages. As I remarked in the last paragraph, any encouragement of debt is undesirable. The only legitimate purposes of an advance are (a) to provide the labourer with an outfit; (b) to provide for his family until he can remit them money; and (c) to pay the expenses of the journey. All these requirements would be more wholesomely met out of the proceeds of previous labour than by the hypothecation of future gains.

558. The advance is not, in many cases, paid to the native immediately before his departure to the mines. Many recruiters let him have the advance and do not require him to proceed to the mines until some time later, the interval varying from one to six months; in fact one recruiter told me that he sometimes had to allow boys eight or nine months. In these cases it is evident that the advance is not expended upon the legitimate purposes mentioned above. It must be largely, if not entirely, exhausted before the native sets out.

559. This postponement of the performance by the native of his share of the contract is a particularly vicious feature of the system. If advances are retained,

I think it should be clearly provided that the native should depart to the work within a specified time after receiving his advance. Fourteen days would be a sufficient interval for the settlement of his affairs. This might be enforced by depriving of the benefit of the compulsory clauses (sec. 14 of Act 15 of 1911) any recruiter who allowed a longer period to elapse without calling upon the native to go out.

560. Abuse of advances might also be checked by substituting for an advance of money the supply of a regulation outfit at a fixed reasonable price, such as is provided by the W.N.L.A., and, if necessary, a bag or two of grain at the current market price.

561. A very great disadvantage attendant upon the advance system is that it offers great temptations and easy opportunity for fraud. It is a very common and increasing offence for a native to get an advance from one recruiter upon a promise to go to work for him and then to repeat the process with other recruiters. Several magistrates in the Territories have declared that the system is depraving the moral standards of the native.

562. The native ground of objection to the advance is usually that it is a trap for the young and foolish, who take advances without the knowledge of their guardians, and waste the money. There is a strong feeling that minors, at any rate, should not be allowed to accept advances except in the presence of their guardians. The Native Council of the Transkei has passed a resolution recommending this. I agree with the recommendation so far as it goes, but I doubt whether it will in practice effect much, owing to the difficulty of determining the age of a native.

563. I learn from many sources that desertion is particularly common among boys who have received heavy advances. The advances having been spent, there is strong temptation to evade giving the labour promised.

564. It is not however necessary to multiply objections to the system of advances. No other class of labour is paid in advance, and the principle of paying any man for work which he has not done, and which, owing to death, sickness, fraud, etc., he may never do, is obviously vicious. Hardly any witness has defended the system upon any other ground than that, in the particular circumstances it is necessary.

565. It has indeed been urged that the advance is a real benefit to the native because it enables him to buy for cash, and therefore to get better terms than if he took credit. No doubt cash is a better basis than credit; but, by taking an advance, the native is not getting on to a cash basis; he is simply taking credit from the labour agent instead of from the trader. The only way to get upon a real cash basis is to earn your money before you spend it, and the advance system encourages the native to spend his money before he earns it.

566. It has also been argued that the abolition of advances will throw the native into the hands of moneylenders, and that his last state of indebtedness will be worse than the first.

567. I do not see how the mere withdrawal of an advance which has, for some time past, not exceeded £5 can have this effect. All the evidence shows that this £5 did not either satisfy the native's desires—he was constantly trying to get more from the recruiting agents—or exhaust his credit, since the recruiters are wiling to, and while allowed to, actually did, advance him much larger usms. If, wanting money and possessing credit he is not in the hands of the moneylenders already, the reason must be sought elsewhere. The evidence goes to show that the true reason is the Cape Usury Act. Witnesses have told me that, before the Act, there was much moneylending in the Territories, but that it has died out because the interest allowed is unremunerative.

568. (7) I do not see anything necessarily degrading in a white man's urging a native to go to work; but undoubtedly it may be, and, under the stress of competition, probably often is, pushed to undesirable lengths. It is certainly not a pleasing spectacle to see half a dozen white men running after the same native.

569. (8) The mines have large sums of money constantly outstanding in advances to natives. This certainly constitutes a handicap on other industries which

cannot afford the same outlay. The Natal industries and the farmers complain greatly of this.

570. (9) There is obvious danger of illegitimate influence being brought to bear upon natives through their chiefs so long as there is any pecuniary advantage to be attained; but I have no positive evidence that this is, in fact, being done.

571. (10) I do not see how complaint No. 10 can have any foundation. Every native sent from the N.R.C. is now examined by a doctor before coming up; and also is examined by a Native Affairs medical officer at the compound at Driehoek, before being sent to his mine. If he fails to pass, he is repatriated at the cost of his recruiter. If he was rejected by the mine for physical reasons, he would return to the N.A.D., which would either compel the mine to carry out its contract or see the native repatriated.

572. Mr. Mostert also is arranging for a medical examination before the departure of the native from the Territories; and his recruits pass through the Driehoek compound.

573. The W.N.L.A. boys are medically examined at Ressano Garcia both by the Association's own doctor and by the Komati Poort District Surgeon; and they undergo a second examination at the Johannesburg compound and a third on the mine. Any boy rejected is repatriated at the expense of the Association.

574. (11) There is certainly an air of probability about this objection, though it can only apply in a limited number of cases.

575. Since objection (10) is unfounded, and it is doubtful whether (3) is really attributable to the recruiting system, it is only necessary to consider the remainder. These constitute quite enough abuses and possibilities of abuse to demand a remedy. Most of them would automatically cease, and all would at least be reduced, if a sufficient supply of voluntary natives could be secured, so that the system of obtaining labour through professional, paid recruiters could be dropped.

Voluntary Labour.

576. As explained in paragraph 539 above, voluntary boys are those who present themselves for employment at the mine itself. Of these, however, only the new arrivals have necessarily got there unaided; the local voluntary has often completed a term of recruited labour on another mine, and could never have reached the Rand at all without extraneous assistance. Some of them no doubt could, and some of the natives classed as recruited would, no doubt, if there were no recruiters, contrive to get to the Rand somehow. There is however, no means of computing the numbers of these two classes; so that the voluntary labourers available can only be stated as the new arrivals *plus* x.

577. In 1913, these new arrivals constituted less than 20 per cent. of the labour supply. The mere statement of this figure is in itself conclusive against any proposal at once to drop recruiting without providing a substitute; the results must be disastrous.

578. Voluntary labour should, however, be encouraged, and I think that more encouragement might be given in some respects. The provision of an official employment bureau at Johannesburg would be useful. At present boys have to wander from place to place seeking work; and employers have to wait until a boy happens to wander their way. Natives so wandering are exposed to all sorts of dangers from illegal labour touts and other undesirables who prey upon the native; and a great deal of this trouble, of which various natives have complained, is removable.

579. All that is wanted is an office, to which employers could notify their requirements by telephone or otherwise, and accommodation for boys awaiting employment. At intervals announcements could be made to the crowd "The So and So Mine wants 50 lashing boys at 1s. 8d. per shift for not less than a three months' contract," and the response could be noted and telephoned to the mine, informing them that a batch of boys was on the way.

580. Something of this kind is already done by the Johannesburg Pass Office; but little publicity has been given to it, and only about 90 cases a month are dealt with. I should like to see it attempted on a much larger scale.

581. It would be a great convenience if a sort of native boarding-house was run in connection with this bureau. At present there is no proper provision for natives seeking work, of whom there are generally about a couple of thousand in the town. It is true that Reg. 41, Proc. 18 of 1903, requires that every pass office shall provide such accommodation at 1s. a day; but this provision is little used, for three reasons. The Johannesburg Pass Office could not accommodate a tenth of the boys needing accommodation; the natives regard the pass office rather as a prison, and won't go there, and 1s. a day is a monstrous charge for a roof and dish of mealie porridge, which latter costs the Government under 1¼d. In fact, the native seeking work lives with any friendly houseboy, which is a contravention of the local by-laws.

582. I have no doubt that a compound with simple sleeping and feeding arrangements and a registry office attached, under the management of the N.A.D., would be a great boon to natives and employers, and would prevent many infractions of the law.

583. Since it is not practicable, at present, to rely upon voluntary labour entirely, it is necessary to consider some other method of meeting the objections above enumerated. These objections admit of some classification. Nos. (4), (5), (7), (9) and (11) all spring from one common cause, the personal financial interest of the recruiter in collecting as many boys as possible, which tends to make him indifferent to the means employed. No (8), monopoly, as a result of No. (6), the advance system; and Nos. (1) and (2) are largely due to the advances and to the payments made to recruiters. It follows that the abolition or reduction of advances and of private interests in recruiting would tend to the abolition or reduction of the abuses complained of.

584. As stated in paragraphs 531 and 533, the W.N.L.A. make no advances, and pay their recruiters in such a manner as to reduce to a *minimum* the personal financial interest of the recruiter. The following suggestions, therefore, refer only to recruiting within the Union, where other conditions prevail.

ADVANCES.

585. Advances, in cash or in kind, are a custom of long standing in the Territories. At one time, owing to the competition of recruiters, sums of £20 to £30, or even up to £60, or their equivalent in cattle, were advanced to a single boy. The Government has, from time to time, restricted the extent of these advances, and, in 1910, the amount which might be advanced was limited to £5. As from 1st January, 1912, it was reduced to £2 and then, in November, 1912, restored to £5 in times of famine only. This was continued until the end of 1913. On 6th January, 1914, a new regulation was published running as follows:—

"(1) It shall be lawful for any person recruiting under the Act to make prior to the contract the following advances, which must be shown separately in the contract:

(a) The cost of transport by rail to the proposed place of employment.

(b) The amount of any taxes due to the Government.

(c) The amount of any fine, not exceeding £5, imposed by a court of competent jurisdiction, provided the convicting magistrate approves thereof in writing.

(d) The Director may, with the approval of the Minister, authorise advances, not exceeding £2, to be made in certain areas for the maintenance of the relatives or dependents of native labourers.

Advances made under this sub-section may be recovered by deductions from the wages of the native labourers concerned.

(2) An employer may during the contract make advances to native labourers in his employ provided that the total amount of indebtedness of any such native labourer on account of advances made under this subsection shall not at any time exceed £2, and provided further that no native shall, by reason of such indebtedness to his employer, be required to extend the period of his contract unless he has specifically agreed to do so before an attesting officer at the time an advance was made. Such advances may consist of payments to the native labourer himself or to any person appointed by him to receive the same. No

deductions from the wages of native labourers shall be made on account of advances given under this sub-section until an official of the Native Affairs Department shall have certified on the passport or passes of the natives concerned that such advances have actually been made.

(3) Any person making advances in addition to or other than those set out in the preceding sub-sections shall be guilty of an offence."

586. The Transkeian General Council has asked that taxes due to them, as well as to the Government, shall be included in sub-section (1) (b). I do not know enough of the circumstances to make any recommendation upon this point.

587. The Council also desires that advances under sub-section (2) shall be made only if required for remittance home. As I have (paragraph 471) expressed my opinion that the native mine labourer needs no credit while on the Rand, I agree with this recommendation, but I would suggest allowing such advances for fines, as well as for remittances, on the terms of sub-section (1) (c).

588. Some objection has been taken to the regulation on the ground that it favours the Government by allowing a preference to claims for taxes and fines. There seems to me to be nothing in this contention. Apart from the consideration that public claims are frequently, and, as I think, rightly preferred to private claims, these preferences apply only to claims which may be enforced by a sentence of imprisonment; and it is certainly desirable to keep natives as far as possible out of prison.

589. The policy hitherto pursued has been to restrict advances, with a view to their final abolition. This policy has provoked much opposition, chiefly from traders and recruiters in the Native Territories. They have objected that, if they like to lend the money, and the native to borrow it, that is their business, and the Government is in no way concerned.

590. The principle that the native must, in many respects, be treated as a minor, and the Government as his guardian is, however, too well established to be open to discussion at this time of day. It is a proper function of the Government to provide that a subject in the undeveloped mental condition of the native shall get his pay under such circumstances as offer him the fewest temptations to fraud and the greatest opportunities for spending it to advantage. I do not share the fears expressed by many witnesses that such provisions will prevent the native from developing the capacity to look after himself in such matters. The expenditure of money offers so many opportunities and temptations which cannot possibly be guarded against that the utmost protection which can be afforded still leaves plenty of room for the training of experience.

591. As I have said before, hardly any one supports the principle of giving advances. The only question, therefore, is one of expediency; whether the system is necessary or offers sufficient advantages to counterbalance its drawbacks.

592. Many witnesses have asserted roundly that the practice of receiving advances is ingrained in the nature of the native, especially in the case of the Pondo, and that he cannot by any means be induced to do without it. It is true that it has now become an established tradition, but it is quite certain that it is of comparatively recent growth. Until a generation or two back, many natives subsisted entirely upon their crops, and, unless they had practised the habit of saving the produce of one harvest until the next, the race would long ago have been extinct. Nature makes no advances.

593. A habit of extravagance and debt which has arisen during the course of, at most, two generations, cannot be so thoroughly established that it is beyond eradication. Opportunity has produced it, and the removal of opportunity can destroy it.

594. There is no doubt at all that the proportion of the native's wages which is spent on the Rand is increasing. Formerly, he often received the whole payment for his contract in the shape of cattle handed to him at the kraal. Even when this was not done, his first object in coming to the mines was to earn money to buy cattle on his return. In those days the acquisition of cattle was the chief pleasure of his life. With increasing experience of the Rand, however, he has learned the delights of the world, the flesh and the devil in many new forms, and his abrupt introduction to such temptations has given him no reasonable chance to develop any power of resistance.

595. A point in favour of advances, mainly urged by the trading community, is that the money so advanced is the only part of the native's wages which he spends in his own district. While this is putting the facts too strongly, the natives are, as stated in the last paragraph, spending an ever increasing proportion of their earnings upon the Rand, and this tendency is likely to continue. The amounts passing through the N.R.C. Remittance Agency show a great falling off. From October, 1912, to February, 1913, about £17,500 was remitted; during the same months a year later, only about £8,000.

596. The trader's interest in the matter is, of course, simply that as much as possible of the native's earnings shall be spent at the trader's store. The trader in the Territories claims that he is entitled to the earnings of the native domiciled in the Territories, just as, when the question of deferred pay for Portuguese natives was under discussion, the Rand trader claimed that he was entitled to the earnings made by the native on the Rand. I cannot see any basis for either claim. The Territories trader did not create the native, nor did the Rand trader create the gold.

597. It is no concern of the country at large whether the native spends his money in one part of the Union or in another, but it certainly concerns the whole community that he should spend it wisely and not foolishly. I think there is no doubt that, on the whole, the money which he spends in his district is better invested than that which he spends on the Rand. The classes from which the mine labourer is drawn are in a state of transition. While at home, they are still largely under the influence of tribal and patriarchal traditions. While at the mines, they are increasingly individualist. As a result, any money paid to the native at home goes, to a great extent, to his family, or is put into stock, either by himself or, perhaps more often, by his father-in-law or intended father-in-law; any money paid to him on the mines is spent on his own personal fancies of the moment, which too often means that it is wasted on unwholesome food, unnecessary clothes or such trash as concertinas; or worse, wasted on intoxicating liquor.

598. This view is largely held among the natives themselves. The native secretary to the paramount chief of the Pondos endorsed the famous *dictum* of the Right Hon. John X. Merriman (whom the secretary describes as "a worthy man") as to the educational merits of Johannesburg. "In the Rand, which is the House of Sin, even the good boys become sinners."

599. Incidentally, any reduction of the proportion of the native's wages spent on the Rand will certainly reduce the extent of the illicit liquor curse, and will limit his indulgence in other local vices, besides diminishing the criminal population which lives by defrauding him.

600. I think the sound conclusion is that the more of a native's wages paid to him at his home, the better both for himself and for the community at large. But this proposition by no means involves the desirability of advances. Wages paid in arrear would, if spent in the worker's own district, be just as well spent as wages paid in advance. In fact, one of the points made by the native spokesmen in the Transkeian districts was that the younger natives wasted their advances in sweets and such like; and it is a matter of universal experience that unearned money is spent with a recklessness very different from the respect with which the product of past labour is treated. Light come, light go.

601. There is a system already in use with tropical natives under which only a part of the native's earnings is paid to him while actually at work on the Rand, the balance being handed to him in a lump sum upon his return home, or remitted to his relatives at home while he is at work on the Rand. This is known as "deferred pay." The above considerations point to the desirability of introducing the same system in respect of natives from within the Union. The advantages of the advance would thus be retained, while its disadvantages would be abolished.

602. The principal argument against the abolition of advances in favour of deferred pay is that it will result in a serious shortage of labour. If this were established, it would certainly constitute a strong case against the change.

603. It is said with considerable force that some natives who are under no economic necessity to leave home are attracted by the prospect of £5 down in immediate cash, and, to obtain it, commit themselves to an undertaking to go to work at some future time, which they would never do unless they had been caught by some such bait. I do not doubt that there are such cases.

604. Another case of which a good deal has been made by the advocates of advances is that of the native who finds himself in immediate need of cash for some specific object, such as the discharge of an old debt, the payment of a fine, damages for seduction or a payment on account of *lobola*. In all these cases, however, the money has got to be found sooner or later. The economic pressure which must drive the debtor to work is already in existence, and there is no necessity for an advance to put it in force. In fact, the system of advances in these cases really postpones the day when the native has to begin working.

605. There is also the case of the native who does not choose for himself whether or not he will go to work, but acts upon the order, advice or persuasion of his father or relatives. In this case it is the family, not the individual native, who have to be persuaded in one way or another; and no doubt the advance is sometimes useful for that purpose. I must, however, point out that this is not really a separate case. Whether the decision rests with the labourer himself or with a relative, the person who decides either is or is not under economic compulsion to decide in favour of work.

606. There are said to be some boys who come to the mines because, after a taste of the delights of the Rand, they are not content to remain at home. Clearly such boys do not need the inducement of an advance.

607. Several witnesses whose experience of natives entitles their views to respect, including Mr. A. H. B. Stanford, who has just retired from the Chief Magistracy of the Transkei, tell me that, in times of famine, many natives will absolutely refuse to leave home until they have made provision for their families and that, in the absence of any advance, they will remain and starve with their families rather than go to the mines. This, however, refers to abnormal periods, when unusual methods may, no doubt, be necessary, and does not support the system of advances as an ordinary and regular transaction. It would be desirable to make some provision, as was done in the regulation of November, 1912, for allowing advances in times of famine.

608. There has been some evidence from witnesses who have actually tried to recruit without giving advances and have totally failed to get any appreciable amount of labour. They were, however competing with other recruiters who were giving advances, so that their failure was only to be expected. Their experience under these conditions is no guide to what may be expected to happen when no advances can be given by anybody.

609. Mr. Saunders, of the Natal Sugar Association, did actually drop the system of advances some years ago, before the big recruiting began, and has never reverted to it. His experience was that the resulting shortage only lasted a few months. The work, however, was surface work, and I understand that Mr. Saunders is exceptionally favourably situated to obtain labour, having long had relations with the native population.

610. The majority of natives whose views I have heard are desirous of retaining the £5 advance. This was to be expected and does not seem to me to be of much consequence. The attractions of cash in hand are great to any class, and one would not expect the native mind to grasp the ultimate disadvantage of the system. What does astonish me is that quite a considerable minority of natives were in favour of abolishing advances, and substituting deferred pay.

611. I think the main line of division—there are many exceptions—is between the actual working native, mostly young, who naturally wants to have his money for himself and to spend it as he pleases, and the elder men who mostly stay at home and who are anxious to conserve as much as possible of their sons' earnings for the benefit of the kraal. The latter will not I think be unwilling to accept the substitution of deferred pay for advances and, though the younger men will at first be averse to the change, the influence of the elders counts for a good deal with them.

612. On the other hand, the Transkeian Native Council, which consists mainly of chief and headmen, has, after a long debate, supported by a majority the principle of local advances as against that of remittances: The question of deferred pay was not, however, raised. The majority of the Select Committee of the Council upon the subject was in favour of abolishing local advances in favour of advances up to £5 to be made in Johannesburg and remitted to the worker's family.

613. It is difficult to say how much weight should be attached to the expressions of native opinion on these matters. In some cases, at any rate, I am sure that the evidence given to me by natives on this point was not an expres-

sion of their own deliberately formed opinion but merely an echo of the views impressed upon them by white men.

614. The deferred pay system has been given an actual trial by Mr. Mostert. Towards the end of 1913 he offered to pay natives engaged by him either in the usual way or at the rate of 5s. to 10s. a month while on the mine and the balance (after payment of the cost of repatriation) on return home. At first only a few accepted the second alternative; but the proportion increased steadily, and now, only five months after the start of the system, half the natives coming forward are upon deferred pay. This argues remarkably well for its popularity; and there can be no doubt that, as soon as the system takes effect, the sight of money being paid into the hands of natives in the Territories will have a very beneficial effect on recruiting.

615. Much depends upon whether the native mine labourer, as a class, has any option about coming to work: whether he is, financially, in a position to remain upon his land if he does not like the terms offered by the mines. Many persons of experience, magistrates, recruiters and traders, including such authorities as Mr. H. M. Taberer and Mr. J. W. Mackenzie, have told me emphatically that he is not—that the question whether or not he comes to the Rand is decided by his domestic circumstances and not by the persuasiveness or the reverse of the recruiter's tout. The native secretary to the paramount chief of Pondoland, speaking on behalf of the chief, replied to my question as to whether the young men would go to work for deferred pay instead of advances. "They go to the mines on account of necessity. If that is the law, they will go up under those conditions." I suppose that this witness is probably as good a judge of what natives are likely to do as any whom I have heard. It seems to be a very widely held opinion that the native mostly goes to work only when he cannot help it, and that until that moment arrives, you may speak with the tongues of men and angels without persuading him to leave his kraal. Mr. Marwick, of the firm of Marwick & Morris, considers that this applies to 90 per cent. of the labour, and that only 10 per cent. consists of natives who might live at home but come out of a desire to earn wages.

616. I do not understand these witnesses to mean that the native comes to the mines because he would starve if he did not: on the contrary, the evidence seems to me to show that, in normal seasons, the country can still produce food for its population. But there are, with the native as with white people, some luxuries which are, for practical purposes, necessaries; their absence is so intolerable to him that he will work to get them. For example, a native must have a wife; he cannot get a wife without money; and he cannot get money without going to work.

617. The weight of evidence seems to me to be in favour of this view. While some part of the labour supply is, no doubt, due to the attractions of the advance, much the larger part appears to be forced out by economic pressure.

618. A good deal of the evidence on the other side, coming from traders and recruiters, must be received with caution. In a circular issued to traders and recruiters, Mr. David Black, of Tsitsa Bridge, states that "if the Government abolish advances, no recruiters will be required, except one in each district to forward boys to the Corporation's (i.e. the N.R.C.'s) agent at the railhead," and he goes on to point out that this means the loss of £90,000 per annum in capitation fees to the traders of the Territory. I have already pointed out their strong interest, as traders, in advances; and, while I do not in the least doubt the good faith of their views as to the probable effect upon the labour supply of the abolition of advances, it is obvious that those views cannot be unbiassed.

619. I am informed—I was not myself interested in the subject at the time that very similar prophecies of destruction to the labour supply were put forward when the cattle advances were abolished in 1910. The result has certainly not borne out those prophecies. It is significant that hardly any recruiters urged an increased advance; the retention of the £5 limit would content most of them.

620. I do not mean that there is anything like unanimity, even among indifferent observers, upon this point. I do, however, consider that the balance of evidence is that the number of recruited natives who will not, sooner or later, be forced to come to work is comparatively small. Even in many cases where the witness expresses the opinion that many natives come out who need not do so, the effect of his evidence, taken together, is to support the opposite view. No-

body denies that the native already has urgent need of money for various purposes and that in future this urgency will increase; nobody has been able to point out any other source from which he can get this money except by coming out to work. I do not see how the conclusion can be avoided that he will come out to work.

621. There is no doubt that the advances had a great effect in bringing the native to work originally, I can well believe that such a stimulus was necessary when he was in a position to remain, practically idle, in his own country. The great loss of cattle which has occurred in recent years has, however, entirely changed this position; the Territories are no longer a wealthy and self-sufficing country. It must be borne in mind, moreover, that the needs of the native are increasing very rapidly. He is, speaking broadly, no longer happy with a blanket and a sufficiency of mealie pap, but requires clothes, tea, sugar, etc. This tendency, which is perfectly certain to continue with increasing force, will operate strongly to bring him to work.

622. Many recruiters have given me figures showing that the reduction of the advance has had a disastrous effect upon their recruiting, the number of boys coming forward this year on the £2 advance comparing very unfavourably with the number in the corresponding months of 1913. I think that the significance to be attached to the present slackness may easily be over-estimated. Any change disturbs the native, who is a conservative person, for the time; it does not follow that the disturbance will be permanent. Also there is just now the doubt whether the advances will not return to the former figure; and, while there is a possibility of a rise in the price of any commodity, vendors are always backward. It may reasonably be anticipated that the passage of time and a definite announcement of future policy will tend to improve the labour supply.

623. It must also be remembered that the natives were very much upset by the industrial disturbances of July, 1913; and the recurrence of this kind of trouble in January, 1914, has not helped them to get over their disinclination to come to the Rand. Also, the last harvest was a good one in many districts, which always results in slack recruiting for a while. In spite of all these drawbacks, there was, in April, 1914, a net gain to the mines of native labour of 2,956, as against a net loss in April, 1913, of 1,608.

624. No doubt the knowledge that a lump sum is waiting for him at home will tend to induce the native to leave the mines directly his contract is over, instead of working on for a time, as he frequently does now. As the average period for which a Union native is recruited is 171 shifts, while the average period for which he stays is 196 shifts, the extreme loss possible on this account is 13 per cent., which would, of course, be very serious. But all will not be affected by this consideration; and so many overstay their time for specific reasons—to wait until a brother's contract has expired, to obtain a particular amount of money, etc.—that there seems no reason to anticipate that the falling off will at all approach this. Against this loss must be set the fact that deferred pay will necessarily reduce desertions. A servant does not readily sacrifice the earnings of past months.

625. On the whole, I think that the change can be effected without any great risk to the labour supply. I do not mean to say that I expect it to be effected without some derangement; on the contrary, I think there will be a temporary shortage, and I am not prepared to define " temporary " with any accuracy. The many experienced witnesses who expressed this opinion gave me very varying estimates; I think the shortest was six months and the longest three years. But it seems to me improbable that there will be any serious permanent shortage.

626. One witness urges that sec. 23 (1) (e) of Act 15 of 1911 gave power to alter, but not to abolish advances. I do not think that this contention, even if sound, is of practical importance; a reduction to 1s. or 1d. would have all the effect of abolition. In any case, there is nothing in my reference to limit my recommendations to matters practicable under the existing statute.

627. It has been argued that the stopping of the advance will necessarily lead to the raising of wages as an alternative inducement. That argument is only sound upon the assumption that to drop advances will result in a shortage of labour; otherwise it has no basis. Further, it assumes that the raising of wages is an evil. I am not going to enter upon a discussion of that very wide question; but the assumption is certainly not universally accepted as an axiom.

628. I therefore think that the policy of gradually abolishing advances should be continued and that the new regulation is a further step in the right direction.

7

I think, however, that its enforcement should be preceded by the institution of the deferred pay system. The change will be attended with some hardship in a community which is, as a whole, steeped in debt. The transition can be made much easier if, for a period, the two are combined, a small advance being given for outfit, provision for families, etc., and, after this is paid off, part of the native's wages being accumulated until his return. The lump sum thus handed to the native at his kraal will give him the opportunity of providing for his next trip without incurring further debt; and if it is definitely announced that, from a specified date, of which a good deal of warning should be given, advances will be finally stopped, I should hope that he will avail himself of this opportunity. I cannot but think that his present indifference to making such provision is largely due to the knowledge that an advance is always waiting for him. Such knowledge is a direct encouragement to improvidence.

629. I think that the advance should remain at £2 for the present. Although this amount is perhaps rather on the small side, in view of the desirability of allowing some opportunity to the native, in his present condition of debt, to get an outfit and to provide for his family, I think it would be highly undesirable to make another change. There is no doubt that the recent variations in the sum allowed, however necessary in the circumstances, have tended to upset the native mind, always averse to change, and have interfered with recruiting. It is of the utmost importance that, whatever policy may be decided upon, it should be definitely announced and rigidly adhered to.

630. I may also note that, when suggesting the abolition of advances, I do not include in the term 'advance" the payment of the recruit's railway fare to the mines or the supply to him of the necessary outfit. These will for a long time be necessary, and they are free from most of the objections taken to the cash advance.

631. The intermediate period, during which both advances and deferred pay are in effect, should be of considerable duration, to allow a substantial amount of money to be accumulated in the Territories. I think that the taking effect of the new regulation should be deferred till the end of the year, at the very earliest. Recruiters say, with a good deal of justice, that they have paid their licensing fee for the year in the expectation that their facilities for recruiting would not be altered.

632. Another reason is that the present season is likely to be a poor one for the crops in most districts, and the additional strain of finally losing the advances would fall heavily upon the natives.

633. At the present time, too, the industry is suffering from the gradual departure of the tropical natives.

634. In fact, there is a good deal to be said for postponing the final abolition of advances for a good deal longer. It will take some time before the advantages of the deferred pay system are thoroughly grasped by the native; and the hope of avoiding a shortage depends to a considerable extent upon his appreciation of those advantages. There is also to be considered the position of contractors who have entered into undertakings upon the assumption that their facilities for obtaining labour would not be diminished. To them even a temporary shortage will be a serious thing. And, if the advance is stopped before the deferred pay has brought a good sum of money into the country districts, there will be danger of a business crisis in the Territories.

635. So long as the policy is definitely laid down and notice given of the date when it will finally take effect, I see no objection to allowing a considerable interval before that date.

636. It is very necessary to secure absolutely that there shall be no default in payment of deferred pay, both as a matter of justice to the native and with a view to recruiting. If a batch of natives were to find, on completing their contracts, that the money was not forthcoming, the result would be disastrous. I think that no one should be allowed to recruit upon this system without giving a bank guarantee or some similar security for the amount to be retained.

Public Control.

637. It is clear that, so long as the business of recruiting is left in private hands, the element of personal financial interest cannot be entirely eliminated. The only course that could have this effect would be for the Government to take the matter upon itself.

638. This course, if adopted, would at once get rid of the objections enumerated above under the numbers (4), (5), (7), (8), (9) and (11). Government officials would have no inducement to obtain native labour by misrepresentation, undue influence or flattery; nor to prefer one employer to another. It would probably also reduce the cost; though Governments are not usually as economical in administration as private persons, yet the saving of the capitation fees now paid should more than make up for this.

639. There can be no doubt that the cessation of any attempt to attract recruits by illegitimate means must, at first, result in some falling off of the supply of labour. It is however, probable that the use of such means, though effective for the moment, ultimately has a deterrent effect by leading natives to discredit even the honest inducements held out by recruiters; so that it may reasonably be anticipated that the cleaner methods will prove the more efficient in the long run.

640. Whether this be so is not, however, a matter of any importance for the present purpose. I do not suppose that anyone will be found to argue that, if legitimate efforts fail to attract a sufficiency of labour, then recourse must be had to illegitimate means.

641. What may reasonably be said is that the abuses are merely the evil results of the element of personal interest and that that element has also good results, such as keenness, etc., which will be lost under the proposed scheme. I have already expressed my opinion that the native is not very susceptible to what may be called legitimate persuasion in such a matter as coming to the mines to work (paragraph 615); and I may add that I doubt very much whether the present recruiters are showing any marked activity in the way of persuasion. They seem, to judge from their own evidence, to rely mainly upon the advance.

642. An experiment in Government labour supply has already been made. In 1910 an attempt was made by the N.A.D. to substitute a system of forwarding Colony to receive applications from natives wishing to work on the mines. Every such native was sent up free, his railway fare and food on the road being provided and the cost thereof afterwards recovered from the particular mine to which he was sent. Natives for mine work were engaged for six months; for the railways for three months.

643. This system (known in the N.A.D. as " Class B ") was an undoubted failure. The total number of native labourers secured for the mines was 233 in four years; for the railways 1,187.

644. At the same time, it would not be safe to conclude that such a system would fail if tried under other conditions. The cause of its failure was the competition of private recruiters, who saw their business threatened.

645. I think the same cause would produce the same result whenever such a system was tried alongside of a competing recruiting system. The latter would be sure to win because it could always offer greater inducements to the native. No Regulations can restrain recruiters from giving indirect advantages of one kind or another, even though direct ones be prohibited. Recruiter-traders, especially, obtain influence over natives by giving them credit; and even though the debts thus incurred were prohibited from figuring on the attestation sheet as advances, nevertheless the power thus obtained would enable the storekeeper to dictate to the native by what channel he should go to work.

646. Some very intelligent natives who came from the E.R.P.M. expressed a strong opinion that the " Class B " system if re-established, would now be eagerly accepted by the natives. I doubt, however, whether these witnesses, who were educated men, are reliable authorities as to what the great mass of uneducated mine labourers would do.

647. It seems that there are only two ways of giving " Class B " a fair trial. Either recruiting must be abolished and the field left open, or the system must be combined with a non-competitive recruiting system.

648. The first alternative is plainly a dangerous experiment. If the labour produced at present by recruiting were entirely abandoned, and the mines had to depend exclusively on "Class B," it is tolerably certain that there would be an immediate shortage, and it is possible that that shortage might prove to be permanent, in which case the recruiting organisation would have to be set up again at a vast expense. For the reasons given in paragraphs 615-623 I do not think this probable, but the risk of the experiment would certainly be increased if the business of recruiting were placed in the hands of a new and inexperienced organisation.

649. The other alternative, if practicable, is far safer. Assuming a non-competitive recruiting organisation, working side by side with "Class B," there is no reason why the former should try to snatch boys who would naturally fall to the latter, which, therefore, could be fairly tested without running the risk incurred by a stoppage of recruiting.

650. Very nearly the whole of the recruiting in Cape Colony is in the hands of the N.R.C. That body is really a branch of the Reef mines; and its ultimate controllers have no interest in recruiting as such. In fact, their interests are the other way; what they want is labour, and, if they can get it by means of forwarding agencies, they will be only too delighted to dispense with more expensive methods such as recruiting. They would therefore readily give orders that their recruiters should not in any way interfere with the working of "Class B."

651. It is, however, a serious question whether they could get those orders obeyed. Every employee of a recruiting organisation has a deep personal interest in the continuance and would certainly do what in him lay to frustrate an experiment which, if successful, must seriously diminish his prospects of earning a living.

652. As a matter of fact, I am pretty certain that the recruiter-traders at present working for the N.R.C. would defeat any attempt of the kind, no matter what instructions they received.

653. There is also to be considered the fact that Mr. A. M. Mostert, the most serious competitor of the N.R.C., is not in the same position as that corporation. His business is to supply native labour to the Robinson Group of mines, and, if a sufficient number of voluntary boys were to come forward under "Class B," his occupation would be gone.

654. I think that, at present, any attempt by the Government to take over the business of recruiting would be unwise.

Capitation Fees.

655. Even though it be impossible, at present, to destroy the element of private interest in recruiting, it may nevertheless be possible to reduce it. If capitation fees ceased to be paid, this would reduce, if not abolish, the objectionable features under (1), (2), (4), (5), (7), (8), (9) and (11). But no prohibition will prevent these fees from being paid; such payments can without difficulty be continued in secret in spite of any repressive legislation, so long as the parties are desirous to continue them.

656. Nor can you remove the desire of the recruiter to receive these fees or his ability to earn them by influencing natives to come to the mines. The great majority of the licensed recruiters are traders, and, apart from that which may be called their moral influence as the comparatively few representatives of the dominant race among a large number of natives, they can always, by giving credit, acquire the power which every creditor has over every debtor.

657. It would, of course, be possible to reduce, if not to abolish, this source of influence by prohibiting credit between Europeans and natives in the Territories, as I have already recommended should be done on the Rand. But this would cause a great deal of hardship; the native at his kraal, being largely dependent upon very variable harvests, has legitimate need of a certain amount of credit.

658. [Since writing the last paragraph I have been informed that debts due by natives to Europeans are not recoverable in Basutoland (evidence before the Native Affairs Commission, 1903-'5. Question 39499). If experience has shown this to work well, the question of extending the system to other Native Territories might well be considered, but it is now too late for me to investigate the point.]

659. I do not, however, see any reason why it should be impossible to destroy the willingness of the mines to pay capitation fees. In fact, I have sought in vain for any sufficient explanation of this willingness. According to Mr. Taberer, the recruiter does no persuading of the native, beyond letting him get into debt on the probability of his getting an advance, and then worrying him to go to the mines and work it off. I think the trader would probably let the native get into debt—though perhaps to a smaller extent, which would be no bad thing for the native—even if there were no capitation fee, and then he would certainly worry him to work it off.

660. The recruiter who is a recruiter pure and simple will not, of course, exert himself to procure labour unless he is remunerated for his efforts. But the trader will; it is entirely in his interest to do so. A trader's business is to sell his goods,

and to do this he must have customers with money to spend. In the Territories, the bulk of his customers are natives, and the only way in which they can get money in any quantity is by going out to work. Capitation fee or none, the trader will always use his influence to induce the natives in his neighbourhood to go and earn wages, provided that those wages are, to a substantial extent, spent with him.

661. It may be objected that, though the trader must desire the native to earn money, it is indifferent to him where the money is earned and that, unless retained in the interest of the mines by the capitation fees, he will send the native elsewhere. I think there are several replies to this.

662. In the first place, there is the natural tendency to labour to go to the most profitable market; and it is the trader's interest to assist that tendency, since the more the native earns, the more he will spend. There can be no doubt that the mines are, for the great mass of native labourers, their best market. The average wage there is about £2 12s. per calendar month, all found. Annexure 14 shows the rates of pay in many other parts of South Africa, and, while there are various cases where these are higher than at the mines, the quantity of labour required to satisfy these cases is not large enough to make a serious inroad upon the total amount available. The demands of the Aliwal North stores and of the East London public works can be filled without imperilling the labour supply of the Rand.

663. I may point out here that it is clearly in the interest of the country as a whole, though sometimes injurious to special classes, that the labour should go in the first instance to those occupations where it is most highly paid. When, as in South Africa, practically all employers are competing for labour, the fact that one trade or place can afford to pay £3 while another can only afford £1, must mean that labour applied to the former is more productive than labour applied to the latter.

664. Of course, if the mines cease to pay capitation fees and other industries take to doing so, this will influence the trader in favour of the latter. Against this, if the mines introduce the deferred pay system, this will act as a bonus to the trader in the Territories. The latter will find a native who spends £10 with him quite as much of an asset as one who brings £2 5s. as a capitation fee and spends his earning elsewhere.

665. I do not think that, if the mines adopt deferred pay, any industry unable to afford higher wages will be able to beat them in competion for labour, for the following reasons. There is a limit to the amount which any industry can afford to pay for its labour. Assuming that limit to be £3 a month, an industry which expends 10s. on capitation fees cannot pay more than £2 10s. in wages. Another industry with the same limit which pays no capitation fee can pay the whole £3 in wages. The £3 thus expended, will have a double effect. The extra 10s. will act as avery strong inducement to the native, while the deferred pay, as explained above, is virtually a bonus to the trader. The capitation fee is an inducement to the trader only, and his influence against the non-feepaying industry will be weakened by his being compelled to urge the native to act contrary to the obvious interest of the latter.

666. A present, the trader gets, by way of capitation fee, about £2 5s. out of the earnings of the native on each trip of 180 shifts. Those earnings amount to about £19, since the native works, on an average, about 196 shifts. If half of this sum were paid in the Territories, the trader would benefit at least as much as by receiving the capitation fee, and, if stress of competition compelled the capitation fees to be added to the native's wages, the trader's interest would be proportionally increased.

667. I am sure that the payment of capitation fees is undesirable, and I do not believe that it is necessary.

Competition.

668. The abuses springing from private financial interest in recruiting are much stimulated by the excessive competition which exists. Annexure 22 shows that, in June 1913, there were 1,347 recruiters at work within the Union, and, as pointed out in paragraph 537 above, each of these is, owing to the system of capitation fees, in active competition with all the others, even though the latter may be working for the same principal. From the same Annexure it appears that these

recruiters employed 1,642 runners, and from Annexure 23 that, during the first half of 1913, recruiters and runners together only obtained an average of from 1·7 (in the Transvaal) to 3·7 (in the Cape) recruits per month for each recruiter or runner employed.

669. Annexure 24 shows the distribution of this army throughout the different districts of the Union. In this Annexure the same recruiter is sometimes shown several times over, as many of them have licences to recruit in two or more districts, but it gives a correct version of the amount of competition in each district. It is apparent that with, e,g., 141 recruiters, and their respective runners, tumbling over each other to get hold of natives in the Kingwilliamstown District, there is great temptation towards the abuses enumerated under Nos. (4), (5), (7), (9) and (11).

670. It seems to me that it would be a good thing to limit the number of licences issued to each district to some definite fraction of the native population. If difficulties as to selection prove insuperable—and I can quite understand that there will be such difficulties—then the solution might be applied which has been applied to a similar difficulty arising in the Transvaal with reference to liquor licences; the grant of new licences can be prohibited until the existing licences have died down to a reasonable proportion.

671. It was suggested by some magistrates in the Territories that each recruiter should be given an exclusive area, so that there should be no competition at all. I am not sufficiently acquainted with the local circumstances to say whether this is practicable, but it would certainly tend to the reduction of the abuses set out in the last paragraph but one.

PART V.

RECOMMENDATIONS.

---

672. I subjoin a summary of my principal recommendations. Various other suggestions, which cannot conveniently be summarised, will be found in the Report itself. It should be understood that the recommendation of a certain course by no means implies that it is nowhere in use at present; on the contrary, many recommendations are taken from the existing practice of one or more of the mines. The numbers in brackets after each recommendation refer to the paragraphs of the Report upon which that recommendation is based.

PART II.

ACCIDENTS.

673. That, if a native complains that his working place is dangerous, he be not required to continue there until the European in charge has consulted another European, preferably a shiftboss, and the latter has agreed that the place is safe. In the event of an accident occurring, the omission to consult such a second opinion should *per se*, constitute negligence (17,18).

674. That Inspectors of the Mines Department be supplied, when evidence has to be interpreted, with interpreters who belong to the Public Service (20).

675. That sections 16, 17 (*a*) and 17 (*b*) of Act No. No. 12 of 1911 be amended to allow of the imposition, in serious cases, of a sentence of imprisonment without the option of a fine (21—23).

676. That more careful examination of " Stulls " be enforced (24).

677. That either all working places be examined before the natives are sent down the mine or steps be taken to compel them to remain at the stations until the Europeans come down (25—30).

678. That every case where any person has been rendered unconscious by " Gassing " be reported to the Mines Department (31).

ASSAULTS.

679. That a licensed underground inspector be attached to the staff of every compound (41—43).

680. That, where practicable, double gates be fixed at stations whence a large number of natives are hauled (48—51).

DELAYS IN HAULING.

681. That, as far as practicable, the size of cages be increased (53—55), shelters be erected near the shafts (56,57) and more cages be run at midday (59—62).

LASHING BY HAMMERBOYS.

682. That, where hammerboys are required to do any lashing, that fact and the amount be set out in their contract (72—78).

683. That, where hammerboys are required to do any serious amount of lashing, they be separately paid for it as a separate job (86—89).

684. That, where practicable, hammerboys be not required to do any serious amount of lashing (65—91).

DRY HOLES.

685. That additional payment upon some uniform principle be made for dry holes (92—95).

INSUFFICIENT DRILLS.

686. That drills be everywhere distributed upon a definite system, providing, where practicable, for a check on the number returned (97—98).

FOOD.

687. That where a limited ration of porridge is at present given, an unlimited supply be substituted (116—118).

688. That a strict system of issuing supplies from the store to the kitchen be adopted, where it is not already in force (120).

689. That special attention be paid to cleanliness in the feeding arrangements (121).

690. That the tastes of special classes of natives be more considered (122).

691. That a hot ration before going to work be made compulsory (123, 124).

WASHING.

692. That a supply of hot water for washing be available upon every mine (130).

FIRING.

693. That firing be always provided (131).

MARRIED QUARTERS.

694. That, by way of experiment, a superior type of location be established where no women are allowed to reside unless the compound manager is satisfied that they are the wives (of course in the native sense), and not merely the concubines, of the men with whom they are living (132—138).

POLICE RAIDS.

695. That police, when raiding a compound, be always accompanied by a representative of the management (139—140).

DELAY IN DISCHARGE.

696. That arrangements be made by which time-expired natives can always get their pay and leave, if they so desire, on the day their time is up (141, 142).

COMPOUND POLICE.

697. That compound police and bossboys be prohibited from carrying sjamboks (146, 147).

698. That police boys be selected, as a rule, from among natives who have worked underground (150, 151).

REDRESS OF GRIEVANCES.

699. That the assignment to a mine of natives of a particular tribe in such small numbers as to preclude the appointment of a police boy for that tribe be avoided as far as possible (161).

EDUCATIONAL FACILITIES.

700. That, in every compound, accommodation be provided for educational and religious meetings (162).

REPATRIATION.

701. That mine medical officers endeavour to arrive at uniformity in dealing with repatriation for medical unfitness (175—177).

702. That where amputation is contemplated, the patient, if conscious, or, if he be unconscious, any available relatives be consulted (178, 179).

DETECTION OF SICKNESS.

703. That the following practices, already in use on many mines, be made universal:—

   (a) Hospital attendants should watch the shifts as they come up and detain any native suffering from visible injuries.

   (b) A check should be arranged by which the compound manager is advised, as early as possible, of the absence of any native from his working gang.

   (c) There should be periodical medical inspection of all natives.

   (d) Voluntary boys should be subjected, on engagement, to the same medical examination as recruited boys (181—187).

SCREENS FOR THE DYING.

704. That the beds of dying patients be screened off (188).

Visiting Hours.

705. That the utmost facilities be given to patients to receive their friends (189).

Malingering.

706. That the medical officer personally see every native who professes to be sick (193—195).
707. That as far as work permits, occasional leave of a day or two be granted (196).

Work in Hospital.

708. That either no work at all be required from patients or that they be paid for what they do (197—199).

Change Houses.

709. That change houses be provided for all natives (200—202).

Medical Attendance.

710. That the employment of whole time medical officers be made compulsory, and that a limit be placed upon the number of patients per medical officer (203—227).
711. That the Government medical supervision of native mine hospitals be increased (228—230).

Nursing Staff.

712. That the position of hospital superintendent be only open, in future, to persons holding proper qualifications (231—233).
713. That arrangements be made for the training of native hospital attendants, that higher pay be offered, and that, when a supply of trained attendants is available, the employment of untrained ones be prohibited (234—239).
714. That the proportion of attendants (European and native) to patients be laid down by regulation (240—243).

Burials.

715. That mine cemeteries be fenced and preserved from other uses (246).
716. That native burials be conducted in accordance with native custom, as far as compatible with health and decency (247).

Wages Generally.

717. That a higher proportion of natives be employed on piecework rates (259—262).
718. That the *maximum* average clause in the N.R.C. schedule of wages be withdrawn (263—271).

Non-Marking Tickets.

719. That no day's pay labourer be refused a ticket except upon a conviction of loafing (287—300).
720. That no hammerboy be refused a ticket for his hole unless the hole has been inspected by the shiftboss as well as by the miner (301—316).
721. That loafer tickets be always bound up in the same book as worktickets (318, 319).
722. That no miner be allowed to mark a rate of pay upon a ticket (320).

Time in Hospital.

723. That all hospital shifts entitled to count against the contract be visibly shown on the native's ticket (322—324).
724. That all shifts spent in hospital as the result of an accident not caused by wilful and serious misconduct be reckoned against the contract (325, 326).

725. That the burden of proving such misconduct rest upon the employer (327).

726. That natives be paid for any day upon which they have begun their day's work, but are disabled by an accident (not arising from their own serious and wilful misconduct) from finishing it (329).

ADMINISTRATION OF ESTATES.

727. That a general instruction be issued that, in cases of accident, valuables upon the injured person shall be secured and reported (336, 337).

CHARGE FOR LOSSES.

728. That the practice of charging natives for lost tickets, badges, etc., be either prohibited or limited (338, 339).

LIMITATION OF LENGTH DRILLED.

729. That any limitation upon the *maximum* to be drilled by a hammerboy be prohibited (340—342).

DEDUCTIONS.

730. That, on pay days, there be always a mine official present to explain to natives the reason of any deductions on their tickets (356).

DESTRUCTION OF RECORDS.

731. That no document bearing on a contract with a native labourer be destroyed until after the native has completed his contract and left (358).

COMPENSATION.

732. That natives be compensated upon the basis of probable loss of earning power; where practicable, the payment to take the form of an annuity (359—385).

733. That every native repatriated be examined for miners' phthisis by a Government medical officer (387—390).

734. That information as to the right to compensation for miners' phthisis be disseminated among the natives (391—401).

RELEASE FROM CONTRACT.

735. That it be a term of the contract that it may be determined by the labourer upon his paying a fixed sum for every unexpired month or obtaining a substitute to work an equivalent period (430—433).

VARIATION OF CONTRACT.

736. That no contract be varied without the knowledge and consent of the Native Affairs Department (439—441).

TAXATION.

737. That, when a labourer claims exemption from the Transvaal tax on the ground that he has paid in the Cape Province, the N.A.D. undertake the verification of the statement, instead of throwing the burden of proof upon the native (442—445).

NATIVE AFFAIRS DEPARTMENT.

738. That the Offices of Inspector and of Protector be separated (447—450).

739. That the civil jurisdiction of Inspectors be restored (451—453).

TRAVELLING.

740. That the number of natives to be carried in each pattern of carriage be laid down, and that the limit be enforced (455—458).

742. That the system of charging Natal natives a higher fare than Cape Colony natives for the same journey be abandoned (466, 467).

LOCAL CREDIT.

743. That debts contracted on the Rand by native mine labourers to Europeans be made irrecoverable at law and any security for such debts invalid (468—474).

744. That mines provide a store for their native labourers' property (473).

ON PART III.

CONTROL.

745. That a dormant force, only for use in emergency, be organised on every mine (474—494).

746. That compounds be in future constructed with a view to their being closed, if necessary (501—503).

747. That a native intelligence department be organised (504).

748. That no compound of any considerable size ever be without a European on duty (507).

749. That it be made an offence in a compound manager that any serious quantity of liquor should be found in his compound (513—522).

750. That possession of the root from which " khali " is made be an offence in a coloured person (524).

ON PART IV.

RECRUITING.

751. That, while advances are permitted, they be permitted to be given only during the 14 days prior to the native's departure for the mine (557—559).

752. That no advance be given to a minor except with the consent of his guardian (562).

ADVANCES.

753. That, if Regulation 24 of 6th January, 1914, be enforced, advances under sub-section (2) be only allowed for remittance home or to pay fines on the terms of sub-section (1) (c) (587).

754. That the system of deferred pay be introduced for Union natives (585—627).

755. That security for due payment of deferred wages be required from anyone recruiting under this system (636).

756. That, after the deferred pay system has become thoroughly established, advances be abolished (585—630).

757. That, pending the abolition of advances, the permissible amount remain at £2 (629).

758. That payment of railway fare and outfit continue to be allowed (630).

759. That a substantial period be allowed to elapse between the introduction of deferred pay and the abolition of advances (631—635).

CAPITATION FEES.

760. That the mines cease to pay capitation fee (656—667).

COMPETITION.

761. That the number of recruiting licences granted in any district be limited to a defined proportion of the native population of the district (668—670).

762. That, if practicable, each recruiter be licensed for a named area reserved exclusively for himself (671).

H. O. BUCKLE,
Commissioner.

Johannesburg,
27th May, 1914.

ANNEXURES

TO THE

REPORT OF THE NATIVE GRIEVANCES INQUIRY, 1913-14.

1. Percentage of cancelled shifts on each mine.

2. Contract and Attestation form used by the Native Recruiting Corporation, Ltd.

3. Contract used by Messrs. Marwick & Morris.

4. Percentage of repatriations for medical unfitness upon each mine.

5. Regulations for change houses.

6. Proportion of whole time medical officers to average daily number of patients and to native population attended.

7. Proportion of part time medical officers to average daily number of patients and to native population attended.

8. Mine Medical Inspectors form of report on compounds.

9. Do. do. do. do. hospitals.

10. Proportion of nursing staff to average daily number of patients.

11. Schedule of rates of pay, May, 1897.

12. Native Recruiting Corporation's Schedule B. as originally laid down.

13. Do. do. do. do. amended to date.

14. Rates of native pay in various parts of South Africa.

15. Percentage of natives employed on each mine at piecework rates.

16. Average cost of repatriation on each mine.

17. Percentage of cases of miners' phthisis reported by each mine.

18. Witwatersrand Native Labour Association " special " ticket.

19. Period for which voluntary natives are engaged by each mine.

20. Portuguese contract (original).

21. Do. (translation).

22. Number of recruiters in the Union.

23. Number of natives recruited per recruiter.

24. Distribution of recruiters throughout the Union.

ANNEXURE 1.

STATEMENT showing (1) Percentage of Cancelled Shifts, or Loafer Tickets, on each Mine among HAMMERBOYS during the twelve months ended the 30th September, 1913, giving figures for each half year separately ; and (2) the percentage of Cancelled Shifts, or Loafer Tickets, on each Mine among OTHER BOYS over the same period.

Mine.	Percentage of cancelled shifts among Hammerboys.		Percentage of cancelled shifts among Other Boys.	
	Half-year ended		Half-year ended.	
	31.3.13.	30.9.13.	31.3.13.	30.9.13.
Randfontein Central :				
Block A	2·0	1·75	1·0	1·0
West	4·0	3·5	1·0	1·0
Ferguson	2·5	1·5	1·5	1·5
Stubbs	5·44	8·1	0·11	0·2
Porges	7·4	10·5	0·36	0·45
South	13·31	11·29	0·4	0·29
North	16·0·	13·0	1·39	1·96
Robinson	5·0	8·0	nil	nil
Durban Roodepoort Deep	8·97	7·26	0·55	0·51
Aurora West	9·97	15·5	0·33	0·39
Roodepoort United Main Reef	9·6	6·96	No record kept, not officially permitted	
Vogelstruis Estates	4·5	5·6	nil	nil
New Unified	4·86	4·46	0·38	0·42
Consolidated Langlaagte	8·8	7·63	0·75	0·44
Robinson	1·2	1·27	0·2	0·22
Langlaagte Estate	0·25	0·2	Practically nil	Practically nil
Crown Mines	0·69	0·34	nil	nil
Witwatersrand Deep	12·37	17·16	0·34	0·22
East Rand Proprietary	9·23	7·95	0·61	0·54
Cinderella	15·65	23·99	nil	nil
New Rietfontein Estate	14·8	13·7	1·3	1·3
May Consolidated	2·48	1·8	0·32	0·38
Glencairn	1·86	1·33	0·39	0·26
Knight's Deep, East and West	4·38	5·06	0·21	0·5
Knight's Central	2·48	1·85	0·43	0·21
Rose Deep, Glen Section	2·95	1·99	0·3	0·15
Rose Deep, Rose Section	2·19	2·22		
Witwatersrand	2·85	3·12	0·89	0·26
Bantjes	5·57	3·99	0·55	0·38
Consolidated Main Reef	2·96	4·63	nil	nil
Durban Roodepoort	nil	nil	nil	nil
Main Reef West	5·7	7·99	nil	nil
Princess Estate	9·04	4·91	0·34	0·31
Geduld	10·0	9·0	0·33	0·25
Springs Mines	*8·76	2·42	nil	nil
Welgedacht	nil	1·18	nil	1·76
Daggafontein	3·4	2·44	0·59	0·40
Clydesdale Colliery	nil	nil	1·88	3·30
East Rand Gold and Coal	No Hammer Boys employed		nil	nil
City Deep	4·51	3·50	nil	nil
New Heriot	14·82	13·11	0·18	0·61
Ginsberg	7·57	10·47	0·33	0·55
Geldenhuis	2·82	1·88	0·32	0·29
Spes Bona	4·92	5·41	0·38	0·49
Nourse	3·17	2·74	0·14	0·19
Wolhuter	2·6	2·13	0·07	0·07
New Goch	5·08	2·42	nil	nil
Luipaards Vlei Estate	5·6	3·1	No record,	about 0·1
York	8·2	4·5	„	„
West Rand Central	0·67	0·55	„	„
West Rand Consolidated	3·18	2·4	„	„
New Kleinfontein	4·26	3·15	0·16	0·14
Modderfontein	3·89	3·42	0·54	0·55
Van Ryn	1·09	0–78	0·34	0·27
Brakpan Mines	1·03	0·16	0·39	0·26
Van Ryn Deep	No record kept	6·3	No record kept	0·18
Modder B.	3·61	4·43	0·58	0·47
Government Gold Mining Areas	2·02	2·1	0·3	0·2
Modderfontein Deep Levels	0·38	0·25	Included with Hammer Boys	
A. M. Mostert, Contractor		Practically Nil		
Meyer & Charlton	9·12	6·23	0·14	0·06
City and Suburban	1·01	1·24	0·81	1·15
Village Main Reef	1·1	0·7	nil	nil
Robinson Deep	3·63	2·94	0·42	0·24
Village Deep	3·14	3·37	nil	nil
Ferreira Deep	1·47	0·78	0·09	0·03
New Primrose	3·86	4·43	1·3	0·53
Simmer and Jack Proprietary	6·46	5·52	0·53	0·72
Simmer Deep	6·89	7·67	0·55	0·36

* This Mine states that all loafer tickets are paid for at rate of 1s. per ticket.

NATIVE RECRUITING CORPORATION, LIMITED.

NOTICE TO ATTESTING OFFICER.—No natives under any circumstances can be given positions other than the ordinary work, the nature of such work to be at the option of the Employer, as provided in Clause 1 of the Agreement.

No labourer not falling within the definition of "native" in the Native Labour Regulation Act, 1911, will be accepted by the Mines.

AGREEMENT.

WE the undersigned natives, hereby agree :

(1) That we will proceed to the Transvaal forthwith and there to work for.............and complete not less than the number of shifts shown opposite our respective names, by day or night, underground or on the surface, on piece-work or day's pay, at the option of our employer, at the rates of wages set forth in the schedule on the back hereof ; that we will proceed to the Mine when called upon to do so, and after arrival will work every working day, that the amounts, if any, set opposite our respective names, being moneys already received by us in respect of advances and rail fares, shall be repaid by deductions from the moneys in excess of 10s. earned by us for each completed ticket of 30 shifts until the whole of such amounts shall have been repaid, after which the full earnings shall be paid to us ; that we shall receive no wages for uncompleted shifts and that such uncompleted shifts shall not count towards the fulfilment of our contract.

AND WE.., through our Agent,....................., hereby agree :—

(2) That we will employ the natives whose names are set forth below for the number of shifts set forth in the schedule on the back hereof in accordance with this contract provided such natives are passed by a Government Medical Officer ; that we will pay the said natives the rates of wages set forth in the schedule on the back hereof at the completion of each thirty shifts worked ; that we will provide the said natives free of charge with the prescribed rations, quarters, and medical attendance from their arrival on the mine until the expiry of their contract ; that all natives on piece-work who have contracted for three months up to six months will be allowed a probationary period of 14 shifts, and all natives who have contracted for six months or over will be allowed a probationary period of 30 shifts, and during such probationary periods will be paid not less than 1/6 per shift irrespective of the amount of work performed.

IT IS AGREED by the parties to this contract that the term "shift" when used with respect to day's pay shall mean work for an unbroken period of time according to the daily working hours of this Mine, as authorised by law, for the work at which the native is employed, and when used with respect to piece-work other than hand drilling shall mean the minimum work as fixed by this Mine for the class of work on which the native is employed, and when used with respect to hand drilling, shall mean the drilling of a hole in hard rock of not less than 30 inches. No native will, however, be entitled to cease work before the expiration of the working hours of this Mine unless he has drilled 42 inches. Any work so performed shall be reckoned as a shift towards fulfilment of this contract.

IT IS FURTHER AGREED that natives under this contract may be called upon to do Sunday work authorised by the Government. Any native falling sick during his period of service shall be removed to hospital if, in the opinion of the Mine Medical Officer, it is necessary for the purpose of medical treatment, and there treated until able to resume work. Should such native, when discharged from hospital, in the opinion of the Mine Medical Officer, not be in a fit condition to resume work, he will, if recommended by the Mine Medical Officer, be repatriated.

Contract No.		

BATCH No........... Recruiter's Name and No.	Travel-ling Pass No.	Name of Native.	Name known by.	Father's Name.	Chief or Headman.	District.	Shifts.	Native's Mark	Not to be filled in by Recruiter			
									G.N.L.B. No.	Passport No.	Min. No.	Contract No.

..........Natives attested on this Contract.

*Attesting Officers are requested to insert in this space the number of Natives attested.

Agents must forward three copies of this form—one to the Government Native Labour Bureau, Germiston, and two to Representative, NATIVE RECRUITING CORPORATION, LTD., G.N.L.B. Compound Germiston.

Place.....................

Signature.....................

Agent Native Recruiting Corporation, Ltd.

Schedule No.....................

Rail Warrant No.....................

All erasures and alterations have been initialled by me. ....

Attesting Officer.

	ADVANCES.				
	Cash.	Kind.	Food.	Rail Fares.	Total. £ s. d.

SCHEDULE OF WAGES (FOR A FULL DAY'S WORK OF AN ABLE-BODIED ADULT.)

All Natives employed on Hand-drilling only will be put on Piece-Work and paid as hereafter stated).

DAY'S PAY.

For a full day's work of an able-bodied adult, according to the accepted standard of the Mine at which they are employed.

PIECE-WORK.

All natives on Piece-Work who have contracted for three months up to six months will be allowed a probationary period of 14 shifts, and all natives who have contracted for six months or over will be allowed a probationary period of 30 shifts, and during such probationary period will be paid not less than 1/6 per shift irrespective of the amount of work performed.

HAND-DRILLERS :—Under 30 inches will not count against the period of service, and will not be paid for. Pay for 30 inches and over in hard rock will be at the following rates for each completed hole :—

TRAMMERS	..	..	1/8 per shift
SHOVELLERS	..	..	1/6 per shift
MACHINE HELPERS	..	..	1/9 per shift on Spanners
" "	..	..	2/- per shift on Handles

ANY OTHER CLASS of work at the usual mine rates in force at the mine at which they are employed

Pay for 30 inches and over in hard rock will be at the following rates 42 inches, 2/6. 37 inches to 41 inches, an additional ⅜d. per inch. 36 inches, 2/-. 30 inches to 35 inches, ½d. per inch. an additional 1d. per inch. and for every inch over and above 42 inches,

TRAMMERS
SHOVELLERS
MACHINE HELPERS
TANK AND DUMP AND ANY OTHER PIECE-WORK NATIVES

Will be paid at the ruling current rates for such classes of work in force at the mine at which they are employed.

ANNEXURE 3.

"KWA MUHLE."

AGREEMENT.—It is hereby agreed between Messrs. John Sydney Marwick and George Abbot Morris, hereinafter called the "Employers," and the undermentioned Natives, hereinafter called the "Labourers," as follows :—

The employers agree to hire the labourers, and the labourers contract to give their services as underground hammer boys on the East Rand Proprietary Mines, Limited, or on any other mines or works to be selected by the employer, for a period of six months, that is to say, one hundred and eighty completed shifts, for wages at the rate of two shillings per shift, a shift to be every completed hole of thirty-six inches drilled in the mine. The labourers agree to do the necessary shovelling to clear the face of the rock before commencing to drill, but the time so occupied shall not exceed two hours.

The labourers shall be paid for the first fourteen days worked in the mine at the rate of two shillings per diem, irrespective of the number of inches drilled by them, but thereafter their time shall be computed on the number of completed shifts only. The employers undertake to provide the labourers with rations and quarters free of cost.

The labourers hereby acknowledge their indebtedness to the employers for advances or value received in the amount set opposite to their respective names hereunder, and they agree to the deduction of such amounts from their wages, and do hereby agree that such indebtedness shall be regarded either as a set off against the wages of the Labourers until the indebtedness is satisfied, or that the Labourers have hereby ceded to the Employers all wages coming due to them until such indebtedness is discharged—whichever course the Employers may deem most expedient.

The Labourers agree to enter upon the terms of this Contract at East Rand, Transvaal, on the.................day of................1914.

Agent's No.	Travelling Pass No.	Passport No.	Name and Clan and Native's Mark.	Father.	Chief.	Residence.	ADVANCES.		Name of Runner.
							Particulars.	Amount.	

Attested by me at......................this.................day of............................

......................Signature of Employer or Agent.

................................1914.

NOTE.—Agents are requested not to put more than one Native name on each Contract Form.

MARWICK & MORRIS' CONTRACT.—SCHEDULE OF WAGES

Hammer Boys.—36 in. hole 2/- per shift. From 36 ins. to 48 ins. 1d. per inch, with bonus of 2d. for 42 ins., and a further bonus of 4d. for 48 ins., i.e., for 42 ins. 2/5, and for 48 in. 3/- per diem.

Tramming and Shovelling.—1/6 per shift.

Machine Boys.—2/- to 3/- per shift (Ispisane).

Winze Boys.—2/9 for 36 inches, including cleaning up (E' Wenjini).

Shaft Boys.—3/- for 36 inches, including cleaning up ('E Dambula).

8

WITWATERSRAND NATIVE LABOUR ASSOCIATION, LIMITED.

East Coast rejects repatriated during year 1913 as being unfit for further work.

Returned by—	East Coast, South of Latitude 28°8.		
	Average Number Employed.	Number of Rejects.	Per Cent.
Apex Coal	286	22	7·69
Apex Gold	148	10	6·75
Aurora West	597	24	4·02
Bantjes Consolidated	407	15	7·68
Brakpan Mines	1,447	108	7·46
**Champ D'Or	..	1	..
Cinderella Consolidated ..	569	58	10·19
City and Suburban	1,627	42	2·58
City Deep	1,543	90	5·83
Clydesdale Colliery	166	14	8·43
Coalbrook Colliery	294	1	0·34
Consolidated Langlaagte ..	492	47	9·55
Consolidated Main Reef ..	1,044	75	7·18
Cornelia Colliery	1,129	95	8·41
Crown Mines	3,635	206	5·66
De Rietfontein Colliery ..	113	2	1·76
Durban Roodepoort Co. ..	510	2	0·39
Durban Deep Ltd.	530	34	6·41
**Dynamite Factory	..	2	..
East Rand Gold and Coal ..	168	2	1·19
East Rand Proprietary Mines ..	3,908	204	5·22
Ferreira Deep	1,979	68	3·43
Geduld Property	970	130	13·40
Geldenhuis Deep	1,423	38	2·67
Ginsberg Co.	852	32	3·75
Glencairn Co.	407	16	3·93
Government Gold Mining Areas ..	577	27	4·67
**Jumpers Co.	..	4	..
Jupiter Co.	961	72	7·49
Knight Central	408	29	7·10
Knights Deep	891	63	7·07
Lancaster West	20	3	15·00
Langlaagte Estate	952	33	3·46
Luipaards' Vlei Estate ..	462	9	1·94
Main Reef West	978	68	6·95
May Consolidated	517	26	5·02
Meyer & Charlton	736	33	4·48
Modderfontein B	355	44	12·39
Modder Deep Leve's	302	23	7·61
New Goch	1,003	63	6·28
New Heriot	364	9	2·47
New Kleinfontein	1,058	39	3·68
New Modderfontein	477	26	5·45
New Primrose	1,044	25	2·39
New Rietfontein Estate ..	555	39	7·02
New Unified	433	26	6·00
**Nigel Co.	..	2	..
Nourse Mines	1,457	58	3·98
Premier Diamond	2,394	122	5·09
Princess Estate	604	22	3·64
Randfontein Group	5,448	262	4·80
Rand Klip	67	7	10·44
Robinson Co.	1,739	50	2·87
Robinson Deep	2,312	91	3·93
Roodepoort U.M. Rf. ..	674	31	4·59
**Rooiberg Minerals	..	1	..
Rose Deep	618	13	2·10
Rose Deep (Glen)	518	38	7·33
Simmer Deep	1,624	144	8·86
Simmer East	220	3	1·36
Simmer Propty.	1,505	88	5·84
South Rand Exploration ..	518	26	5·01
**Spes Bona Tribute	..	3	..
Springs Mines	177	8	4·51
Sub-Nigel	293	10	3·41
Van Ryn Deep	868	48	5·52
Van Ryn Mines	676	58	8·57
Village Deep	551	85	15·42
Village Main Reef	1,538	80	5·20
Vogelstruis Estates	543	14	2·57
Welgedacht Explor.	298	4	1·34
West Rand Consolidated ..	362	5	1·38
Witwatersrand Co.	723	38	5·25
Witwatersrand Deep	607	41	6·75
Wolhuter Company	1,053	34	3·22
**York G.M. Co.	..	13	..
	..	3,398	..

** Figures not obtainable—non-members of W.N.L.A.

REGULATIONS for the Construction and Control of Change Houses and the Treatment of Tropical Natives generally, sanctioned by the Native Affairs Department.

ALL MINE MANAGERS WILL BE HELD RESPONSIBLE FOR SEEING THAT THE FOLLOWING REGULATIONS ARE CARRIED OUT ON THEIR MINES.

---

1. A change house shall consist of :

   (a) A part fitted with pegs or pigeon holes for surface clothes, a counter or trough and sufficient space with benches for natives to change. The pegs or pigeon holes shall be clearly numbered with the identification numbers of all natives using the change house.

   (b) A part fitted with pegs for mine clothes, a counter or trough and sufficient space with benches for natives to change. The pegs shall be clearly numbered with the identification numbers of all natives using the change house.

   (c) A passage with a row of baths, shower or otherwise, ranging from hot to cold. Where necessary two or more rows of baths must be provided.

   (d) A coffee stall inside the change house properly equipped with appliances for serving hot drinks to all natives passing through the change house without delay.

2. There shall be a covered way from the change house to the shaft where the intermediate distance exceeds 100 feet. Where the covered way is impracticable, a shelter, in charge of a native policeman, must be provided at the shaft head where natives going on shift must wait until called to go down the shaft. In this case, natives, in addition to their underground clothing, must be provided by the mine with an extra blanket for protection between the change house and the shaft, and *vice versa*.

3. Change houses shall be kept at an even temperature of not less than 60 degrees.

4. A European attendant, assisted by an adequate number of native police, shall be in constant attendance at the change house while such change house is being used by natives.

5. The change house and covered way shall be kept in a clean and sanitary condition by the attendant in charge. The attendant shall be responsible that all underground clothes are thoroughly dried between shifts, and shall see that natives remain in the change house not less than twenty minutes after coming off shift. No one, except the attendant and his assistants or Government inspector or person duly authorised by the Management, shall be allowed access to clothes deposited in the change house. The building must be securely locked when left by the attendant and his assistants.

6. On arrival at the mine the mine management shall supply every tropical native with an overcoat or heavy blanket. Such overcoat or heavy blanket shall be clearly marked with the native's identification number, and shall remain the property of the mine, and the native will be liable to punishment by the Government authorities in case of loss. The Compound Manager shall be responsible for each native being clad in this surface outfit, especially when proceeding between the compound and the change house, and *vice versa*, when going on or coming off shift.

7. Each tropical native before employment underground shall be supplied with adequate mine clothing for wear underground, such clothing to consist of either shirt and loin cloth, or sweater and loin cloth. These clothes shall be clearly and distinctly marked with the native's identification number. They shall be the property of the native, and the cost shall be deducted over two months, out of the wages paid to him locally. As they wear out they must be replaced at the expense of the native. No native shall proceed underground unless adequately clad.

8. Underground clothes must be kept in the change house, and must not be removed therefrom except for the purpose of wear underground until the native's discharge from the mine.

9. Every tropical native before going on shift underground must be provided with a hot meal, and must be provided with a loaf of bread to take underground unless arrangements have been made to feed him underground. He shall leave the compound in his surface clothes, with the heavy blanket or overcoat referred to above, and proceed to the change house nearest the shaft by which he descends. He must enter the change house by the door prescribed for the purpose and must there show his identification badge and deposit all his surface clothes with the attendant, who shall place them on the pegs or in the pigeon holes bearing the number shown on the badge. The native shall then pass through the connecting door, show his badge, and draw his underground clothes, which he must immediately put on.

10. Every tropical native on coming up from work underground must on arrival at the surface proceed to the change house forthwith by the covered way (where such exists). He must enter the building by the door prescribed for the purpose and must divest himself of all his underground clothes and hand them to the attendant, who will hang them on the peg bearing his identification number. The native must then pass through the row of baths from hot to cold, and presenting himself at the surface clothes-counter, draw his surface clothes. He shall, before leaving the building, receive a mug of hot cocoa, coffee or soup. Every native passing through the change house when coming off shift must remain in that building for not less than fifteen minutes after passing through the baths.

11. There shall be as little delay as possible in the transit of natives between the levels in which they are working and the surface. Steps must be taken, as far as possible, to protect natives, while waiting to ascend, from the drafts from down-cast shafts.

12. No native shall expectorate or commit a nuisance in the change house, covered way, or in proximity thereto, or damage the Company's property.

13. Natives passing through the change house shall obey all reasonable commands of the attendant in charge of the building or his assistants.

14. Natives must be warned not to leave money or valuables in their clothing at the change house.

15. Tropical natives shall not be employed on surface dumps.

16. While occupied by tropical natives, compound rooms must be properly heated during the winter months.

WHOLE-TIME MEDICAL OFFICERS.

Mine.	Number of Doctors.	Number of Natives on Mine.	Average daily number in Hospital.	Population per Doctor.	Cases per Doctor.
Ferreira Deep .. .. Robinson G.M.	1	6,848	134	6,848	134
Randfontein Central (North) .. .. Randfontein Central (South)	2	24,719	553	12,359	276
New Unified .. .. Consolidated Langlaagte	1	4,401	108	4,401	108
Durban Roodepoort .. .. .. Bantjes Consolidated	1	5,776	84	5,776	84
Geldenhuis Deep .. .. .. New Heriot	1	6,157	168	6,157	168
Nourse Mines .. .. City Deep	1	8,140	265	8,140	265
Apex Mines .. .. New Kleinfontein	1 ·	5,015	120	5,015	120
Van Ryn Deep .. .. Government Areas	1	4,266	197	4,266	197
New Modder .. .. Modder " B "	1	5,278	135	5,278	135
	10	70,600	1,764	7,060	176.4

PART-TIME MEDICAL OFFICERS.

Mine.	Number of Doctors.	Number of Natives on Mines.	Average daily number in Hospital.	Population per Doctor.	Cases per Doctor.
*Spes Bona Tribute	1	527	7	527	7
Roodepoort U.M. Reef	1	2,563	43	2,563	43
Geduld Proprietary .. .. Springs Mines .. .. Daggafontein G.M. .. .. Clydesdale Colliery .. .. .. De Rietfontein	2	2,932	169	1,466	84·5
Luipaardsvlei Estates .. .. .. West Rand Central	1	1,935	45	1,935	45
Glencairn Main Reef .. .. .. Rose Deep .. .. New Primrose	1	5,414	111	5,414	111
Witwatersrand Deep .. .. .. Knights Central	1	6,125	270	6,125	270
City and Suburban .. .. .. Village Deep .. .. Village Main Reef .. .. .. Turf Mines	1	8,614	352	8,614	352
Modder Deep	1	517	19	517	19
Crown Mines	2	13,105	440	6,552·5	220
Aurora West	1	1,506	22	1,506	22
Wolhuter G.M.	1	2,383	68	2,383	68
Jupiter G.M. .. .. Simmer Deep .. .. Simmer & Jack	3	10,063	518	3,354·3	172·7
Consolidated Main Reef & Main Reef West	1	4,733	109	4,733	109
May Consolidated Witwatersrand G.M. ..	1	3,072	84	3,072	84
E.R.P.M.	2	14,298	516	7,149	258
Vogelstruis Estates, Durban Roodepoort G.M.	1	2,601	34	2,601	34
Brakpan Mines	1	3,704	125	3,704	125
Knights Deep .. .. Simmer East	1	4,321	194	4,321	194
Ginsberg G.M.	1	1,413	38	1,413	38
New Goch	1	2,299	96	2,299	96
Princess Estates	1	2,519	42	2,519	42
†New Rietfontein Estates and Rose Deep (Glen Section).	1	3,407	85	1,703·5	42·5
Meyer & Charlton	1	903	26	903	26
Robinson Deep	1	3,869	149	3,869	149
West Rand Consolidated	1	3,634	73	3,634	73
Van Ryn Estates	1	2,017	40	2,017	40
Langlaagte Estates	1	1,847	99	1,847	99
Welgedacht Exploration	1	353	17	353	17
Jumpers	1	1,002	26	1,002	26
York Syndicate	1	990	13	990	13
East·Rand G.C. & Estate	1	240	4	240	4
Cinderella G.M.	3	900	101	300	33·7
	39	113,806	3,935	2,918·1	100·9

*Have two wards in Goch Hospital.

†Dr. Perkins, of Ginsberg, helps also at New Rietfontein.

COMPOUNDS.

1. Date of inspection ....

2. Date of previous inspection..

3. Alterations and improvements since previous inspection ....
....
....
....
....

4. Name of Company ....

5. Name of Compound ....

6. Number of Compounds on Mine ....

7. Number of Natives housed in this Compound ....

8. Name of Mine Manager ....

9. Name of Compound Manager ....

10. Name of Native Protector ....

11. Site of Compound ....
....

12. Drainage and how disposed of ....
....
....

13. Number of Change Houses ....

14. Number of Shafts ....

15. Age of Compound ....

16. Ventilation of rooms ....
....

17. Light ....

18. Heating ....

19. Bunks (kind of, etc.) ....
....

20. Disinfecting bath for bunks ....
....

21. Condition of floors of rooms ....
....

22. Condition of walls of rooms ....
....

23. Condition of inside open space of compound..
....
....

24. Surroundings of Compound..
....

25. Cook House :
    (a) Kind of ....
    (b) Condition of ....
    (c) Storage rooms for food...

26. Bathing accommodation :
    (a) Shower   Hot ....
                 Cold ....
    (b) Plunge   Hot ....
                 Cold ....
....
....
....

27. Latrines :
    (a) No. of buckets ....
    (b) General conditions ....
....
....

28. Scale of diet..
....
....
....

29. Time of different meals ....
....

30. Time of Shifts ....
....

ANNEXURE 8—*continued*.

31. Labourers supplied from which source :
    (*a*) G.N.L. Bureau ....
    (*b*) W.N.L. Association ....
          (1) East Coast ....
          (2) Tropical
          (3) Local ....
    (*c*) Contractors ....
32. Location or not, and general conditions........................
....
....
....
....
....

33. Source of water supply..
....

34. General health conditions of Compound...........................
....
....

35. Remarks and Recommendations by Medical Inspector...............
....
....
....
....
....
....
....
....
....
....
....
....
....
....
....
....
....
....
....
....
....
....
....
....
....
....

ANNEXURE 9.

HOSPITALS.

---

1. Date of inspection...
2. Date of previous inspection...
3. Alterations and improvements since previous inspection...........................
....
....
....
....

4. Mine Hospital for following Mines...
....
....

5. Name of Hospital..
6. Name of Medical Officer...
....
7. Name of Superintendent of Hospital..
8. Number of European Attendants...
9. Number of Native Attendants...
10. Are the Surgical and Medical Wards separate ?...................................
11. How many surgical beds ?..
12. How many medical beds ?...
13. Number of beds...
14. Number of Natives depending on this Hospital..................................
15. Distance of Hospital from (*a*) Compound ....
                (*b*) Shafts ....

105

ANNEXURE 9—*continued*.

16. What kind of ambulance is kept ?...
....
17. Telephone ....
18. When was Hospital erected ?
19. Condition of the Mine ....
20. What kind of building...
....
21. Site ....
22. Drainage ....
....
23. Ventilation ....
....
24. Light· ....
25. Heating..
....
26. Accommodation for Convalescents...
27. Isolation Ward ....
....
28. Operating Theatre ....
....
29. Instruments ....
30. Sterilising apparatus ....
31. Dispenser ....
32. Dispensary ....
....
33. How is dispensing done ?...
....
34. Mortuary ....
35. Incinerator ....
36. Latrines ....
....
37. Bath-room ....
38. Clothes-room ....
....
39. Verandahs ....
40. Corridors..
41. Case-book ....
....
42. Post-mortems ....
43. Source of Water Supply..
44. Kitchen ....
....
45. Disinfectants ....
46. Temperature Charts...
....
47. Poisons ....
....
48. Conditions of (a) Floors...
....
        (b) Walls ....
....
        (c) Ceilings ....
....
49. What kind of beds...
....
50. Condition of Equipment...
....
51. How is Hospital kept ?..
....
....
52. Condition of surroundings ....
....
53. Death-rate compared with other Hospitals...............................
....
54. Predominating diseases at time of inspection............................
....
....

Annexure 9—*continued.*

55. Prevalence of Miners' Phthisis ....

....

....

Tuberculosis ....

....

....

Mixed Phthisis and Tuberculosis..

....

....

Pneumonia ....

....

Pleurisy ....

....

Other forms of Pulmonary diseases.....................................

....

....

Worms

....

....

Typhoid ....

Dysentry ....

Circulatory ....

Nervous ....

Venereal ....

....

....

Skin ....

Septicaemia ....

....

....

Surgical Cases (except due to accidents).................................

....

....

56. Remarks and recommendations by Medical Inspector ....

....

....

....

....

....

....

....

....

....

....

....

....

....

....

....

....

....

....

....

....

....

....

....

....

....

....

....

....

....

....

....

NURSING STAFF.

Mine.	European Attendants.	*Native Attendants.	Average daily number in Hospital.	Cases per European Attendant.	Cases per Native Attendant.
May Consolidated	1	5	33	33	6·6
Witwatersrand G.M.	1	7	51	51	7·3
New Heriot	1	3	38	38	12·7
Geldenhuis	4	14	130	32·5	9·3
Vogelstruis Estate	1	2	4	·4	2
Durban Roodepoort G.M.	1	3	30	30	10
Brakpan Mines	3	19	125	41·7	6·6
Knights Deep	2	14	123	61·5	8·8
Simmer & Jack (East)	2	10	71	35·5	7·1
Ginsberg	1	6	38	38	6·3
New Goch	2	6	96	48	16
Princess Estate	1	4	42	42	10·5
New Rietfontein Estate	2	8	51	25·5	6·4
Rose Deep (Glen)	1	8	34	34	4·2
Meyer & Charlton	1	4	26	26	6·5
Robinson Deep	2	8	149	74·5	18·6
West Rand Consolidated	2	8	73	36·5	9·1
Van Ryn Estate	1	6	40	40	6·7
Langlaagte Estate	1	5	51	51	10·2
†Spes Bona Tribute	..	..	7	..	..
Roodepoort U.M. Reef	1	4	43	43	10·7
Geduld Prop.	3	9	95	31·7	10·6
Springs Mines	1	4	41	41	10·2
**De Rietfontein Collieries	none	..	..	..	..
**Daggafontein G.M.	,,	1	12	..	12
**Clydesdale Collieries	,,	2	14	..	7
**Luipaardsvlei Est, East Section (Old Windsor)	,,	5	37	..	9·4
**West Rand Central	,,	1	8	..	8
Glencairn Main Reef	1	4	20	20	5
Rose Deep (Rose)	2	15	62	31	4·1
New Primrose	1	6	29	29	4·8
Wit. Deep	3	24	210	70	8·7
Knights Central	2	7	60	30	8·6
‡City and Suburban					
Village Deep	3	26	352	117·3	13·5
Village Main Reef					
Modder Deep	1	3	19	19	6·3
Crown Mines	5	21	440	88	20·9
Aurora West	1	2	22	22	11
Wolhuter G.M.	1	3	68	68	22·7
Jupiter G.M.	3	15	130	43·3	8·7
Simmer Deep	3	20	253	84·3	12·6
Simmer & Jack	2	19	135	67·5	7·1
Consolidated Main Reef	2	11	109	54·5	9·9
Main Reef West					
Ferreira Deep	3	4	69	23	17·2
Robinson G.M.	2	6	65	32·5	10·8
Randfontein North	3	22	284	94·7	12·9
Randfontein South	4	23	269	67·2	11·7
New Unified Main Reef	1	2	19	19	9·5
Consolidated Langlaagte	2	6	89	44·5	14·8
Durban Roodepoort Deep	2	7	43	21·5	6·1
Bantjes Consolidated	2	7	41	20·5	5·9
Nourse Mines	4	11	144	36	13·1
City Deep	3	13	121	40·3	9·3
E.R.P.M.	4	27	516	129	19·1
§Apex	..	1	3	..	‡3
Kleinfontein	2	14	117	58·5	8·4
Van Ryn Deep	2	8	107	53·5	13·4
Government Areas	2	4	90	45	22·5
New Modder	4	15	90	22·5	6
Modder "B"	2	9	45	22·5	5
**Welgedacht Expl.	none	1	17	..	17
Jumpers	1	3	26	26	8·7
**York Syndicate	none	3	13	..	4·3
**East Rand G.C. & Estate	,,	1	4	..	4
Cinderella	2	8	101	50·5	12·6
	110	537	5,644	51·3	10·5

* Native Attendants include Cooks, Sweepers, etc.
† Have same staff as Goch ; have two wards in Goch Hospital.
‡ Had no whole-time Hospital Superintendent—have same doctor with separate hospital and and staff of native attendants.
§ Use Kleinfontein Hospital.
** Compound Manager also acts as Hospital Superintendent.

CHAMBER OF MINES.

REVISED SCHEDULE OF NATIVE WAGES.

MAY, 1897.

Mine.	s.	d.	Mill.	s.	d.
Machine Helpers	1	8	Elevator Boys	2	0
Hammer Boys	1	6	Vanner Boys	2	0
Shovel Boys	1	3	Mill Boys (12 hours)	2	0
Tram Boys (10 ft. Trucks)	1	2	Mill Boys (8 hours)	1	4
Tram Boys (16 ft. Trucks)	1	6	Blanket and Sluice Boys	2	0
Dry Shaft and Winze Boys	1	8	Crusher Boys	1	4
Wet Shaft Boys	2	0	Surface Trammers	1	9
Wet Shaft Boys (when developing only)	2	6	Mule Drivers	2	6
Boys Cutting Hitches for Timber ..	1	6			
Timber Boys	1	2	Cyanide.		
Stope Ganger's Assistants	2	0	Solution Shed Boys	1	4
Station Boys (where White Man employed)	1	2	Boys (Filling and Discharging).. ..	1	9
Station Boys (where no white man em-			Zinc Cutters	1	6
ployed	2	6	Tramming Residues	1	4
Air Hoist Drivers	2	0			
Pumpman's Assistants	1	8	General.		
Platelayer's Assistants	1	6	Fitter's Boys	1	6
Pipeman's Assistants	1	6	Blacksmith's Boys (Strikers)	2	6
			Blacksmith's Boys (Helpers)	1	4
Surface.			Carpenter's Boys	1	2
Stokers (12 hours)	2	6	Mason's Boys	1	4
Stokers (8 hours)	1	8	Police	2	6
Engine Cleaners	1	6	Compound Cooks	2	0
Sorting Boys	2	0	Drill Packers	1	0
Head Gear Boys (where White Man			Drill Sorters	1	6
employed)	1	4	Surface Labourers	1	2
Head Gear Boys (where no White man			Office and Store Boys	2	6
employed)	2	6	Assay Office Boys	2	6
			Coal Boys (off-loading)	1	6

Notes.—Timber Boys assisting in timbering shafts to be paid at the rate of Wet and Dry Shaft Boys.
Seven and one-half per cent. of the natives employed may be paid at special rates.
Month to be reckoned as consisting of at least thirty working days.

SCHEDULE B.—SCHEDULE OF RATES OF PAY.

(1) NATIVES EMPLOYED IN HAND DRILLING IN HARD ROCK.

Under 30 inches not to count against the period of service, and not to be paid for. Pay for 30 inches and over to be at the following rates for each completed hole :—

30 inches to 35 inches	½d. per inch.
36 inches..	2/-
37 inches to 41 inches .. .. an additional ½d. per inch.
42 inches..	2/6

and 1d. per inch for every inch over 42 inches.

Natives not to be allowed to come out of the Mine before the end of the shift unless they have completed not less than 42 inches.

Boss Natives .. .. An average of 2s. 3d. per shift.

(2) NATIVES EMPLOYED IN MACHINE DRILLING.

Handle and Spanner Natives (including special Natives engaged rigging machines, but excluding drill carriers), 1s. 9d. to 2s. per shift.

Handle and Spanner Natives on bonus-plus-day's-pay, such rates of pay that the average pay of such Natives as a class on any member's property shall not exceed 2s. 3d. per shift, *excluding drill carriers.*

Drill Carriers .. .. 1/- to 1/6 per shift.

The question of pay of machines Natives on bonus-plus-day's-pay may be reopened at any time by any member of the Board of Management upon such member giving one month's notice of his intention to do so.

(3) NATIVES EMPLOYED IN SHOVELLING AND TRAMMING.

Trammers	1/8 to 2/- per shift.
Shovellers	1/6 to 1/8 per shift.

Trammers and Shovellers on contract, such rates of pay that after 31st of January, 1913, the average pay of such contract Natives as a class on any member's property shall not exceed 2s. 3d. per shift.

Natives employed on both Shovelling and Tramming may be paid at the tramming rate.

Sweepers	1/- to 1/6 per shift.
Boss Natives	a maximum of 2/3 per shift.

(4) All natives on piece work who have contracted for three months up to six months to be allowed a probationary period of 14 shifts, and all natives who have contracted for six months or over to be allowed a probationary period of 30 shifts, and during such probationary periods to be paid not less than 1s. 6d. per shift irrespective of the amount of work done.

(5) NATIVES EMPLOYED IN OTHER CLASSES OF WORK.

(A) UNDERGROUND.

CLASS OF WORK.	Maximum rate of pay for natives other than head and boss natives. (Per shift.)	Maximum rate of pay for head native and boss natives. (Per shift.)
Mine Captains' Natives	2/3	—
Shift Bosses' Natives	2/-	—
Surveyors' Natives	2/-	2/3
Samplers' Natives	1/9	2/3
Platelayers' Natives	2/-	2/3
Timbering : Shafts and Stopes Natives	2/-	2/3
Rockwalling Natives	1/9	2/3
Stopefilling Natives	1/9	2/3
Pump Natives	2/3	—
Pipelaying Natives	2/-	2/3
Skips and Onsetters' Natives	2/-	2/3
Underground Hoists Natives	2/-	—
Mechanical Haulage Natives	2/-	2/3
Station and Drill Distribution Natives	2/-	2/3
Sanitation Natives	1/9	2/3
Ventilation Natives	2/-	—
Underground Rock Drill Fitters' Natives ..	2/-	—
Underground Truck Repairers' Natives	2/-	—
Other classes of underground natives	1/9	2/3

ANNEXURE 12—(continued).

(B) SURFACE.

CLASS OF WORK.	Maximum rate of pay for natives other than head and boss natives. (Per shift.)	Maximum rate of pay for head natives and boss natives. (Per shift.)
REDUCTION RATE.		
Sorting	1/– to 1/8	2/–
Crushers	1/– to 1/8	2/–
Waste Rock Transport	1/– to 1/8	2/–
Ore Transport	1/– to 1/8	2/–
Stamp Mill :		
General	1/– to 1/8	2/–
Cam floor	1/8 to 2/3	—
Tube Mill	1/– to 1/8	2/–
Extractor House :		
General	1/– to 1/8	2/–
Zinc lathes	1/8 to 2/3	—
Tanks :		
General	1/– to 1/8	2/–
Slimes vats	1/6 to 1/10	2/–
Slimes Dam :		
General	1/– to 1/10	2/–
Return Pump	1/6 to 2/–	—
Filling and Discharging Tailings, Dumping Tailings, Ashes or Waste Rock	No rate fixed.	
Samples and General	1/– to 1/8	—
Assay Office	1/6 to 2/–	2/3
ENGINEERING ;		
Smiths :		
General	1/– to 1/10	—
Strikers	1/8 to 2/6	—
Drill Sharpeners (including underground) :		
General	1/– to 1/10	—
Strikers	1/8 to 2/6	—
Boiler Makers	1/– to 2/–	—
Fitters	1/– to 1/8	2/–
Carpenters	1/– to 1/6	2/–
Electricians	1/– to 1/8	2/–
Riggers	1/– to 2/–	2/3
Masons	1/– to 1/8	2/–
Fire	1/6 to 2/6	—
Ash	1/– to 1/8	2—
Surface Gangers	1/– to 1/8	2/–
Plate Layers	1/– to 1/8	2/–
Engine Room Attendants	1/– to 1/8	—
Boiler and Condenser Cleaners	1/6 to 1/10	2/–
Compressors	1/– to 1/8	—
Other classes of surface engineering boys	1/– to 1/8	—
Compound :		
Police Natives and Night Watchmen	No rate fixed.	
Cooks	1/– to 2/–	2/6
Beer Natives	1/– to 2/–	2/6
Sweepers	1/– to 1/6	2/–
Sanitary	1/– to 1/8	2/–
Whitewashers	1/– to 1/8	2/–
GENERAL :		
Office and Store	1/– to 2/–	2/6
Banksmen	1/– to 1/8	2/–
Change House	1/– to 1/8	—
Headgear	1/– to 1/8	2/–
Hospital	1/6 to 2/–	3/–
Stables (excluding head natives and special drivers)	1/– to 2/–	Not limited.
Ventilation	1/– to 1/8	—
Other classes of surface natives	1/– to 1/8	—
Under age natives	4d. to 1/–	—

(6) VERTICAL SHAFTS.

It is permissible to pay Natives employed in vertical shafts in process of sinking a rate of pay exceeding the schedule rate of pay for similar Natives on ordinary work by not more than 1s. per shift.

(7) DEVELOPING MINES.

No extra payment is allowed to Natives working on mines developing only.

8) NATIVES FEEDING THEMSELVES.

Payments to Natives for feeding themselves are not to exceed 4d. per shift, in addition to the loaf of bread supplied daily by the Mines to every underground Native.

No payment of bonus in kind such as meat, etc., is to be given to any Native.

(9) NATIVES RE-ENGAGING.

It is permissible to pay underground Natives a bonus in the way of increased pay during any period of re-engagement *without break of service*, after having completed 180 shifts or their contracted period of service, whichever is the longer, such bonus not to exceed 5s. per month in the case of Natives re-engaging on monthly engagements, and to be paid monthly in one sum in the form of a bonus, and not in any way included in the payment per shift. Further, in the case of Natives re-engaging for a period of three months or more, it is permissible to pay the bonus as a lump sum on re-engagement (*i.e.*, 15s. for a three months' Native, 20s. for a four months' Native, and so on), and in the case of Natives re-engaging for six months or more to make an additional lump sum payment of 10s. (*e.g.*, a total of 40s. for a six months' Native, 45s. for a seven months' Native, and so on), in both cases in place of the monthly bonus.

(10) LOCAL AND VOLUNTARY NATIVES.

It is not permissible for any mine to pay rail fare or travelling expenses or to give any other inducement in cash or kind to voluntary or local natives.

(11) PAY OF COLOURED LABOURERS OTHER THAN PASSPORT NATIVES.

SCHEDULE C.

Apex Mines, Limited.
Afrikander Proprietary Gold Mines, Limited.
Aurora West United Gold Mining Company, Limited.
Bantjes Consolidated Mines, Limited.
Brakpan Mines, Limited.
Benoni Consolidated Gold Mines, Limited.
Cinderella Consolidated Gold Mines, Limited.
City Deep, Limited.
Crown Mines, Limited.
Consolidated Langlaagte Mines, Limited.
Consolidated Main Reef Mines and Estate, Limited.
Cloverfield Mines, Limited.
Durban Roodepoort Deep, Limited.
East Rand Proprietary Mines, Limited.
Ferreira Deep, Limited.
French Rand Gold Mining Company, Limited.
Geldenhuis Deep, Limited.
Geduld Proprietary Mines, Limited.
Glencairn Main Reef Gold Mining Company, Limited.
Ginsberg Gold Mining Company, Limited.
Government Gold Mining Areas (Modderfontein) Consolidated, Limited.
Jupiter Gold Mining Company, Limited.
Knight Central, Limited.
Knights Deep, Limited.
Lancaster West Gold Mining Company, Limited.
May Consolidated Gold Mining Company, LiDited.
Main Reef West, Limited.
Meyer and Charlton Gold Mining Company, Limited.
Modderfontein B. Gold Mines, Limited.
Modderfontein Deep Levels, Limited.
New Boksburg Gold Mines, Limited.
New Goch Gold Mines, Limited.
New Kleinfontein Company, Limited.
New Modderfontein Gold Mining Company, Limited.
New Primrose Gold Mining Company, Limited.
New Rietfontein Estate Gold Mines, Limited.
New Unified Main Reef Gold Mining Company, Limited.
Nourse Mines, Limited.
Princess Estate and Gold Mining Company, Limited.
Rand Collieries, Limited.
Rand Klip, Limited.
Randfontein Deep, Limited.
Robinson Gold Mining Company, Limited.
Roodepoort United Main Reef Gold Mining Company, Limited.
Rooiberg Minerals Development Company, Limited.
Rose Deep, Limited.
Simmer and Jack Proprietary Mines, Limited.
Simmer and Jack East, Limited (in Liquidation).
Simmer Deep, Limited.
Springs Mines, Limited.
Sub Nigel, Limited.
Treasury Gold Mines, Limited.
Tudor Gold Mining Company, Limited.
Van Dyk Proprietary Mines, Limited.
Van Ryn Gold Mines Estate, Limited.
Van Ryn Deep, Limited.
Village Deep, Limited.
Village Main Reef Gold Mining Company, Limited.
Vogelstruis Consolidated Deep, Limited.
West Rand Consolidated Mines, Limited.
Witwatersrand Deep, Limited.
Witwatersrand Gold Mining Company, Limited.
Wolhuter Gold Mines, Limited.

SCHEDULE B.—SCHEDULE OF RATES OF PAY.

Under 30 inches not to count against the period of service, and not to be paid for. Pay for 30 inches and over to be at the following rates for each completed hole :—

30 inches to 35 inches	½d. per inch.
36 inches..	2/-
37 inches to 41 inches	an additional ½d. per inch.
42 inches..	2/6

and 1d. per inch for every inch over 42 inches.

Natives not to be allowed to come out of the Mine before the end of the shift unless they have completed not less than 42 inches.

As little shovelling as possible to be done and not to exceed 2 hours per shift.

Boss Natives .. .. An average of 2s. 3d. per shift.

(2) NATIVES EMPLOYED IN MACHINE DRILLING.

Handle and Spanner Natives (including special Natives engaged rigging machines, but excluding drill carriers), .. 1s. 9d. to 2s. per shift.
See attached Circular.

Drill Carriers .. .. 1/- to 1/6 per shift.

The question of pay of machines Natives on bonus-plus-day's-pay may be reopened at any time by any member of the Board of Management upon such member giving one month's notice of his intention to do so.

(3) NATIVES EMPLOYED IN SHOVELLING AND TRAMMING.

Trammers .. .. 1/8 to 2/- per shift.
Shovellers .. .. 1/6 to 1/8 per shift.
See attached Circular.

Natives employed on both Shovelling and Tramming may be paid at the tramming rate.

Sweepers .. .. 1/- to 1/6 per shift.
Boss Natives .. .. a maximum of 2/3 per shift.

(4) All natives on piece work who have contracted for three months up to six months to be allowed a probationary period of 14 shifts, and all natives who have contracted for six months or over to be allowed a probationary period of 30 shifts, and during such probationary periods to be paid not less than 1s. 6d. per shift irrespective of the amount of work done.

(5) NATIVES EMPLOYED IN OTHER CLASSES OF WORK.

(A) UNDERGROUND.

CLASS OF WORK.	Maximum rate of pay for natives other than head and boss natives. (Per shift.)	Maximum rate of pay for head native and boss natives. (Per shift.)
*Mine Captains' Natives	2/3	—
*Shift Bosses' Natives	2/-	—
Surveyors' Natives	2/-	2/3
Samplers' Natives	1/9	2/3
Platelayers' Natives	2/-	2/3
*Timbering : Shafts and Stopes Natives	2/-	2/3
*Rockwalling Natives	1/9	2/3
*Stopefilling Natives	1/9	2/3
*Pump Natives	2/3	—
Pipelaying Natives	2/-	2/3
*Skips and Onsetters' Natives	2/-	2/3
Underground Hoists Natives	2/-	—
Mechanical Haulage Natives	2/-	2/3
Station and Drill Distribution Natives	2/-	2/3
*Sanitation Natives	1/9	2/3
Ventilation Natives	2/-	—
Underground Rock Drill Fitters' Natives ..	2/-	—
Underground Truck Repairers' Natives	2/-	—
Other classes of underground natives	1/9	2/3
Natives cleaning up Inclines	1/6 to 2/-	—
Natives cleaning Sumps	2/-	2/3
Natives on underground crushers	2/-	2/3

Natives filling sands tanks with hoses to be considered as filling and discharging tailings.
Natives bagging concentrates may be paid not more than 2s. per shift.
Natives on filter presses in discharging ordinary slimes may be paid not more than 2s. 3d. per shift.
Natives on construction work to be paid ordinary surface rates.

ANNEXURE 13—*(continued.)*

(B) SURFACE.

CLASS OF WORK.	Maximum rate of pay for natives other than head and boss natives. (Per shift.)	Maximum rate of pay for head natives and boss natives. (Per shift.)
REDUCTION WORKS :		
Sorting	1/– to 1/8	2/–
Crushers	1/– to 1/8	2/–
Waste Rock Transport	1/– to 1/8	2/–
Ore Transport	1/– to 1/8	2/–
Stamp Mill :		
General	1/– to 1/8	2/–
Cam floor	1/8 to 2/3	—
Tube Mill	1/– to 1/8	2/–
Extractor House :		
General	1/– to 1/8	2/–
Zinc lathes	1/8 to 2/3	—
Tanks :		
General	1/– to 1/8	2/–
Slimes vats	1/6 to 1/10	2/–
Slimes Dam :		
General	1/– to 1/10	2/–
Return Pump	1/6 to 2/–	—
Filling and Discharging Tailings, Dumping Tailings, Ashes or Waste Rock	No rate fixed.	
Samples and General	1/– to 1/8	—
Assay Office	1/6 to 2/–	2/3
ENGINEERING :		
Smiths :		
General	1/– to 1/10	—
Strikers	1/8 to 2/6	—
Drill Sharpeners (including underground) :		
General	1/– to 1/10	—
Strikers	1/8 to 2/6	—
Boiler Makers	1/– to 2/–	—
Fitters	1/– to 1/8	2/–
Carpenters	1/– to 1/6	2/–
Electricians	1/– to 1/8	2/–
Riggers	1/– to 2/–	2/3
Masons	1/– to 1/8	2/–
Fire	1/6 to 2/6	—
Ash	1/– to 1/8	—
Surface Gangers	1/– to 1/8	2/–
Plate Layers	1/– to 1/8	2/–
Engine Room Attendants	1/– to 1/8	—
Boiler and Condenser Cleaners	1/6 to 1/10	2/–
Compressors	1/– to 1/8	—
Other classes of surface engineering boys	1/– to 1/8	—
Compound :		
Police Natives and Night Watchmen	No rate fixed.	
Cooks	1/– to 2/–	2/6
Beer Natives	1/– to 2/–	2/6
Sweepers	1/– to 1/6	2/–
‡Sanitary	1/– to 1/8	2/–
Whitewashers	1/– to 1/8	2/–
GENERAL :		
Office and Store	1/– to 2/–	2/6
*Banksmen	1/– to 1/8	2/–
Change House	1/– to 1/8	—
*Headgear	1/– to 1/8	2/–
Hospital	1/6 to 2/–	3/–
Stables (excluding head natives and special drivers)	1/– to 2/–	Not limited.
Ventilation	1/– to 1/8	—
Other classes of surface natives	1/– to 1/8	—
Under age natives	4d. to 1/–	—

‡Where difficulty is experienced in obtaining sanitary natives Mines have permission to pay up to 2s. 6d. per shift.

*Mines have discretion to pay up to 2s. 6d. per shift for hospital boys.

(6) VERTICAL SHAFTS.

It is permissible to pay Natives employed in vertical shafts in process of sinking a rate of pay exceeding the schedule rate of pay for similar Natives on ordinary work by not more than 1s. per shift.

(7) DEVELOPING MINES.

No extra payment is allowed to Natives working on mines developing only.

(8) NATIVES FEEDING THEMSELVES.

Payments to Natives for feeding themselves are not to exceed 4d. per shift, in addition to the loaf of bread supplied daily by the Mines to every underground Native.

No payment of bonus in kind such as meat, etc., is to be given to any Native.

(9) NATIVES RE-ENGAGING.

It is permissible to pay underground Natives a bonus in the way of increased pay during any period of re-engagement *without break of service*, after having completed 180 shifts or their contracted period of service, whichever is the longer, such bonus not to exceed 5s. per month in the case of Natives re-engaging on monthly engagements, and to be paid monthly in one sum in the form of a bonus, and not in any way included in the payment per shift. Further, in the case of Natives re-engaging for a period of three months or more, it is permissible to pay the bonus as a lump sum on re-engagement

ANNEXURE 13—*continued.*

(*i.e.*, 15s. for a three months' Native, 20s. for a four months' Native, and so on), and in the case of Natives re-engaging for six months or more to make an additional lump sum payment of 10s. (*e.g.*, a total of 40s. for a six months' Native, 45s. for a seven months' Native, and so on), in both cases in place of the monthly bonus.

(10) LOCAL AND VOLUNTARY NATIVES.

It is not permissible for any mine to pay rail fare or travelling expenses or to give any other inducement in cash or kind to voluntary or local natives.

(11) PAY OF COLOURED LABOURERS OTHER THAN PASSPORT NATIVES.

It is permissible for Mines to make their own arrangements *re* pay for such labourers.

(12) NATIVES WORKING 12-HOUR SHIFTS.

It is not permissible to pay such natives in excess of Schedule Rates.

(13) SUNDAY WORK.

Work of Sundays must be avoided as far as possible, but, where necessary, only Schedule Rates are to be paid.

NATIVE RECRUITING CORPORATION, LIMITED.
JOHANNESBURG.

MINES.
Circular Letter No. 118.   11th February, 1914.

TO ALL MINE MANAGERS.

Dear Sir,

For some little time my Board has been considering the question of the rates of pay for natives employed on Tramming and Shovelling Piece-work and Machine Piece-work, and you have already been advised of certain of their decisions in the matter (*vide* Circular Letters Nos. 112, 113 and 116), but I now quote below all the decisions come to in this connection, which, you will note, include certain alterations in the rates for machine piece-work, of which you have not yet been advised.

NATIVES EMPLOYED ON MACHINE PIECE-WORK.

The present maximum average of 2s. 3d. for machine boys on day's pay plus bonus has been abolished and the following maximum rates have been adopted, which may be paid at your discretion :—

RECIPROCATING DRILLS (LARGE AND SMALL).
Stoping.

Handle Boys.—2s. for the first 24 feet drilled, and an additional one and one-third pence per foot drilled thereafter, with a minimum of 2s. per diem.

Spanner Boys.—1s. 9d. for the first 24 feet drilled, and an additional one penny per foot drilled thereafter, with a minimum of 1s. 9d. per diem.

RECIPROCATING DRILLS.
Developing.

In developing with reciprocating drills it shall be optional with the Mines to pay the above rates, or to pay 2s. and 2s. 3d. per shift to the spanner and handle boy respectively in cases where the drilling of the round is completed during the shift.

HAMMER DRILLS.

In the case of hammer drills of the jack hammer type, when used for stoping, or of the Waugh drill type, when used for stoping or raising, either when mounted on a bar or otherwise, and run by one boy, the maximum rate shall be one penny per foot drilled with a bonus of sixpence to any native drilling 18 feet or over in one shift.

In the case of hammer drills of the jack hammer type when used for foot-walling, and run by one boy, the rate shall be one penny per foot drilled with a minimum of 2s. per diem.

In the case of water-fed hammer drills (other than drills of the jack hammer or Waugh drill type), as these drills are still in the experimental stage, a final standard cannot be fixed at present, but, in the meantime, a minimum standard of 30 feet per shift has been fixed, for which 1s. 9d. and 2s. per shift may be paid the spanner and handle boy respectively, but any Mine may raise this standard to meet its particular conditions or requirements, and for each additional foot drilled above whatever standard is adopted, a maximum rate of five-sixths of a penny and one penny per foot may be paid the spanner and handle boy respectively.

With regard to the above rates of pay for hammer drills, it is understood that natives employed on such drills must be paid the same minimum wage per diem as those on reciprocating drills, *i.e.*, 1s. 9d. for spanners and 2s. for handles.

NATIVES EMPLOYED ON TRAMMING AND SHOVELLING PIECE-WORK.

Up to the 31st January, 1914, the maximum average for tramming and shovelling on piece-work, irrespective of the percentage of natives employed on such work, was fixed at 2s. 3d. This has now been abolished and, as from the 1st February, 1914, it is permissible to pay natives employed on this work according to the following sliding scale :—

Number on Contract, being percentage of all natives employed on Tramming and Lashing.		Maximum Average. Per Shift.	Equivalent Amount Per 30 Shifts.
Not more than 25 %	.. ..	2/9	82/6
,, ,, 37.5%	.. ..	2/8	80/-
,, ,, 50 %	.. ..	2/7	77/6
,, ,, 62.5%	.. ..	2/6	75/-
,, ,, 75 %	.. ..	2/5	72/6
,, ,, 87.5%	.. ..	2/4	70/-
,, ,, 100 %	.. ..	2/3	67/6

DAY'S PAY RATES.

The Day's Pay rates for natives employed on machines and tramming and shovelling remain as at present laid down in the Corporation's Schedule of Wages.

Yours faithfully,
E. MARTIENSSEN, Secretary.

AVERAGE Rates of Pay earned by Natives per month in certain parts of South Africa outside the Witwatersrand.

District.	Stores.	Public Works.	Railways.	Mines and Industrial Works.	Harbour Works.
	£ s. d.	£ s. d.	£ s. d.	£ s. d.	£ s. d.
Pietermaritzburg	1 0 0 / 1 10 0	1 10 0 / 2 5 0	1 10 0 / 2 0 0	1 10 0 / 2 0 0	..
Durban	2 0 0	1 15 0	2 0 0	..	*3 0 0
Pinetown	2 0 0	2 10 0	2 10 0	2 0 0	2 10 0
Ladysmith	1 10 0	2 5 0	2 5 0	2 10 0	..
Dundee	1 0 0 / 2 0 0	1 0 0 / 2 0 0	1 10 0 / 1 15 0	1 5 0 / 3 0 0	..
Harding	3 0 0	1 15 0	..	..	..
Port Shepstone	1 10 0 / 2 0 0	2 0 0 / 2 5 0	1 15 0 / 2 0 0	..	..
Graaf-Reinet	*3 0 0	..	*3 15 0	..	..
Grahamstown	2 10 0	3 0 0	1 0 0	3 0 0	..
Zululand	2 0 0	2 0 0	1 18 0	2 10 0	..
King William's Town	*3 0 0	*3 15 0	*3 15 0	..	..
Mafeking	2 0 0 / 4 0 0	..	4 0 0 / 6 0 0	2 8 0 / 3 0 0	..
Queenstown	*2 8 0	*4 10 0	*3 15 0	..	..
Umtata	0 10 0 / 2 0 0	2 5 0	2 5 0	..	..
East London	*3 0 0 / 5 5 0	*3 4 0	3 0 0 / *6 0 0	3 0 0 / *3 15 0	3 0 0 / *4 0 0
Kokstad	1 0 0 / 1 10 0	2 5 0	2 5 0	..	..
Aliwal North	*3 10 0 / 4 10 0	*3 15 0	3 0 0	..	..
Cradock	*2 0 0 / 3 0 0	*3 0 0 / 4 0 0	*3 0 0 / 3 15 0	..	..
Indwe	*2 0 0 / 2 10 0	..	*3 0 0 / 4 10 0	*1 17 6 / 4 10 0	..
Cape Town	4 10 0	4 10 0	4 10 0	4 10 0	4 10 0
Port Elizabeth	*3 0 0 / 5 0 0	*3 15 0 / 4 10 0	*3 0 0 / 4 0 0	*3 12 0 / 4 0 0	*3 15 0 / 6 0 0
Pietersburg	2 5 0	3 0 0	3 0 0	3 10 0	..
Rustenburg	2 0 0	2 0 0	2 10 0	..	..
Potchefstroom	3 0 0	3 0 0	2 10 0	..	..
Lydenburg	2 0 0	2 10 0	3 0 0	3 0 0	..
Standerton	3 0 0	2 15 0	2 10 0	2 10 0	..
Bechuanaland	*£1 0 0 / 3 0 0	0 15 0 / 1 10 0	..	*2 0 0 / 5 0 0	..
Swaziland	1 10 0 / 2 0 0	1 15 0	..	1 10 0 / 2 0 0	..
Basutoland	2 0 0 / 5 0 0	2 5 0	..	..	..
Bulawayo	1 10 0	1 5 0	1 5 0	1 15 0	..
Salisbury	1 7 6	1 5 0	1 5 0	1 0 0 / 1 10 0	..
Gwelo	0 15 0	1 10 0 / 2 0 0	1 0 0	1 10 0 / 2 10 0	..
Victoria	0 15 0 / 1 15 0	0 15 0	..	0 10 0 / 2 5 0	..
Umtali	1 0 0 / 2 0 0	0 10 0 / 1 10 0	0 10 0 / 2 0 0	1 2 6 / 3 0 0	..
Gwanda	1 10 0	1 10 0	1 10 0	1 10 0 / 5 0 0	..
Lourenco Marques	3 10 0	2 12 6 / 3 7 6	2 12 6	..	2 12 6
Totals ..	120 10 6	99 9 0	107 5 6	89 10 0	29 7 6
Averages ..	2 6 4	2 7 4	2 13 6	2 11 2	3 13 5

* Signifies without rations.

PERCENTAGE of Natives employed on Piecework on Mines.

District.	Mine.	Percentage.
Randfontein North	Randfontein Central G.M. Company, Northern Division	52·01
Randfontein South	Stubbs	53·93
,, ...	Porges	32·14
,, ...	South	40·71
,, ...	North	44·22
,, ...	Robinson	40·5
Krugersdorp	Luipaardsvlei Estate	37·6
,, ...	West Rand Central	54·2
,, ...	West Rand Consolidated	27·5
,, ...	York	..
,, ...	Nolan's Lime Works	..
,, ...	Champ d'Or	..
Roodepoort East	Bantjes Consolidated	45·0
,, ...	Consolidated Main Reef	27·0
,, ...	Durban Roodepoort	35·34
,, ...	Main Reef West	35·0
,, ...	Princess Estate	29·34
Roodepoort West	Aurora West	40·2
,, ...	New Unified	40·2
,, ...	Vogelstruis Estate	42·0
,, ...	Roodepoort United Main Reef ..	29·51
,, ...	Durban Roodepoort Deep	30·0
Johannesburg West	Consolidated Langlaagte	43·73
,, ...	Crown Mines	35·5
,, ...	Langlaagte Estate	23·58
,, ...	A. M. Mostert	29·0
,, ...	Robinson	24·8
Johannesburg Central	Ferreira Deep	20·81
,, ...	Village Deep	31·7
,, ...	Village Main Reef	13·8
,, ...	Meyer & Charlton	44·68
,, ...	City and Suburban	16·1
,, ...	Robinson Deep	41·8
Johannesburg East	City Deep	31·9
,, ...	New Goch	47·7
,, ...	Spes Bona	49·0
,, ...	Wolhuter	40·13
,, ...	Nourse Mines	27·37
,, ...	New Heriot	25·0
,, ...	Jumpers	..
Germiston West	Geldenhuis Deep	40·0
,, ...	Jupiter	..
,, ...	New Primrose	31·0
,, ...	Rose Deep	28·6
,, ...	Simmer & Jack	24·42
,, ...	Simmer Deep	37·0
,, ...	Palmers North Rand	7·0
Germiston East	Knights Deep	18·7
,, ...	Glencairn	38·83
,, ...	New Rietfontein Estate	31·25
,, ...	Knights Central	19·47
,, ...	Witwatersrand	42·41
,, ...	Rose Deep (Glen)	16·9
,, ...	May Consolidated	36·95
,, ...	Dynamite Factory	..
Boksburg	Witwatersrand Deep	32·3
,, ...	East Rand Proprietary	30·48
,, ...	Ginsberg	40·89
Benoni West	New Kleinfontein	33·67
,, ...	Brakpan Mines	32·0
,, ...	Van Ryn Deep	0·7
,, ...	Apex Gold	..
,, ...	Apex Coal	40·4
Benoni East	New Modderfontein	21·2
,, ...	Van Ryn	41·0
,, ...	Government Areas	48·74
,, ...	Modderfontein " B "	37·48
,, ...	Modderfontein Deep	7·44
Springs	Geduld	19·2
,, ...	Daggafontein	66·0
,, ...	Clydesdale Colliery	39·81
,, ...	Welgedacht	43·69
		2,190·53

Average .. 33·7

STATEMENT showing average cost of Repatriating Natives, from 1st January, 1912 (date of coming into force of Labour Act) to 30th September, 1913.

Mine.	Average Cost of Repatriation.		
	£	s.	d.
Randfontein Central :			
Block A	1	11	0
West	1	11	0
Ferguson	1	11	0
Stubbs	1	10	0
Porges	1	10	0
South	1	10	0
North	1	10	0
Robinson	1	10	0
Durban Roodepoort Deep	1	7	6
Aurora West	0	17	9
Roodepoort United Main Reef	4	5	7
Vogelstruis Estate	1	5	0
New Unified	1	16	2
Consolidated Langlaagte	0	18	6
Robinson	1	4	0
Langlaagte Estate	0	19	8
Crown Mines	1	2	4
Witwatersrand Deep	1	5	10
East Rand Proprietary	1	7	11
Cinderella Consolidated	0	18	0
New Rietfontein Estate	0	17	6
May Consolidated	1	0	0
Glencairn	0	19	5
Knights Deep, East and West	1	10	11
Knights Central	0	18	0
Rose Deep, Glen Section	(1	19	3)
Rose Deep, Rose Section	(1	10	10)
Witwatersrand	0	17	7
Bantjes	1	2	6
Consolidated Main Reef	1	3	6
Main Reef West	0	18	8
Princess Estate	1	4	8
Geduld	0	18	0
Springs Mines	0	17	9
Clydesdale Colliery	0	18	0
City Deep	1	4	8
New Heriot	0	17	6
Spes Bona	1	10	10
Nourse	0	17	9
Wolhuter	0	18	0
New Goch	1	5	0
Luipaardsvlei Estate	1	7	6
York	1	7	6
West Rand Central	1	7	6
West Rand Consolidated	1	7	6
New Modderfontein	1	0	0
Van Ryn	1	0	2
Brakpan Mines	1	3	5
Van Ryn Deep	0	16	6
Modderfontein " B "	1	0	0
Government Gold Mining Areas	1	10	0
Modderfontein Deep Levels	0	19	0
A. M. Mostert, Contractor	1	12	0
Meyer & Charlton	0	17	6
City & Suburban	1	0	0
Village Main Reef	1	2	6
Robinson Deep	1	4	8
Village Deep	1	5	9
Ferreira Deep	1	2	0
New Primrose	0	17	6
Simmer & Jack Proprietary	0	17	4
Simmer Deep	1	6	0
Geldenhuis Deep	2	0	0
Ginsberg	0	16	6
Durban Roodepoort		..	
Daggafontein		..	
Welgedacht (Coal)		..	
East Rand Gold and Coal		No records kept.	
New Kleinfontein			
	£80	2	5

Average .. £1 5 0

RETURN showing the number of cases of silicosis

(1) Amongst native labourers employed on Mines included in the list published under Section 2 of the Miners' Phthisis Act, which have been dealt with by the Department of Native Labour :
(a) for the period 1 ·8 ·12 to 31 ·12 ·13.
(b) For the period 1 ·1 ·14 to 31 ·3 ·14.

(2) Amongst natives employed on Mines and Works *not* included in the List published under Section 2 of the Act.

Group.	Period 1/8/12 to 31/12/13.				Period 1/1/14 to 31/3/14.			
	Average No. of natives.	Cases reported.	Cases not reported.	Total on record.	Average No. of natives.	Cases reported.	Cases not reported.	Total on record.
East Rand Proprietary Mines..	14,100	8	1	9	12,677	5	..	5
Group total ..	14,100	8	1	9	12,677	5	..	5
Farrar Anglo-French								
New Kleinfontein	4,642	4	1	5	4,345	..	..	..
Apex Gold Mine	187	..	..	..	156	..	..	..
Rand Klipfontein ..	257	..	1	1	..	..	..	..
Group total ..	5,086	4	2	6	4,501	..	..	..
General Mining and Finance.								
Aurora West	1,459	6	1	7	1,169	..	..	..
Cinderella Consolidated ..	2,034	1	2	3	14	1	..	1
Meyer & Charlton	963	7	3	10	916	2	..	2
New Goch	2,297	20	3	23	2,652	..	1	1
Roodepoort United Main Rf.	2,762	8	..	8	2,725	..	1	1
West Rand Consolidated ..	3,318	12	2	14	3,537	..	..	..
Rand Collieries	80	..	1	1	..	..	..	..
Van Ryn G.M.	2,388	6	2	8	2,420	3	..	3
Group total ..	15,301	60	14	74	13,433	6	2	8
Rand Mines.								
Durban Roodepoort Deep	2,617	..	3	3	2,174	1	3	4
Geldenhuis Deep	4,927	8	..	8	3,871	2	..	2
Rose Deep	2,650	8	1	9	2,460	2	..	2
Crown Mines	12,505	3	2	5	10,575	14	7	21
Ferreira Deep	3,550	3	3	6	3,047	1	..	1
Group total ..	26,249	22	9	31	22,127	20	10	30
Consolidated Mines Selection.								
Brakpan Mines	3,677	9	2	11	3,332	1	1	2
Group total ..	3,677	9	2	11	3,332	1	1	2
Consolidated Gold Fields.								
Jupiter	1,987	2	..	2	11	..	..	..
Knight's Deep	2,903	22	3	25	3,466	2	..	2
Luipaardsvlei Estate ..	1,328	11	2	13	1,479	1	..	1
Sub-Nigel	215	7	..	7	533	1	..	1
Robinson Deep	3,437	27	1	28	2,579	..	..	..
Simmer and Jack	3,128	7	..	7	2,761	3	1	4
Simmer Deep	3,790	1	..	1	2,883	..	..	..
Group total ..	16,788	77	6	83	13,712	7	1	8
Sundry Mines.								
Durban Roodepoort ..	1,068	2	..	2	1,058	..	..	..
Nigel	2,007	5	3	8	2,112	2	1	3
West Rand Central ..	478	4	2	6	494	..	..	..
York	899	14	3	17	82	..	1	1
Ferguson Champ D'Or ..	202	..	..	..	98	..	..	..
Vogelstruis Estate ..	1,514	1	1	2	1,396	1	..	1
Ariston	157	..	..	..	..	..	..	..
Quest..	306	1	..	1	257	..	..	..
Warren Hill	495	..	..	..	413	..	..	..
Spes Bona Tribute.. ..	556	4	1	5	454	2	..	2
Group total ..	7,682	31	10	41	6,364	5	2	7

ANNEXURE 17.—(continued).

Group.	Period 1/8/12 to 31/12/13.				Period 1/1/14 to 31/3/14.			
	Average No. of natives.	Cases reported.	Cases not reported.	Total on record.	Average No. of natives.	Cases reported.	Cases not reported.	Total on record.
Neumann & Co.								
Consolidated Main Reef ..	2,390	6	3	9	1,852	..	..	..
Knights Central	2,142	4	..	4	1,547	..	..	..
Main Reef West	1,894	..	..	..	1,447	1	..	1
Witwatersrand Deep ..	3,444	3	..	3	2,862	4	..	4
Wolhuter	2,389	23	2	25	2,586	5	..	5
Group total ..	12,259	36	5	41	10,294	10	..	10
Goerz & Co.								
May Consolidated	1,137	5	..	5	787	1	..	1
Princess Estate	2,595	1	1	2	2,647	3	..	3
Geduld Proprietary ..	1,572	3	1	4	1,377	1	..	1
Modderfontein Deep ..	482	9	..	9	887	1	..	1
Lancaster West	1,160	4	2	6	..	..	..	..
Group total ..	6,946	22	4	26	5,698	6	..	6
J. B. Robinson.								
Langlaagte Estate	4,871	45	8	53	4,701	10	1	11
Randfontein Central ..	22,644	24	3	27	20,776	2	..	2
Group total ..	27,515	69	11	80	25,477	12	1	13
Campagnie Francaise.								
Jumpers	974	1	3	4	101	1	..	1
Group total ..	974	1	3	4	101	1	..	1
H. Eckstein & Co.								
City Deep	4,017	..	..	..	3,882	..	..	..
City and Suburban ..	2,621	10	4	14	2,363	..	..	..
New Heriot	1,253	5	..	5	1,223	..	..	..
New Modderfontein ..	3,236	2	..	2	2,307	2	1	3
Nourse Mines	4,277	8	1	9	3,106	..	..	.
Robinson	3,152	3	3	6	2,813	..	..	..
Village Deep	3,497	5	1	6	3,173	..	..	..
Modderfontein " B " ..	2,031	3	..	3	1,865	1	..	1
Village Main Reef ..	2,815	5	2	7	2,321	2	..	2
Bantjes Consolidated ..	2,822	..	5	5	2,354	..	1	1
Group total ..	29,712	41	16	57	25,407	5	2	7
Consolidated Investment.								
Consolidated Langlaagte ..	3,195	..	..	..	2,559	..	1	1
Ginsberg	1,369	5	..	5	1,076	..	..	..
Glencairn	1,225	1	..	1	1,155	..	..	..
New Primrose	1,693	8	4	12	1,495	2	1	3
New Rietfontein Estate ..	1,774	14	2	16	1,245	3	1	4
New Unified	1,035	..	1	1	854	..	..	..
Witwatersrand	2,567	6	1	7.	2,307	3	..	3
Modderfontein Consolidated	1,471	2	2	4	1,476	3	..	3
Van Ryn Deep	1,848	1	1	2	2,325	1	1	2
Group total ..	16,177	37	11	48	14,492	12	14	16
Sundry Mines and Works. not included under the Act	..	30	28	58	..	..	3	3

W.N.L.A., LTD.-LOURENCO MARQUES AGENCY.

The bearer has produced his *Transvaal Native Labour Badge No. 2430 attached herewith, showing he has worked on the New Kleinfontein Gold Mine, to which he desires to return. He has brought with him ......brothers, who desire to go to the same Mine. Of these, ... are in my opinion genuine, and ...... doubtful.

W. FITCHETT,
Recruiter.

*NOTE.—If Native has not Transvaal Labour Passport, but has old Portuguese Passport or Aluminium Ticket, the Recruiter should strike out the words " Transvaal Native Labour Passport " and substitute " Portuguese Passport (or Aluminium Ticket) No........." This will be verified on arrival at Johannesburg.

STATEMENT showing minimum period for which each Mine will accept a Voluntary Native.

Mine	Period.	Remarks.
Randfontein Central :		
Block A	30 shifts	One month when scarcity of natives, otherwise one month plus one month's notice.
West	30 ,,	
Ferguson	30 ,,	
Stubbs	30 ,,	,,
Porges	30 ,,	,,
South	30 ,,	,,
North	180 ,,	
Robinson	180 ,,	
Durban Roodepoort Deep	60 ,,	
Aurora West	120 ,,	
Roodepoort United Main Reef	30 ,,	Plus one month's notice
Vogelstruis Estates	90 ,,	
New Unified	120 ,,	
Consolidated Langlaagte	30 ,,	
Robinson	120 ,,	
Langlaagte Estate	30 ,,	
Crown Mines	60 ,,	
Witwatersrand Deep	120 ,,	
East Rand Proprietary	30 ,,	
Cinderella	30 ,.	
New Rietfontein Estate	30 ,,	
May Consolidated	30 ,,	
Glencairn	60 ,,	
Knights Deep (East and West)	30 ,,	
Knights Central	30 ,,	
Rose Deep (Glen Section)	60 ,,	
Rose Deep (Rose Section)	60 ,,	
Witwatersrand	120 ,,	
Bantjes	30 ,,	
Consolidated Main Reef	150 ,,	
Durban Roodepoort	30 ,,	
Main Reef West	90 ,,	
Princess Estate	30 ,,	
Geduld	90 ,,	
Springs Mines	30 ,,	
Daggafontein	60 ,,	
Welgedacht Ex. (Coal)	30 ,,	
Clydesdale Colliery	30 ,,	
East Rand Gold and Coal	90 ,,	
City Deep	30 ,,	
New Heriot	120 ,,	
Spes Bona	30 ,,	
Nourse	30 ,,	
Wolhuter	180 ,,	
New Goch	30 ,,	
Luipaardsvlei Estate	180 ,,	
York	30 ,,	
West Rand Central	30 ,,	
West Rand Consolidated	90 ,,	
New Kleinfontein	120 ,,	
New Modderfontein	90 ,,	
Van Ryn	30 ,,	
Brakpan Mines	30 ,,	
Van Ryn Deep	30 ,,	
Modder B	90 ,,	
Government G.M. Areas	90 ,,	
Modderfontein Deep	60 ,,	
A. M. Mostert (Contractor)	30 ,,	
Meyer & Charlton	30 ,,	
City and Suburban	90 ,,	
Village Main Reef	120 ,,	
Robinson Deep	90 ,,	
Village Deep	30 ,,	
Ferreira Deep	30 ,,	
New Primrose	120 ,,	
Simmer & Jack Propy.	90 ,,	
Simmer Deep	90 ,,	

(Modelo J.A.)

GOVERNO GERAL DA PROVINCIA DE MOCAMBIQUE.

Districto de.................................

No. ....do acampamento de.................   N. geral do contracto......

O engajador...................subdito..............ao serviço e sob a responsabilidade da WITWATERSRAND NATIVE LABOUR ASSOCIATION contracta, em harmonia com os preceitos do Regulamento de Emigração,..........indigenas constantes do presente contracto para, durante o prazo de um anno, a contar da saída de territorio Portuguez, trabalharem nas industrias mineiras do Transvaal, com o salario minimo de...........shillings por cada dia util de trabalho e por adulto ou de oito pence mesmas condições para menores, salario no qual não será feito qualquer desconto sem autorização do Governo Portuguez, com excepção da somma maxima de uma libra esterlina para cobrir as despesas de transporte, vigilancia e alimentação dos mesmos durante a viagem até Ressano Garcia quando hajam de regressar á Provincia ; ser-lhes-á fornecida alimentação, assistencia medica e domicilio gratuitos desde que estejam contractados.

Obrigo-me, quer por mim, quer pela entidade acima citada, ou ainda em nome das minas a que cedo estes indigenas, a cumprir todas as condições do regulamento acima citado, e especialmente : a empregar os contractados exclusivamente em territorio do Transvaal e nas minas pertencentes a WITWATERSRAND NATIVE LABOUR ASSOCIATION ; a facilitar-lhes o communicarem com o seu Curador ou representantes ; a emprehender e custear a sua repatriação em harmonia com as obrigações por elles abaixo contrahidas e de accordo com os compromissos por nós tomados para com o Governo Geral da Provincia ; e ainda ás seguintes condições :

1.ª—A notificar ao Curador : *a*) todos os fallecimentos de trabalhadores, a causa e data do fallecimento em cada caso e os dados necessarios relativos aos fallecidos ; *b*) todos os casos de deserção, com todas as informações que possam ser uteis ; *c*) todos os casos de emigrantes Portuguezes clandestinos, empregados além dos trabalhadores legalmente recrutados ;

2.ª—A adoptar todos os meios para evitar a perda ou destruição do passe portuguez, notificando os casos de trabalhadores que nao tenham esse passe ;

3.ª—A auxiliar e facilitar a cobrança dos emolumentos de emigração que possam ser impostos aos trabalhadores ;

4.ª—A empregar todos os trabalhadores exclusivamente em serviço proprio, não os utilizando para outros fins que nao sejam aquelles para que foram recrutados ;

5.ª—A fornecer ao Curador todos os dados á nossa disposição com o fim de se encontrarem os interessados nos espolios dos trabalhadores fallecidos.

.............................,......de..................de 191..

O ENGAJADOR,

....

NÓS INDIGENAS CONSTANTES DO PRESENTE CONTRACTO, OBRIGAMO-NOS :

1.°—A regressar a territorio Portuguez, por via Ressano Garcia, logo que termine o prazo d`este contracto ou dos subsequentes periodos de re-engajamento que ulteriormente hajamos effectuado ;

2.°—A não trabalharmos senão em minas pertencentes a WITWATERSRAND NATIVE LABOUR ASSOCIATION, quer durante o primitivo periodo de contracto, quer durante os de re-engajamento, obrigando-nos a fazel-o na medida das nossas forças e saude, e em harmonia com os preceitos dos regulamentos que nos sao applicaveis ;

3.°—A não permanecermos por caso algum em territorio de Transvaal por mais de dois annos, contados da data de saída do territorio Portuguez, ao qual regressaremos nas condições acima citadas logo que esse periodo haja expirado ;

4.°—A consentir que nos salarios do nosso primitivo periodo de engajamento nos seja feito pela WITWATERSRAND NATIVE LABOUR ASSOCIATION um desconto nao superior a uma libra esterlina para cobrir as despesas de conducção, alimentação e fiscalização durante a viagem desde a mina em que trabalharmos até Ressano Garcia, a qual faremos aproveitando sempre os meios postos ao nosso dispôr para esse fim pela mesma entidade e em harmonia com o que acima é dito.

OS INDIGENAS CONSTANTES DO PRESENTE CONTRACTO TOMARAM PERANTE MIM, E DE LIVRE VONTADE, OS COMPROMISSOS ACIMA DETERMINADOS, QUE SE OBRIGAM A CUMPRIR RIGOROSAMENTE E A QUE DOU A VALIDADE, ASSIGNANDO POR ELLES ESTE CONTRACTO.

.............................,......de....................de 191..

O (*a*).................,

....

(*a*) Governador do Districto, Commandante Militar, Chefe de Circumscripçao, ou Fiscal de Emigraçao.

Numeros.		Nomes.					Indicaçoes eventuaes.		
Do passe.	De ordem	Do indigena.	Do pae.	Commando ou circumscripçao.	Regulado.	Nome do induna ou do secretario.	Nome do regulo.		Observvaçoes.

CONTRACTO N.º............DO POSTO DE EMIGRAÇAO EM

Logar do carimbo

Foram-me presentes........................indigenas constantes d'este contracto, faltando os n.ºˢ.......................................que desertaram, e os n.ºˢ......................
...................que foram rejeitados.
Seguem, portanto, para o Transvaal...................................indigenas, na data de......de........................de 191..

O FISCAL,

....

Recebi do engajador..indigenas constantes do presente contracto que me obrigo a apresentar ao Curador em................................, ao mesmo tempo que este, salvo se tiver autorizaçao para os levar directamente para...........
.........................come é permittido pelo fiscal.

CONCEDIDO.

O CONDUCTOR TRANSVAALIANO,   O FISCAL,

Logar do carimbo

....

Foram-me presentes.......................................indigenas em..:.........de
...................de 191.., faltando os n.ºˢ..dos quaes os n.ºˢ......................................morreram.

O CURADOR (ou quem suas vezes faça)

....

DISTRIBUICAO.

Nome das minas.	Districto mineiro.	Numero dos passes.

TRANSLATION OF PORTUGUESE NATIVE CONTRACT.

FORM J—A.

GOVERNMENT GENERAL OF THE PROVINCE OF MOZAMBIQUE.

District of..

No.......of.......................Camp.   General No. of Contract...............

The Recruiter......................, ...Subject, in the service and under the responsibility of the......................................hereby does contract, in compliance with the provisions of the Regulations of Emigration,..................natives, as detailed herein, to, during the period of one year, counting from the date of departure from Portuguese Territory, work for the mining industries of the Transvaal, at a minimum salary of 1½ shillings per useful day's work and per adult, or eightpence under the same conditions for minors, from which salary no deduction whatever shall be made without authorisation from the Portuguese Government, with the exception of the maximum sum of One Pound Sterling to cover the expenses of transport, surveillance and feeding of same during the journey to Ressano Garcia when they may have to return to the Province ; food, medical assistance and quarters shall be supplied to them free of charge from the time they have been contracted.

I undertake the obligation, in my name, or in the name of the above-mentioned party, or further, in the name of the mines to which I cede these natives, to comply with all the conditions of the above quoted regulations, and especially to employ the contracted natives exclusively in the territory of the Transvaal and the mines petaining to the........................ ; to facilitate their communication with their Curator or representatives ; to undertake and defray the cost of their repatriation in compliance with the obligations at foot hereof undertaken by them and in accordance with the obligations undertaken by us towards the Government-General of the Province ; and further to the following conditions :—

1.—To notify to the Curator : (a) all deaths of labourers, the cause and date of death in each case, and the necessary data relative to the deceased ; (b) all cases of desertion, with all information that may be of use ; (c) all cases of Portuguese clandestine emigrants, employed besides the labourers lawfully recruited ;

2.—To employ all means to prevent the loss or destruction of the Portuguese pass, notifying any cases of labourers who are not in possession of such pass ;

3.—To aid and facilitate the collection of the emigration fees which may be imposed on the labourers ;

4.—To employ all the labourers exclusively in our own service, never utilising them for other purposes beyond those purposes for which they have been recruited ;

5.—To supply to the Curator all the data at our disposal for the purpose of tracing the parties interested in the estates of deceased labourers, and to respect the conditions established in the Convention of 1st April, 1909, and in the memorandum attached thereto.

Ressano Garcia....................of..................19..

THE RECRUITER,

....

WE, THE NATIVES APPEARING IN THE PRESENT CONTRACT, UNDERTAKE THE FOLLOWING OBLIGATIONS :

1.—To return to Portuguese territory, via Ressano Garcia, immediately the period of this contract, or the subsequent periods of re-engagement which we may effect, shall have expired.

2.—To work only for the mines of the........................, either during the original period of contract, or during the periods of re-engagement, undertaking to do the work according to our strength and health, and in accordance with the provisions of the regulations in so far as they apply to us.

3.—Not to remain in any case in the territory of the Transvaal for more than two years, counting from the date of departure from Portuguese territory, to which we shall return under the above quoted conditions, immediately that period shall have expired.

4.—To consent that from our salaries of our original period of engagement a deduction be made by the........................of not more than One Pound Sterling to cover the expenses of conducting, feeding and surveillance, during the journey from the mine where we shall be working to Ressano Garcia, which journey we shall always do, availing ourselves of the means placed at our disposal for that purpose by the said party and in accordance with the foregoing.

THE NATIVES, AS DETAILED HEREIN, HAVE TAKEN BEFORE ME, AND OF THEIR OWN FREE WILL THE ABOVE-MENTIONED OBLIGATIONS, WHICH THEY UNDERTAKE TO THOROUGHLY COMPLY WITH AND TO WHICH I GIVE THE DUE VALIDITY BY SIGNING FOR THEM THIS CONTRACT.

...............................of..................19..

The (a) ....

....

(a) Governor of the District, Military Commandant, Head of Sub-District, or Fiscal of Emigration.

Following on are two ruled pages, with headings, for particulars of not more than one hundred natives.

ANNEXURE 22.

RETURN, covering the twelve months, July, 1912 to June, 1913, showing the number of :

(a) Holders of Labour Agents' and Employers' Licences, and of Runners Permits, within the Union, on the last day of each month, and

(b) natives recruited for labour on mines and works in the proclaimed labour districts of the Transvaal (exclusive of natives Recruited for contractors, with the exception of natives recruited for Mr. A. M. Mostert at Randfontein), during each such month.

Month.	(a) Licence Holders.					(b) Recruited Labourers.					(c) Comparative Statement.	
	No. of persons holding Labour Agents' Licences.	No. of persons holding Employers' Licences.	Total No. of Licence Holders.	No. of persons holding Runners' Permits.	Total No. of individuals recruiting within Union.	Cape.	Transvaal.	Natal and Zululand.	Orange Free State.	Total.	No. of labourers recruited per Licence Holder.	No. of labourers recruited per individual (Labour Agent, Employer and Runner).
1912.												
July	1,626	23	1,649	3,309	4,958	4,103	831	717	29	5,680	3·4	1·1
August	1,646	23	1,669	3,445	5,114	5,293	749	822	28	6,892	4·1	1·3
September	1,696	27	1,723	3,511	5,234	5,971	499	736	8	7,214	4·2	1·4
October	1,732	28	1,760	3,634	5,394	6,328	636	1,062	8	8,034	4·6	1·5
November	1,763	30	1,798	3,682	5,475	7,504	619	1,140	8	9,271	5·2	1·7
December	1,767	31	1,798	3,685	5,483	8,674	798	1,219	5	10,696	5·9	2·0
Monthly Average	1,705	27	1,732	3,544	5,276	6,312	689	949	14	7,964	4·6	1·5
1913.												
January	1,038	12	1,050	427	1,477	13,352	1,045	1,566	13	15,976	15·2	10·8
February	1,181	14	1,195	1,014	2,209	8,676	1,050	1,154	26	10,906	9·1	4·9
March	1,265	16	1,281	1,265	2,546	5,336	905	969	29	7,239	5·7	2·8
April	1,312	17	1,329	1,492	2,821	4,030	741	971	14	5,756	4·3	2·0
May	1,330	19	1,349	1,578	2,927	2,917	559	654	15	4,145	3·0	1·4
June	1,347	19	1,366	1,642	3,008	2,558	669	538	11	3,776	2·7	1·2
Monthly Average	1,246	16	1,262	1,236	2,498	6,145	828	975	18	7,966	6·3	3·2

ANNEXURE 23.

RETURN, covering six months, January to June, 1913, showing the number of :

(a) Holders of Labour Agents' and Employers' Licences and Runners' Permits, and

(b) Natives recruited for labour on mines and works in the proclaimed labour districts of the Transvaal (exclusive of Natives recruited for contractors, with the exception of those recruited for Mr. A. M. Mostert at Rand-fontein) in each Province of the Union.

Month.	No. of persons holding		Total No. of Licence Holders.	No. of persons holding Runners' Permits.	Total. No. of persons recruiting within the Province.	Re-cruited. Labour-ers.	No. of Native Labourers Recruited.	
	Labour Agents' Licences.	Em-ployers' Licences.					Per Licence Holder.	Per indi-vidual. (Licence Holders. and Runners.)
1. Cape Province.								
January	845	2	847	242	1,089	13,352	15·8	12·3
February	954	3	957	577	1,534	8,676	9·1	5·7
March	1,014	3	1,017	704	1,721	5,336	5·2	3·1
April	1,040	3	1,043	812	1,855	4,030	3·9	2·2
May	1,051	4	1,055	859	1,914	2,917	2·8	1·5
June	1,061	4	1,065	894	1,959	2,558	2·4	1·3
Monthly Average	994	3	997	681	1,678	6,145	6·2	3·7
2. Transvaal.								
January	106	2	108	130	238	1,045	9·7	4·4
February	118	3	121	272	393	1,050	8·7	2·7
March	125	4	139	350	479	905	7·0	1·9
April	139	4	143	411	554	741	5·2	1·3
May	144	5	149	430	579	559	3·8	1·0
June	148	5	153	450	603	669	4·4	1·1
Monthly Average	130	4	134	340	474	828	6·2	1·7
3. Natal.								
January	86	8	94	55	149	1,566	16·7	10·5
February	108	8	116	161	277	1,154	9·9	4·2
March	124	9	133	206	339	969	7·3	2·9
April	130	10	140	264	404	971	6·9	2·4
May	132	10	142	282	424	654	4·6	1·5
June	135	10	145	291	436	538	3·7	1·2
Monthly Average	119	9	128	210	338	975	7·6	2·9
4. Orange Free State								
January	1	..	1	..	1	13	13·0	13·0
February	1	..	1	4	5	26	26·0	5·2
March	2	..	2	5	7	29	14·5	4·1
April	3	..	3	5	8	14	4·7	1·8
May	3	..	3	7	10	15	5·0	1·5
June	3	..	3	7	10	11	3·7	1·1
Monthly Average	2	..	2	5	7	18	9·0	2·6

RETURN SHOWING THE NUMBER OF RECRUITERS AND

District.	Baerecke & Kleudgen.	Barnato Group.	Ballengeich Colliery.	Bray & Pearce.	City & Suburban.	Consolidated Goldfields.	Cooper, R. H.	Corte & Gibello.	De Beers Consolidated.	Denny & Roberts.	De Rietfontein Colliery.	Dundee Coal Co.	Durban Navigation Colliery.	Elandslaagte Colliery.	Fairleigh Colliery.	Glencoe (Natal) Colliery.	Glynn's Lydenburg.	Hadley's Organisation.	Harris Bros.	Hatting Spruit Colliery.	Hlobane Collieries.	Jorrisen, van Tilburg & England.	Kleinfontein Group.	Knollys & Co.	Koffyfontein D. M.	Lawless, J.	Lazarus, P. H.	Luipaardsvlei Estate.	Marwick & Morris.
Cape.																													
Bizana	3				1	2		1							1			1				1						1	
Butterworth	4					1	1								1		1	1											
Elliotdale	2				1													15											
Engcobo	3																												
Flagstaff	3				1																							2	
Glen Grey	8				3										2			4							1	1		2	
Herschel																													
Idutywa	6					1												2											
Kentani	1							1							1														
Kingwilliamstown															1			4											
Kuruman																													
Libode					1													2											
Lusikisiki	5		1		2													1										1	
Maclear		1		2																									
Matatiele				2																								1	
Mount Ayliff																													
Mount Fletcher																													
Mount Frere	1	1																										1	
Mafeking																													
Mqanduli	1																	11											
Ngqeleni	6					1												3											
Nqamakwe	3						1											2							1				
Peddie	3																												
Port St. John's	2				1													1											
Qumbu		1			1													1											
St. Marks	14				2												1	3							1				
Tabankulu	1																											2	
Taungs																													
Tsolo					1													1											
Tsomo	10																	1											
Umtata	4																	2											
Umzimkulu														2													1		
Victoria East																													
Vryburg																													
Willowvale	9						1									1		4										2	
Wodehouse																		2							1				
Xalanga																		5							1				
East London																													
Fort Beaufort																													
Komgha																													
Mount Currie																													
Queenstown	5				2											2		2								1	1		
Total	94	3		1	2	17	2	2	4				3		9			66				1		2	6		1	10	
Transvaal.																													
Zoutpansberg	20	7																										1	
Lichtenburg																													
Lydenburg	4										1						1												
Marico		1																											
Middelburg	1																												
Pretoria	2	2															1												
Rustenburg		1																											
Waterberg	4																											1	
Piet Retief	1																												4
Pietersburg																													
Barberton																													
Total	32	11								1							1	1										2	4

NAMES OF THEIR PRINCIPALS IN EACH OPEN AREA.

Mackenzie, G. B.	Mackenzie, J. W.	Mackenzie, R.	McPhee, H. H.	Messina Develop. Co.	Mostert, A. M.	Natal Cambrian Collieries.	Natal Navigation Collieries.	Natal Steam Coal Co.	Native Recruiting Corporation.	Newcastle Collieries.	New Heriot.	New Jagersfontein.	Northern Lime Co.	Oogies Colliery.	Orton, W. F.	Premier Diamond Mine.	Prior & Tracey.	Randfontein Cent. & Langlaagte Est.	Robinson Group.	Rubin, N.	Scott & Co.	Sheba G.M. Co.	Simmer & Jack.	Smith, W. S.	Snyman, T. T.	South African Collieries.	South African Railways.	South African Tin Mines.	St. George's Collieries.	Still Bros.	Transvaal G.M. Estate.	Vryheid Rly. Coal & Iron Co.	W.N.L.A.	Wallsend (Natal) Collieries.	Warren & Co.	Western Lime Co.	S. F. Drake and about 50 Farmers.	Total.
	1				1				27														1															38
					11				20		1												1							1								42
					16				17															1						1								52
					19				35																	1			1						1			59
	1				2				28																1				1						1			38
					14				40	1			1													1			1						1			77
									2	1																												3
					10				12																													31
					9				35																													47
					54				82																													141
					11				37																													51
	1				4		1		38																													54
					1				6																													8
					5				21																													28
					1				7																													9
					9				18																													27
	1				9				26																													38
					1				5								3	1	4																			15
					19				23																													54
					23				33																													66
					9				22	1																												39
					4				7																													14
					5	1			24																													34
	1				8			1	37																													50
					9				35	2		1																		1				1		1			70
	1				5				33																													42
																																					..
					12				23																													37
									17	1																												29
					20				36																													62
	1							1	15	1																					1							22
					3				13																				1									17
																1	1																					2
					14				23																													54
					8				13																													24
					7				15																													28
					12				8																													20
					2				5																													7
					13				11																													24
									5																													5
									12		1		1																	1	1				1		1	31
	7				350	3		1	866		1	8				3	4	1		5		1		1	1	1		6			1		1		4		1	1,489
		1	2						52		1				10		23												1									118
																																					..
		1			3				17						5																	1						33
									2				1		1																							5
		2							8				1		5											1												18
									8						4																			1		1		19
																				1																		2
									10		1		5		2			1											1									24
									5																													10
											1		1		1																							3
																								1														1
		2	2		5				102				3	1	30	1	26	1	1		1			1				2			1		1		1		233

ANNEXURE 24—*continued.*

RETURN SHOWING THE NUMBER OF RECRUITERS AND

District.	Baerecke & Kleudgen.	Barnato Group.	Ballengeich Colliery.	Bray & Pearce.	City & Suburban.	Consolidated Goldfields.	Cooper, R. H.	Corte & Gibello.	De Beers Consolidated.	Denny & Roberts.	De Rietfontein Colliery.	Dundee Coal Co.	Durban Navigation Colliery.	Elandslaagte Colliery.	Fairleigh Colliery.	Glencoe (Natal) Colliery.	Glynn's Lydenburg.	Hadley's Organisation.	Harris Bros.	Hatting Spruit Colliery.	Hlobane Collieries.	Jorrisen, van Tilburg & England.	Kleinfontein Group.	Knollys & Co.	Koffyfontein D. M.	Lawless, J.	Lazarus, P. H.	Luipaardsvlei Estate.	Marwick & Morris.
Natal.																													
Hlabisa														1															
Ingvavuma			1											1						1									6
Mahlabatini			1									1	1	2							1								3
Mapumulo			1																										3
Impofana														1															
Ndwandwe	1			1																									1
Ubombo				1																									4
Alfred	4						1																						1
Emtonjaneni		1																											1
Eshowe		1												1															2
Helpmakaar	2			1									1	4							1								1
Krantzkop							1							1															1
Nqutu	1			1								2	1												1				
Polela												2								1	1		1						2
Umlazi		3		1										4		3		4											
Lower Umzimkulu	4																												
Richmond		2					1						1					3											
Ixopo							1			1																			1
Dundee	1											3	1							1	1		1		1				2
Ngotshe	1											2	1							1	1								1
Vryheid	1											2	1							1	1								2
Nkandhla	1											1	1								1								4
Newcastle															1	1					1				1				3
Ladysmith														1		1													
Umgeni							1																						
Alexandra							1																						
Weenen							1																						
Estcourt							1																						
Total	16	7	3	5			8			1		13	8	16	1	5		7		5	8		2		3				38
Orange Free State.																													
Bloemfontein																													
Thaba 'Nchu					1																						1		
Harrismith																													
Total					1																						1		
Summary.																													
Cape Province	94	3		1	2	17	2	2	4					3		9		66				1		2	6	1		10	
Natal	16	7	3	5			8			1		13	8	16	1	5		7		5	8		2		3				38
Orange Free State					1																						1		
Transvaal	32	11									1						1	1										2	4
Total	142	21	3	6	3	17	10	2	4	1	1	13	8	19	1	14	1	74		5	8	1	2	2	9	1	1	12	42

ANNEXURE 24—*continued.*

NAMES OF THEIR PRINCIPALS IN EACH OPEN AREA.

Mackenzie, G. B.	Mackenzie, J. W.	Mackenzie, R.	McPhee, H. H.	Messina Develop. Co.	Mostert, A. M.	Natal Cambrian Collieries.	Natal Navigation Collieries.	Natal Steam Coal Co.	Native Recruiting Corporation.	Newcastle Collieries.	New Heriot.	New Jagersfontein.	Northern Lime Co.	Oogies Colliery.	Orton, W. F.	Premier Diamond Mine.	Prior & Tracey.	Randfontein Cent. & Langlaagte Est.	Robinson Group.	Rubin, N.	Scott & Co.	Sheba G.M. Co.	Simmer & Jack.	Smith, W. S.	Snyman, T. T.	South African Collieries.	South African Tin Mines.	South African Railways.	St. George's Collieries.	Still Bros.	Transvaal G.M. Estate.	Vryheid (Natal) Rly. Coal & Iron Co.	W.N.L.A.	Wallsend (Natal) Collieries.	Warren & Co.	Western Lime Co.	S. F. Drake and about 50 Farmers.	Button, E. A.	Total.
1									7																														16
									5																														11
1							1		12	1																							1						26
									1																														1
1						1	1		9	2																							1						23
									5																														7
	1				1				5																														13
1									4																														9
1									7																											1			17
								1	1																														9
									1																									1					5
							1		8	1																1			1					1					23
									3																														3
	1						1		8																								1		3				29
	1				1	1	1		5																														13
	1						1		5																														16
	1						1		6																														12
		1						1	2																	1			1										16
1						1	1		11	1																1			1	1									24
	1						1		16	1																1			1	1									30
1							1		6																				1										16
1																																							3
																																							1
																																							1
																															1								2
																															1								2
8	5	1			3	8	6	1	128	6																6			5	2		2		5					332
																																						1	1
																																							2
									2																														2
									2																													1	5
	7				350	3		1	866		1	8			3	4	1		5		1		1	1	1		6		1		1		4		1				1,489
8	5	1			3	8	7		128	6																6			5	2		2		5					332
									2																													1	5
			2	2	5				102				3	1		30	1	26	1	1		1				1		2				1		1		1			233
8	12	1	?	?	358	11	7	1	1,098	6	1	8	3	1	3	34	2	26	6	1	1	1	1	1	2	6	2	6	5	3	1	3	1	5	4	1	1	1	2,059